When Kumbaya Is Not Enough

When Kumbaya Is Not Enough

A Practical Theology for Youth Ministry

DEAN BORGMAN

HENDRICKSON
PUBLISHERS

© 1997 by Hendrickson Publishers, Inc.
P. O. Box 3473
Peabody, Massachusetts 01961-3473
All rights reserved
Printed in the United States of America

ISBN 1-56563-247-8

Third Printing – July 1999

Library of Congress Cataloging-in-Publication Data

Borgman, Dean, 1928–
    When Kumbaya is not enough: A practical theology for
youth ministry / Dean Borgman.
    Includes bibliographical references.
    ISBN 1-56563-247-8
    1. Church work with youth. I. Title
BV4447.B674 1997
259′.23—dc21   97-20785
                                                        CIP

Dedication

I am thankful to Bill Koerner, Joe Kantor, and Joe Gyana, who first got me into youth ministry, and to the many colleagues who have helped me grow. This book is also dedicated to my students over many years and finally to my faithful family—Gail, my loving partner, and my children, who instructed me through their adolescence: John, Debbie, Matt, and Christy.

TABLE OF CONTENTS

PREFACE: OVERVIEW OF THE THEOLOGICAL TASK

A Youthful Perspective

This book is a theology of youth ministry, or theological reflections on the youth culture, for those who love God and young people—those who want to know what in the world God is doing with young people these days. It is for those who love God's Word and want to have a practical understanding about today's popular and youth cultures and an ability to recognize both their negative and their positive features.

The book of Proverbs was intended to give guidance to the simple, knowledge and prudence to the youth, and further learning and discretion to those already wise (Proverbs 1:4-5). The wisdom of Proverbs was based on the principles of the Torah or Jewish Law, on wise interpretation of traditional culture by keen observers, and on the illumination of God's Spirit. This book seeks God's wisdom; together we will seek to understand God's truth and work in our society.

I have written these theological reflections over several years of teaching those who care about young people. I hope that youth workers and teachers, parents and pastors, will here find encouragement, help, and hope. The worldwide cultural and youth crises demand global and cross-cultural perspectives, and I write from my global and urban experiences. Only through cross-cultural collaboration and cooperation can we all become more effective guides in these complex times.

An underlying assumption of this book is that those who bring a love for God's Word and for young people to a study of current music, media, and human issues will come to "have more understanding than [their] teachers" (Psalm 119:99, NRSV), who may be isolated in academia. The seemingly lowly understanding from the streets and the marketplace can be of more value than lofty pronouncements from scholarly realms.

Academics continue an ongoing debate as to the age range of youth and the exact meaning of related terms. We will generally use the terms *youth, adolescents, teenagers,* and *young people* interchangeably referring to that age group between childhood and adulthood. Most of what is written here considers junior-high through college students with particular focus on teenagers in their high school years.

We face today both a youth crisis and a cultural crisis. Many of us tend to overreact to dangerous trends, to oversimplify, to separate ourselves from what we see as the sources of our troubles. In times of change cultures manifest recurrent cravings for oversimplified politics and oversimplified theologies, which often lead to polarization. Today's societies are in danger of being paralyzed by their polarization.

Jesus astounded the teachers and theologians of his time by defying the current categories in his lifestyle and teaching. His radical entrance into the subcultures of sinners and outcasts brought inside wisdom to outsiders. Today we seek a practical wisdom with that same radical boldness—for the sake of those oppressed or confused. We best help young people discover God's way by loving them, not by judging them. In so doing we bring back the central message of God to fractured cultures and individuals, whatever their situation.

Those who are not learning and growing are beginning to die. Learning demands humility and openness to challenge and change. Dogmatism is supported by egocentrism and ethnocentrism—a "me (or us) against them" mentality. Remember how Jesus brought a child into the presence of the contentious disciples (Mark 9:36). Being with the young enhances humility, vulnerability, and a learning spirit. The encouragement of such a spirit is one goal of this book.

THEOLOGY OF YOUTH MINISTRY

This book is not a theology of youth; it is *a theology* of youth *ministry*. No adult can claim an authentic youthful perspective on culture or God; only young people can. They are our experts on themselves and their constantly changing culture. As we listen to their music and conversations, whether they are religiously committed or not, we hear deep and dynamic stirrings of the human heart and of divine intentions. Cries of frustrated human beings often point to the divine ideal and intent. Adolescents may not be a religious lot, but they possess deep spirituality. High school and college students drift away from institutional religion, but they are concerned with matters of morality and ultimate meaning. Young people must give us their own theology of youth. From that we must faithfully attempt a theology of youth ministry.

This work is not a popular theology of culture. It does not seek its norms from popular consensus or from cravings for fulfillment or from easy "how to's." Its quest for truth begins in the mystery of the triune God and in God's revelation through creation, Christ, and Scripture. It does attempt new insights into popular culture from God's perspective—expecting to find relevancy and fresh challenges.

A theology of youth ministry or of popular culture does think about God's views and activity from within the youth culture and popular culture. In order to interact seriously with the dynamic popular and youth cultures today, leaders must be able to conceptualize about what they are doing— able to draw on the behavioral sciences and theology. Although youth leaders, teachers, and pastors do not need to be social scientists, they do need to be theologians.

You may not be a systematic, biblical, or historical theologian, but if you are reflecting seriously about God in your work you are already a practical or pastoral theologian. Your calling and work demand that you think carefully about

God in reference to human growth and cultural dynamics. You are constantly seeing God in the lives of young friends. From this observation should come a theology of popular culture and youth ministries.

Thinking about God's Word in a troubled world and considering what the gospel is saying to today's youth culture is theological reflection. To ask what God is about in John's or Maria's or Yung Lee's life is to do theology. As a youth minister you *are* a practical theologian. You have insights needed in theological circles, and you are in need of consultations with others in your field. This book is intended to aid you in your theologizing.

If Bob and Mary are living together, how can you minister to them while remaining true to biblical and church teaching? If Juan is caught up in a gang that demands the taking of human life, how do you approach him and his group regarding the basic worth of human life as expressed in the commandments? If Jennifer is addicted to television, obsessed with images of fashion magazines, or seems bordering on anorexia, what can you do to help her? I maintain that these are theological as well as sociological questions. This book is about such questions because that is what youth ministry is about.

OVERVIEW OF THEOLOGY AND MINISTRY

The following propositions lay out the theological overview of this book. Take time to consider what may be challenging and provocative statements about this theology of popular culture and youth ministry. Whether you agree or disagree, this exercise should at least help clarify various theological positions and ways of integrating theology and ministry.

Theological Setting

1. *Cultural Context:* We always do theology in a particular cultural situation. Christian theology is the interpre-

tation of the eternal Word or Son of God by particular persons in a particular cultural situation. That Word is forever established in heaven. In a way, the original manuscripts of the Bible represented a "translation" of heavenly, divine truth into a language of human culture. A main task of theology is to make divine revelation (the Bible and especially Jesus Christ) relevant and coherent to any particular age and society. To fulfill that task with regard to young people, we must learn a great deal about culture.

2. *Communal Dimension:* You cannot do relevant theology by yourself; theology is not a private affair. It is always, in some sense, a community effort arising from and influenced by particular cultural and religious needs. Divine revelation, the illumination of the Holy Spirit, human reason, the wisdom of the past, and interaction within the faith community are all involved in the theological task. Youth ministry is always community building, and youth leaders understand the value of doing things together.

Theological Style

3. *Compassionate:* Good theology flows from a heart of compassion. Theology defines how we can best minister to, or care for, human beings. Theology that tends to serve scholars, elevate the status of its practitioners, or divide the church not only damages rather than edifies the church but also fails to speak to the world outside. You cannot even start to do youth work without compassion. That is why good teachers and youth ministers have a bias toward tolerance and an applied and compassionate view of God's work in the world.

4. *Narrative:* Think of theology first of all as a story. Theology begins as narrative—it arises from the biblical story and prepares us for telling the great story, the good news. Theology gathers together the whole story of Scripture from Genesis to Revelation, from creation to eschatology. Theology always moves toward being told as story; the gospel is a proclamation and a sharing of our theology.

Theology, and therefore the gospel we proclaim, is an account of God's wonderful works. Theology ought then to be good news to those around us. An effective communicator to young people tells stories. Youth ministers, teachers, and preachers should recognize the priority of theology in narrative form. Our narratives and biblical stories must then be interpreted by propositions that come after or along with stories.

5. *Christocentric:* From our first to our final theological step—including all leaps of faith—we follow Jesus Christ. The good news was proclaimed most clearly and successfully in the incarnation of the Son of God (John 1:1-18). What the Law and the Prophets tried to convey was communicated most successfully by the Son of God (Deuteronomy 18:15-18; John 1:17). We need to understand how difficult it is for young people to clarify their personal identities in today's world and how critical relationships are to them. Then we will understand why our presentation of the faith must be Christocentric rather than bibliocentric or theocentric. Adolescent Christian spirituality should be centered not on an institution but on a relationship with Jesus Christ as Savior, Lord, and friend.

6. *God-Inspired:* Theology is a human activity; it is human reflection on God—especially God's wonderful works in our world. But it is attempted at God's initiative. Only those drawn toward God and only those who respond to God's gracious revelation can reflect on the divine nature and divine presence. The ultimate object of theology is unknowable in its fullness; God's definition and full essence must remain a mystery to the human mind. Theologians ought to be humble people; they ought to realize they do not know much about their divine subject. Sometimes they forget this. Being with young people can remind us of how much we do not know.

7. *Incarnational Model:* Jesus Christ is our model. As Christ left heavenly status and security to enter human life and a particular human culture, our Lord has sent all Chris-

tians (incarnationally) into specific cultures. ("As the Father has sent me, even so I send you," John 20:21, RSV.) Youth ministry takes its model from the incarnation in a special way. It must continually reflect on the radical demands of cultural immersion and relational sacrifices. Those who want to enter the youth culture and communicate with young hearts should carefully study the model of Christ's incarnational ministry (as in Philippians 2:5ff. and John 4:4ff.). Such incarnational theology affirms the primacy of the Father (as articulated by Jesus), the power of the Holy Spirit, and the centrality of the cross. These doctrines are heightened as we fully appreciate the incarnation of our Lord.

Theological Process

8. *Theology and Ministry:* As you serve Christ in young people, you will understand your Lord better; you will grow theologically. Theology has traditionally been seen as informing ministry. But for a growing number of theologians—especially from the two-thirds world—ministry precedes systematic theology. The apostles set out to follow what they had seen and learned from Christ. Theirs, at first, was a very rudimentary biblical theology. They were doing theology before they sat down to reflect (and be inspired) to write letters back to their churches. The creeds would come later. Throughout the world, the gospel is received into a given situation, the Spirit builds the church, and the community considers the nature of God's working in their culture. Over decades in youth ministry many of us have found application coming before or along with exegesis and practice preceding reflection. Some theologians become comfortable and do not want to continue the effort and risks involved in doing theology for each generation and place, and traditionalists may take offense at what sounds like a radical departure from customary theological methodology. But there is historical precedent for theology stemming from ministry.

9. *Interdependence:* Theologians need one another. We should humbly work together. Theology is done as biblical theology, historical theology, systematic theology, and pastoral or practical theology. The last draws heavily on the behavioral sciences and pastoral situations in contextualizing the Christian faith into the life of specific cultures. The great challenge of theology should create a need for greater interdependence among theologians than is the case at most theological institutions. Systematic theologians need to hear much more from practical theologians. Practical theologians should turn to biblical, historical, and systematic theologians. We all need input, balance, and correction to fulfill our particular tasks. Understanding teenagers, popular culture, and the Word of God is too great a task for any of us. To keep a divine balance, we must learn from each other's particular areas of expertise.

The complexity of our world and the theological task demand special interdependence among theologians of different genders, races, and places. Male and female; young and old; black, brown, and white; rich and poor; and those of northern and southern hemispheres should be talking and working together. All have unique perspectives on creation, rebellion, reconciliation—the great truths. None of us can afford to be unaware of the perspectives of those from other classes, races, genders, or ages. Our mutuality is one of our greatest witnesses to the world: "they will know we are Christians by our love." Most young people—even those in cliques or gangs—have a great desire for coming together. This is especially true among Christians.

Theological Integrity

10. *Test of Authenticity:* Most Christians judge the orthodoxy of theologies by their faithfulness to Scripture and to church creeds. Among the Orthodox, Roman Catholic, and Protestant communions are several varieties of more or less orthodox theologies. Youth leaders around the world, working with young people from all sorts of religious back-

grounds, insist on an appreciation of various perspectives as long as they are within what we might call "historic orthodoxy": Any theology not accepting scriptural authority and the centrality of the cross as the place where the unique Son of God died for our sins lacks the proper foundation for youth ministry. Any weakening of the blessed Trinity and the power of the Holy Spirit is likewise unacceptable. Church, tradition, Scripture, the incarnation, the cross, and the Holy Spirit—none of these can be slighted.

Nonetheless, the acid test of relevancy for any given theology lies in the way it is lived out by mission communities—how a biblical theology is done by a particular community of faith. An orthodox theology may become racist, materialistic, sexist, or egotistical. There may be truth in such a theology, but it is not good theology. Theologies may be judged, as Christians may be, by their fruits.

11. *Holistic Exegesis:* It follows (especially from a Christocentric theological style, number five above) that theologians ought to understand the importance of three kinds of exegesis or interpretation necessary to the theological task:

- the exegesis of Scripture (faithfulness to the Word of God),
- the exegesis of (youth) culture (relevance and sensitivity to the world),
- the exegesis of self and community (awareness of self).

We who theologize from the standpoint of youth are especially aware that such a threefold process of interpretation will make application holistic. In this way we can seek to address all of youth's needs—physical, emotional, academic, social, spiritual.

12. *Faithful Hermeneutics:* Faithful interpretation of Scripture means, among other things, an understanding of the original languages, the intent of the author, the context (the relation of any part of the Bible to the whole of Scripture), and the application of the text in history and in today's world. In this sense we must all be biblical, historical, systematic, and practical theologians—though not

necessarily scholars! Faithful hermeneutics must be followed by careful exegesis of the text and application of it into real life. Faithful hermeneutics accepts the biblical emphases on the corporate or systemic as well as the individual, on social justice as well as personal salvation and piety, on works as well as faith. Faithful interpretation of the Bible finds and emphasizes the unity, balance, and practicality of Scripture for all faith and practice. Youth leaders emphasize that the laity, that young people, can understand Scripture and theology. All are needed in our common endeavor.

Theological Perspectives

13. *Personal Stories:* Youth ministry may be seen as providing young people with a safe place with caring mentors where personal stories can be told and seen in perspective of the great story. Youth leaders should grow in appreciation of their own life stories. The interpretation of self means an awareness of our personal values. It involves an understanding of our personal histories and identities. This process should help us acknowledge the personal baggage we bring to our theological task. It also means we are maturing in our ability to help others think about themselves and grow. We are saved from self-centeredness by acknowledging theology to be a community enterprise. A recognition of "our community" is essential. Theology brings an appreciation of *God's story* as it intersects *our story* and makes sense of *my story.* For instance, since our stories arise from our experience in communities, gender and ethnicity are important elements in the theological process. Those in the human community who feel marginalized by gender or ethnicity will be very sensitive to the cultural origin of any theology and will want their theology to speak specifically to their human condition.

14. *Critical Perspectives:* Not enough has been made of theological location. It makes a great deal of difference whether you are writing theology uptown or downtown, in an ivory tower or from a storefront theological center. All

theologians bring their own personal and cultural histories to their tasks. They do their theology in terms of particular cultural concerns because they are writing out of specific cultural milieus. The perspective and agendas of feminist, black, and liberation theologies are quite clear and well known. The perspectives and agenda of male, white, and European theologies, however, are more subtlely concealed. European white males sometimes deny the cultural bias of their theologies. (While many discuss "black theology," people rarely refer to "white theology.") It is always the responsibility of Christians, particularly those in privileged places, to take the initiative of meeting Christ in those who are different and to learn from them. Men must listen to women; whites to blacks; older to younger, West to East, and North to South—and the other way around as well.

15. *Socioeconomics of Community:* In addition to ethnicity, culture, and gender, class also enters into the theological perpsective. Our interpretation of community means that we know where we come from and how our socio-economic station affects all we do. In many European countries class divides people more than race does. Those who drive nice cars down a freeway have a different perspective from those who live in the neighborhoods divided by that freeway. In a sense economics rules our world. The financial bottom line has incredible power—even in Christian organizations and churches. We must recognize how class, economics, and institutional pressures affect the theological community.

16. *Deeper Insight:* Our interpretation of self leads further to a critical interpretation of the cultures that grow and shape the self. In sharing personal insights with young people, we gain greater wisdom for our theological task. We understand that God made us with basic needs to survive and grow, to produce and reproduce. God made us to find significance in our existence and relationships with others. Ultimately, we all crave union (love) and significance (worth). These themes are important both in Scripture and

in popular culture. Each young person possesses a critical need to love and be loved, to achieve, to serve, and to be affirmed. Effective family and youth ministries are meant to provide opportunities to have these needs met.

Theology of Christian Care

17. *Human Needs and Family:* As we consider human needs theologically, we realize that God has created human beings as needful creatures. God is the great parent and shepherd who provides for our basic needs and who would give love and significance to all. Such images and emphases occupy a great deal of Scripture. They provide theological understanding and impetus for youth ministry. In the case of a newborn child, God gives to parents the divine (godly) responsibility of nurturing the child. Fathers and mothers are to provide for the child's security and growth. With love and discipline they are to encourage the child's sense of worth and emerging responsibility. The love and affirmation given children offer a foundation for a lifetime of growth and development. That foundation has never been more important than it is today, yet the family itself has never been under greater stress. Thus youth ministry must give new attention to creative interaction with, and service to, the family.

18. *Socialization and Nurture:* Family life does not take place in a social vacuum. Many other systems contribute to the socialization of the child, and society may help or hinder parents' ability to raise their children with dignity and real possibilities for adult success. The Creator gave responsibility for raising children to parents; God also holds society's leaders responsible for making life fair for all. It is a serious matter when politicians and business leaders fail poor children. What is our theological position if citizens vote for an anti- immigration bill that punishes innocent children rather than their parents (who brought them in) or employers (who need cheap labor)? In deciding, we must remember God's anger toward those who hinder the

growth of children or undermine the basic dignity of all. No faithful reading of the Bible can miss its emphasis on righteousness and justice. Youth ministers are called to intervene, to be advocates, to reflect theologically, and to shape future ministers as faithful prophets and pastors.

19. *Ministry of Christian Care and Empowerment:* We understand theologically that God made us needy creatures. As parents and leaders we find ourselves placed by God—in the very place of God—ministering to those in need. The biblical model is that of the good shepherd. False shepherds angered God because they did not minister faithfully to the needs of people. Ministering to youth today involves the awesome responsibility of picking up slack left by parental and social failures. In a sense youth ministers assume some of the godly role of parents, of teachers, even of social leaders. Youth ministers are adult role models in a young person's growth process. This process often demands deep healing before adult development can come. Compassion these days demands the skills of helping professions. Beyond relating, teaching, and proclaiming, youth ministers are on the side of liberation and healing in order to bring about empowerment and service.

YOUTH MINISTERS: LISTENERS, LEARNERS, INTERVENERS, PASTORS, AND ETHICISTS

Sound theology should lead to positive ministry. Our theology and ministry ought to be true to Scripture, faithful to our Christian traditions, and relevant in our current situations. No theology confined to an ivory tower can be relevant. You are seeking a theology that is true to God, faithful to your Christian community, and relevant to the times—especially to the young people you serve. You and your colleagues will be working out a practical theology as you function as missionaries, social workers, and pastors. Here are some characteristics of these functions.

Listeners and Learners

Compassion for young people soon leads to a deep sense of awe toward God's creation of an individual *and* toward the dynamic youth culture. We begin by using two ears before opening our one mouth. We need help from young people! The missiological aspect of youth ministry requires that we be students of the culture. We recognize culture as being created, judged, and redeemed by God. That means we acknowledge what is positive and what is negative in all cultures. As youth ministers we look, with young people, for the positive and negative in pop music, television, movies, magazines, commercials, clothes, adolescent humor and behaviors—as well as in the larger economic and political systems that shape our lives. Where is a postmodern, post-Christian youth culture to find moral authority in pluralistic and secular societies? You will build an answer to that critical question as you read on and struggle with complex and often conflicting issues.

Interveners

In the midst of a confusing world, young people struggle to find their own identities, to develop relationships, and to establish lives for themselves. They move from a family of origin to a family of transition (their friends or peer groups) to a family of creation (their lives as a couple or as parents). They thus move from being parented, to parenting themselves (a sign of adulthood), to parenting others. The task of parenting oneself is not simple. Still, the nurturing of oneself, the giving of love and significance to self, is necessary for a whole, full life. Where families and the larger community have failed young folk, many young people find it easier to accept substitute nurturers such as celebrity figures, or to rely on sex, food, or drugs. Your wise and appropriate intervention in helping young people to develop socially can be critical. On what principles do you counsel and how do you step into the life of a young person?

Pastors and Ethicists

How can a generation programmed to act out individual indulgence, violence, and sexual promiscuity move back to responsible behavior and regard for the common good? How can young people make good choices when they seem to have no good options? Our society provides many false answers to these questions. Your ministry can provide a safe place during a confusing transition to a complex adult society.

The challenge to be listeners, learners, interveners, pastors, and ethicists may appear overwhelming to an already overburdened youth minister. But understanding can relieve hidden anxieties, render help in setting clearer goals, and provide youth workers with needed affirmation. You are called to be a theologian in a supportive, theological community. If you fail to understand your task and its professional foundation you will feel drained, but theological insights are invigorating. This book is intended to provide an antidote for burnout and to help you grow personally and professionally. Its theology is meant to encourage a ministry that is truthful, faithful, and relevant.

INTRODUCTION TO A THEOLOGY OF YOUTH MINISTRY

Theology from a Practical Perspective

The destiny of any nation, at any given time, depends on the opinions of its young men and women under twenty-five years of age.

—*Source unknown*

Where there is no vision, the people perish.

—*Proverbs 29:18,* KJV

And it will come about . . . That I will pour out My Spirit on all mankind; And your sons and daughters will prophesy, Your old men will dream dreams, Your young men will see visions.

—*Joel 2:28,* NASB

Where in the world is God? If God's glory is not fully expressed by any denomination or Christian communion, if the teaching of Christ is not at the heart and core of the our political platforms, if no ethnic tradition captures the fullness of the divine intention, and if no theology has all the answers, then how are we to know God? What is God about these days?

Many are looking—and still have not found what they're looking for. The cries and longings of people today reveal a church-wide as well as a society-wide crisis. The problem involves a youth crisis and a crisis of adult leadership. In a world of indifference and cynicism, among those who are dogmatic and polarized, we need to know where God is and what Christ is doing. Articles and books have been written about these critical times. Those who care for young lives are especially aware that we are in a crisis. But beyond praying for revival (which our world and churches certainly need), how are we to think and what ought we to do? And how are we to sense what God thinks and is doing? John Wiley Nelson once wrote an important book with a long title: *Your God Is Alive and Well and Appearing in Popular Culture.*[1] That assertion is a premise of this book: God is in this world overruling distinctions between secular and Christian, conservative and liberal, old and young. And we have to find out what God is doing.

THE SPECIAL PLACE OF THE YOUNG

The young and the impressionable are close to the heart of God. The poorest and most vulnerable among children are special targets of divine concern. Jesus made this point clear several times in his ministry (Mark 10:13-16). His amazingly strong statement about anyone who leads a child astray further illustrates and reinforces this truth (Mark 9:42). Jesus' selection of some relatively young people to be the leaders of his church points to his trust in youthful potential.

God is the Creator of all young lives. God watches over the development of these lives and cares about their futures. The Creator who made human beings so needy and (inter-)dependent has given shepherding responsibilities to all caregivers of children and youth. It is the Creator who has placed in young hearts the powerful needs for relationships, justice, and a quest for truth. Excitement about their lives and quests must be understood theologically. This chapter is an introduction to this theology. It calls for serious thinking and great effort.

THE CHALLENGE OF MINISTERING TO YOUNG PEOPLE

Around the world today concerned adults want to be more effective in encouraging and guiding young people. In

---

[1] Philadelphia: Westminster, 1976.

the Philippines, Australia, Kenya, South Africa, Great Britain, Russia, Costa Rica, Canada, the United States, and elsewhere, rapid changes are taking place among young people and in the popular (or pop) culture. Those who care about youth are coming together in an unprecedented way, forming networks, and asking for resources that will make them more effective in their work. This book is about new and exciting theological reflections coming to those who serve the young. We will first consider the challenge of youth in a changing world, and then we will think about the theological task of reaching young people more effectively.

The challenge of youth ministry involves an estimated one billion teenagers (thirteen to nineteen years of age) in the world today, an astonishing 25 percent of the global population (more than half the population of the second and third worlds is under eighteen years of age). Much of the international pop culture and media is driven by the young. Pop culture and the revolution in world communications are bringing all cultures closer and closer together.

The challenge of youth ministry involves the suffering of children. The question will continue to be raised: Where is God when a child cries out while being sexually abused? According to the United Nations, two million children have died in war over the last ten years.[2] Many more have suffered crippling injuries. An estimated one hundred million active land mines, some insidiously disguised as toys, make this world a dangerous place for children. No statistics can tell the extent of infant neglect and child abuse. Millions of children are today being kept as slaves, toiling in forced labor, or forced into prostitution. Worldwide, children and their parents suffer from natural catastrophes, epidemics, terrorism, and social upheavals. Their loss is the world's loss; those who survive will take possession and leadership of the world. God knows the loss and the potential of childhood better than anyone.

---

[2] UNICEF, *State of the World's Children* (New York: UNICEF, 1995).

Youth are not only our hope for the future; they are a key to present development. They are always either a great liability (in terms of criminal justice costs, remediation, etc.) or an asset to any society. Around the world young people have, in recent times, precipitated significant political changes. Where an adult generation had given up in South Africa, in the Middle East, in China, and in Eastern Europe, young adults and sometimes children came forward as prophets, revolutionaries, and even warriors. Where there is significant social, political, and even economic change, young people are often in the forefront.

In terms of world missions, young people form the largest, most crucial, and most dynamic "unreached people group" in the world. In terms of national prosperity, youth are the work force and leadership of the near future.

For all their present and future importance, young people are not well served. Family systems, town and school systems, even national systems and churches can all benefit from the dreams and aspirations of youth—if they would only listen to what young people are feeling and saying! Young people the world over are being told things adults think they ought to know. But what teenagers want most are adults who will help them discover and use the truth and skills they really need for life.

The primary tasks of young people or adolescents are not serving the church or youth group—though such may become one goal in their busy lives. The life tasks of young people begin with clarifying their personal identities, developing significant relationships, and participating in the world about them. We must begin, therefore, by looking at how young people are being socialized in our various cultures. For example:

- Suicide is a problem among youth internationally, with the problem being most severe in the following nations:[3]

---

[3] United Nations Children's Fund, *Progress of Nations* (New York: UNICEF, 1994).

New Zealand	15.7 per 100,000
Finland	15.0 per 100,000
Canada	13.5 per 100,000
Norway	13.4 per 100,000
United States	11.1 per 100,000

- The FBI reports a striking number of juvenile homicides:[4]

  7-12 years of age—120 homicides
  13-16 years of age—944 homicides
  17-19 years of age—2,308 homicides

- Well over a million teenage girls become pregnant each year in the United States. According to the *Statistical Abstract,* twenty-seven thousand girls under fifteen and 938,000 from fifteen to nineteen became pregnant in 1991.[5]

Such statistics indicate that social systems are not doing well in promoting growth and welfare. Those closest to young people see many more indicators of pain and rage. Malevolent intention could hardly construct more efficient programs to turn human beings toward antisocial behavior than the mixed messages and frustrations that family, media, schools, or friends present to many children. The prenatal damage done by crack or alcohol to babies, rampant child neglect and abuse from the initial figures of trust in a child's world, the contradictory messages from each system meant to socialize our young, and the media's encouragement to engage in premature sex and senseless violence—all these factors are far more the fault of adult systems than of delinquent juveniles.

THE NEED FOR APPRECIATION OF THE YOUTH WORKER

Such a world of the young calls for role models with special understanding and skills. These adult leaders must

---

[4] United States Department of Justice, *Unified Crime Report* (Washington, D.C.: US Government Printing Office, 1994).

[5] United States Department of Commerce, *Statistical Abstract* (Washington, D.C.: US Government Printing Office, 1992).

give stronger attention and support to family and neighborhood systems than ever before. Parents need to see beyond
the home situation and school report cards. Teachers must be
interested in more than their own subject. Youth ministers
cannot attend only to traditional youth groups. More than
ever, today's youth ministers must function first as missionaries, then as social workers, and finally as pastors. Furthermore, these professional roles are effective only if youth
ministers have proved themselves as real friends of particular individuals *and* groups. Communities and churches
need to see youth leaders as critical bridges to youth culture.

If youth workers are not to burn out in the process,
they need to reflect on the nature of their friendship with
young people from a biblical point of view. Burnout comes
from unrewarding and unfruitful labor. Youth leaders need
network support, ongoing training, opportunities to expand professionally and to train others as antidotes to
burnout. As youth ministers grow professionally, it is critical that they reflect theologically about themselves and
their task. Too few conferences and books have provided
the challenge to do this theological reflection.

Since church and society do not give a great deal of
respect or reward to youth leaders, they themselves must
possess a deep sense of their own worth and the value of
the theological reflections that flow from the grass roots of
youth work. Youth ministers often feel somewhere near the
lowest rungs of pastoral ministry and the ecclesiastical
hierarchy. Isn't youth ministry commonly considered to be
a starting point or stepping-stone to real, grown-up, fully
professional ministry? Along with new sensitivity toward
the young, we—parents, teachers, counselors, and youth
leaders—must have a new appreciation for those who serve
the emerging generation.

THE NEED FOR NEW THEOLOGICAL PERSPECTIVES

What can those who minister to youth possibly have to
offer the church's theological endeavor? Aren't youth lead-

ers too busy with young people and too unsophisticated in their thinking to bother about theology? Aren't they relational people with little interest in theory?

Some theologians have declared, and most of us would agree, that all Christians are theologians, that we must all see our Christian lives theologically—as God's work and the embodiment of God's truth in the world. Theologians do not construct their theological systems in cultural or social vacuums. Their work always reflects the spirit of the times, the issues of an age, and the cries or questions of a particular people. The cries of young people today are for acceptance, belonging, security, love, and justice. Theology must be seen, to some degree, as social history, a family affair, and a community's reflections. Because the challenge of growing a new generation is so great, the whole community of believers is needed to make sense of it all.

When we approach the study of those who are weak or hurting, oppressed or in need—or just misunderstood—we approach holy ground. We are moving to the place neglected by the powers of this world but where God is specially at work. Adolescence is often confusing and painful. We must theologize about this critical transition in human existence, and we should listen to theological questions and issues raised by adolescents themselves. We approach God's Word to the world from the perspective of children and youth who are sometimes in crisis or confusion. Inundated by stories and conflicting messages, they need and long for the true story.

STATIC AND DYNAMIC THEOLOGIES

Is theological reflection about young people and the youth culture merely the application of a theology codified in the sixteenth century or is it the arena in which exciting theology is now being done? We can think of the principles of youth ministry as an aftermath or appendix to our theological system, or we can do theology from within the youth culture. Some seminarians spend three or more years getting a theological education from the perspective of library shelves and then go out to apply it to various pastoral ministries—youth ministry probably last of all. To view adolescent development in terms of psychological principles somehow informed by the truth of theology would be like building a computer and then asking God's blessing on the new technology. To discover theology through biblical reflections on adolescent development, however, to begin with a passionate understanding of adolescent development as divine creation and providence; that would be like building computers prayerfully as partners in God's creative process. The latter perspective approaches theology as an interdisciplinary task—theology and social sciences working hand in hand.

To watch a baby or to tend a garden is to appreciate growth. Theology of growth is stimulated by this appreciation and by praying through the biblical stories of growth. A theology of growth involves experience with youthful growing and, negatively, watching society stunt that growth. As observers of human growth and students of the Scriptures, we find solemn principles as to the nature, significance, and responsibility for human maturation. The dynamism and complexity of it all can be missed by theologians and students locked up by academic pressures; it is the challenge of a theology of youth ministry.

A narrow theological perspective sees our life in the world merely as a stage for an eternal decision. Some Christians and theologians are so wrapped up in the issues of conversion and their own (personal and institutional) survival that they miss the bigger picture of what is happening in the whole world. The corrective for narrow theology, in my own and many other lives, has been urban and global experiences. Cross-cultural involvement challenges previous biases and securities. Narrow and parochial boundaries are broken down. Such urban and global Christians find themselves working on common ground despite denominational and creedal differences. Similarly, they are able to collaborate for peace and justice with secularists and those of other religions. Today's demand for a new global responsibility needs Christians with global perspective who are able to look beyond their own communities.

Still, some Christians are retreating, drawing the wagons into a tight circle for protection against worldly attack. Isolated communities make for a narrow theology. Narrow theologies pay little attention to the world outside the walls of their faith community. They give little notice to those who "although they have no law, . . . are their own law, for they display the effect of the law inscribed on their hearts" (Romans 2:14-15, NEB). They have little sense of needing to learn from the secular world and receiving the kindness from those such as "the natives [of Malta, who, according to the writer of Acts,] showed us extraordinary hospitality; they lit a fire and welcomed all of us because it had begun to rain and was cold" (Acts 28:2, NAB). Nor do they appreciate God's surprising anointing of the pagan Cyruses of this world (Isaiah 45:1).

Narrow theologies are often intracultural and see little need to move beyond their own safe and comfortable compound. According to Erik Erikson:

> Man as a species has survived by being divided into what I have called *pseudospecies*. First each horde or tribe, class and nation, but then also every religious association has become *the* human species, considering all the others a freakish and gratuitous invention of some irrelevant deity. To reinforce the illusion of being chosen, every tribe recognizes a creation of its own, a mythology and later a history.[6]

"Tribal theology" is comfortable as long as it stays within the species. It tends to be closed to the larger community. It talks to itself and at the larger world. It does not understand the need and practice of dialogue. It thus becomes dysfunctional in the larger world. "Tribal theology" becomes a scandal and offense for many outside the faith. Theology must be broad and relevant enough to reach into every pseudospecies of human culture, but also then

---

[6] *Identity, Youth, and Crisis* (New York: Norton, 1968) 41.

able to speak to specific issues. Theology begins with God's perspective and work; it continues with our translation and application. Sensitive young people in particular demand this emphasis and breadth. Theology provides the only means by which human beings can find their true identity, be liberated from false divisions, and attain the universal longings of the human heart.

Narrow theologies can miss the balance displayed in a theological process that moves from theory to *praxis* as well as *praxis* to theory. *Praxis* is the exercise of theology and obedience, and it implies reflection. In narrow theology we often see a strictly cognitive endeavor moving from propositions to application and practice. That systematic theology needs practical theology, that thinking needs prior doing for contextualization and relevance, is often missed. There can be a greater balance of propositions, images, stories, feeling, practice, and reflection in broader theologies.

Broader theologies do not rest in dogmatic complacency nor are they adrift in uncertainty. They trust the Word of God in Scripture and in the living Christ; they accept change and the "relativities" of life trusting in the sovereignty of God and the amazing power of God's Spirit. Rooted in God's certainty, they are able to deal with the ambivalence and ambiguities of life.

Jesus knew the human situations of his time, and during storms or around a death he would say something like: "Fear not . . . believe in me." Sustained by personal and institutional faith in Christ, broad orthodox theologies should be secure enough to venture out into the heavy seas of human crises and ideological conflicts, not tied to land or to the security of a theological ship. The context of theology—and this is especially true as we watch God at work in youth culture—is not just a serene sea but is troubled water as well. We should be willing to be there with Jesus without fully understanding the storm or the working of divine grace.

Unless we have a keen sense of the context of the audience with and for whom we do theology, we will miss some of the cultural context of Scripture and of Jesus Christ. As Christopher Sugden has cautioned: "The goal of interpreting the Bible is to find the meaning of the Scriptures for our obedience in our context. . . . In order to have meaning and power for every situation, Scripture must have meaning in each situation."[7]

Narrower and broader Christian perspectives are distinguished by the questions they ask, by the fears and dreams that drive them, and by the emphasis they give to various doctrines. Is human life summed up merely in terms of its response to the Christian message, or is it meant to express God's creativity in various earthly forms? Do we find a quest for the divine in all cultures—whether the divine impulse is understood as such or not? Does Christian responsibility include helping all people become better persons, in addition to encouraging a specific faith commitment?

The broader view does not deny the critical nature of a personal salvific decision, but it also sees in all human existence a quest for cosmic union and significance—by God's grace or in opposition to that loving intent. From this standpoint, all life is acceptance or rejection of God's creative and redemptive purposes. The world and its culture cannot be lightly denounced or dismissed. All serious considerations of our lives, music, television, advertising, families, and politics should move to the ultimate *Why,* which is theological. It is the ultimate question of ends, the question that the secular world seeks to avoid. For the powers of this world (financial, political, military), the means of profits and power have become their ends. Freeing themselves from the authority of God's Word and law, they become slaves to their own ends, a tyranny of deified means.

A Theological Ear to Our Cultural Ground

Every youthful quest for truth (whether at a youth group, the movies, or listening to rap) is a theological

---

[7] *Radical Discipleship* (London: Marshalls, 1981) 143.

question. To ask why is human; theology directs us to the source of all meaning. Children ask the basic questions, adolescents ask the difficult and ultimate questions, and adults get tired of questions. Some may object to the notion of a theology of youth ministry, theology from the perspective of those who work with adolescents: "Theology is theology, period." These may smile at our endeavor and sigh, "What next?" Objectors to a theology of youth ministry may also dismiss, out of hand, African-American theologies, Asian theologies, liberation theologies, and feminist theologies.

Those who dismiss a theology of youth ministry may also forget that historic theologies emerged from the cultural crises of their own days. Roman dominance and persecutions inspired the apostles and early church fathers. Those who fled the worldliness and compromise of Christianity as the state religion produced a spirituality and theology of the desert. The medieval situation allowed for a great Christian synthesis. Issues of commerce and nationalism, along with a new spirit of academic independence and spiritual renewal, were all contributing factors in the theologies of the Reformation.

It is impossible to exclude social history from a study of any theology, whether Puritan theology or the theologies of liberation in the Americas. Puritan hopes for a final realization of the kingdom of God were mixed with disdain for the church and society in the Old World and a desire for a better life in the New. Liberation theologians are part of the drama of decolonization and development. They have also pointed out ethnocentric, personal, or even professional values that subtly influence Western scholars.

Today's youth culture presents another social crisis. Those who would dare to theologize about today's youth scene will provide the Christian church with new emphases—lessons fascinating and instructive for societies entering the twenty-first century. It is vital that you who are with young people on urban streets, in suburban malls, or in rural towns have your voices heard in this theological endeavor.

To understand the world of youth is to feel the cutting edge of cultural change. Each new kind of music, new genre of movie, new fad, and new advertising pitch is a challenge to those who would understand the beauties and pitfalls of our culture and the ups and downs of adolescent years. To do theology in youth culture forces one to be in touch with the spirit of the age and the trends of the times. Questions raised by each twist of contemporary history must be taken to the faithful truth of Scripture. Fidelity to Scripture and creeds, relevance to the times, and integrity of self are the threefold responsibilities of Christian theology.

Theology is done in various cultural contexts; cultures raise the questions and suggest the needed styles. American individualism and European dichotomies have led many Western theologians to separate the Old and New Testaments, the individual and community, the material and spiritual, the culture and salvation in a way never intended by the Hebrew mind or the biblical spirit. To reach urban, suburban, and rural young people today requires a holistic gospel, relevant for a wide range of human pain and needs.

In Jesus, the individual and corporate entities, the material world and spiritual realities, the culture and salvation meet. As the central focus of the Old and New Testaments, Christ cannot be understood except as the incarnation of God into our human culture.

If Christian theology is taught and preached in its intended wholeness—if we understand that God's heart is set on the salvation and fulfillment of every young life—it can speak to both secular audiences and people of faith. Our Creator and final Judge asks church and society to promote individual growth, expects society to encourage youthful faith and freedom of religion (Acts 17:24, 26-27), and commands the church to help citizens serve the state in a godly manner. Such theology teaches the glory of the Creator and creation along with a powerful sense of sinful depravity and redemptive power. The power of the cross is required for the healing and transformation of both individuals and social systems.

Our theological effort starts with a questioning human being, takes place in a particular cultural setting, and points in the critical direction (to God). The one who does theology—and this is particularly evident in theological reflection from the perspective of young people—must do a threefold exegesis: an exegesis of the Word, an exegesis of the culture, and an exegesis of self and the community. Some theologians deny gender and ethnic bias. Other theologians are obsessed and controlled by certain social issues. Both groups may be blind to the extent that their autobiographies influence their theological emphases. Therefore the emphasis on exegeting Word, world, and self is needed in current theological dialogue.

THEOLOGICAL TOLERANCE

Today's youth leaders minister among a great variety of theologies and serve young people from diverse traditions. A youth rally or camp may include people from Orthodox, Catholic, Reformed, Pentecostal, Zionist, Wesleyan, Anabaptist, Dispensational, and other faith traditions. Theologians of these persuasions all argue the historicity and legitimacy of their systematic understanding of the faith. Those who minister across the lines of the various faith communions recognize important emphases and contributions to the work of systematic theology from each tradition. It is possible to encourage the faith tradition in all young people we serve if we appreciate all theological perspectives and maintain a critical eye on the human and cultural limitations of each.

As any particular stream of theology becomes enculturated or ingrown, it may gradually miss or distort the dynamic truth of the gospel. In early modern times European nationalists came to resent the imperial bias and institutional accretions of medieval theology. In this century African-American pastors began to sense how inadequately Anglo theologies spoke to their oppressed condition. Christian leaders around the globe continue to remind European theologians about the need for indigenous thinking.

EMPHASES IN A THEOLOGY OF POPULAR AND YOUTH CULTURES

How can we sum up the unique contributions of doing theology within the youth culture? What do the challenges of global theological dialogue have to do with youth ministry? What possible contributions do faithful youth leaders bring to theological reflection? Some theological principles arise out of reflection on these questions.

- There is a need for a theology of growth and development.
- There is a need to increase our sensitivity regarding the egocentric and ethnocentric influences in all systems of theology.
- There is a need to assert the necessity for a threefold interpretation: the exegesis of Word, world, and self in community.
- There is a need to reaffirm the personal and christocentric nature of ministry and the gospel.
- There is a need for a balance between individual and community, between relational spirituality and social justice issues.
- There is a need for new theological reflections on prophetic cultural analysis.

In developing a theology of Christian care for the young, we must search for clarity on several issues.

- We must understand how young people grow up in youth and dominant cultures and youth subcultures.
- We must formulate a Christian perspective on pop, youth, and dominant cultures.
- We must develop an understanding of service for and with youth.
- We must grow in an appreciation for the youth ministries profession.

We proceed on this critical task by investigating:

* the Bible,
* the behavioral or social sciences,
* various traditions of theologies,
* various subcultures of youth.

THE SPIRIT OF THEOLOGY AMONG YOUTH

A valid theology of youth ministry must proceed with constant input from the behavioral sciences as well as from biblical scholarship. Historians, ethicists, Christian educators, practical theologians in other fields (pastoral counseling), and systematic theologians are all needed to produce holistic and relevant theology. What is written here will be useful if it promotes honest interdependence among academicians in theological studies and youth ministers at the grass roots. The effort will be worthless if it does not liberate, encourage, and empower young people themselves.

God loves young people. By nature they are making fresh discoveries about what it means to be created in culture, what it means to be a unique individual, how to relate in their own way, to give and receive, to feel unfairness, to yearn for perfection, to decide. These are awesome theological matters.

Theology from an adolescent perspective does not know it all; it realizes that it knows very little. The heart of such theology is knowing Jesus so that we may better know youth—which leads to better knowing ourselves. As we seek to be faithful theologians in the service of young people, we will always be a bit behind the rapidly changing youth culture. Humbly, we continue to learn from them and return to the Word of God so that the gospel and our ministry may be as relevant as possible. Above all, we seek to understand how God is loving young people in our times and how Jesus would move through the crowd today.

QUESTIONS FOR REFLECTION AND DISCUSSION

1. Do you consider yourself a theologian? If so, how would you describe yourself as a theologian?
2. Do you see the divisions of theology as biblical, historical, systematic, and practical (and pastoral)? What kind of theologian would a professor of youth ministry be?
3. Do relationships with young people, their culture, and their leaders provide anything unique to theological discussion? What would you suggest as examples?
4. Do you agree that the ideas presented here (pp. 6–16) are examples of contributions youth ministries can make to the theological establishment?
5. What is the place for theological reflection on your ministry with young people? What might be a danger of not reflecting in this way, and the benefit of doing so?
6. With whom are you able to do such theological reflection?

2 CONTEXTUALIZING THEOLOGY

Doing Theology on Young People's Turf

The true light ... was coming into (our) world. . . . the Word became flesh and lived (intimately) among us.
—John 1:9, 14, NRSV, *author's additions*

How can you, a Jewish man, ask me for a drink?
—John 4:9, *author's paraphrase*

You shall be . . . in Jerusalem, in all Judea, in Samaria, and in all the ends of the earth.
—Acts 1:8, *author's paraphrase*

Contextualization is an overexpressed and underused theological term. Context is crucial to the theological task in two related ways. First, it points to the mission of the church and of theology. Every missionary movement and each church must interpret its own "Jerusalem, Judea, Samaria, and ends of the earth" (Acts 1:8). Theology needs a target and moves toward larger contexts. Second, good theology ought to be formulated out of a particular context; it needs to be based in mission and praxis. The term *praxis* connotes ministry plus theological reflection. Practical theology is built on the rock of the Word and on the clay of a culture. (Yes, it always includes the human element, as we will continue to see.) It moves from obedience to the Great Commission in ministry, to scholarly reflection, and back to praxis in a continuing process.

The context for us is the dynamic world of young people. Some of us were trained in one or another school of theology. We followed its implications out into the youth culture—in suburban, rural, and urban situations. There, dramatically, we realized how our theologies did not have all the answers—did not even raise some of the right questions. We looked back at the indexes of our old theology texts and found no references to suffering, the poor, or women among the pages on decrees and predestination. On urban streets or in rural towns around the world we began thinking in new theological terms. The challenge of new contexts brings theological growth and maturity.

Theology as a Translation and a Presence

Theology is a work of translation: the wisdom of God must be translated into a given culture in a particular time and place. "Inspiration" describes the initial work of translating the word of God into human languages, those of Hebrew, Aramean, and Greek cultures. But further translations—into tribal and technological societies—are needed. The Word must be encountered, in flesh and in word, in each new culture. A living witness, a written Word, and a contextualized theology are the results. Theology must be understood in terms of relationships, communication, and presence; young people have taught us this. They remain mostly unconvinced by the classic arguments for the existence of God; they understand God's existence as they hear stories of Jesus, watch how he relates to people, see the relationship of love to communication, and experience the presence of God in the lives of friends.

To be heard, the Word must come into the world of young people. Presence precedes preaching, and listening precedes speaking. A hundred preachers will fail to break through to those kids over there on the corner. But the street worker who has hung out with them for months may be able to penetrate to the heart of their concerns and gain an audience.

Theology flows out of the biblical account of God's saving activities among those in need—physically, socially, economically, politically, and spiritually. God works with those who are humble enough to recognize their need of divine grace. To those close to God and to those God loves, God will give special insights for the theological task. This closeness to God and humility of spirit should be hallmarks of the practical theologian.

CONTEXTUALIZATION: THE NEED AND THE COST

Systematic and practical theologians need each other. The ivory towers of academia need to be in touch with the streets, and the streets need the resources of scholarship and reflection. The cries of the world need to be heard; the lessons of historical analysis must be remembered. Such interdependence will not happen if academia does not appreciate the full meaning of contextualization.

Many academics give lip service to the need for contextualizing the gospel into the culture of a people, but talking the talk is not walking the walk of contextualization. Most fail because they are not willing to relocate among the poor and oppressed, really to listen to women or to spend adequate time with the young. They fail because they do not have the opportunity to make themselves culturally vulnerable (as Jesus did with the woman at the well or with tax collectors) so as to realize the risks, costs, and benefits of genuine contextualization. It is difficult for adults to give up adult defenses or for professionals to give up professional security. Youth workers have to learn Jesus' style of ministry early on. They and other practitioners may help academics to find challenging and creative ways to contextualize their work.

The four Gospels show Jesus radically relocating himself away from the powers, synagogue, and temple. Although Christ had contact with the upper classes and the learned, his life centered on common people, women, and outcasts. He took himself to the streets and to those of lesser repute. Like many prophets, he spoke in the language and style of the common folk.

Some charged that Jesus was not just a friend of sinners but himself a sinner (Luke 7:34). Their condemnation stemmed from the people who interested him, the way he enjoyed their activities, and the places that attracted him. Those who truly serve sinners may be similarly condemned, for one cannot genuinely contextualize the gospel without running the risk of being identified with those to whom one ministers. Such a one lives in the tension of a difficult paradox: trying to avoid scandal and the appearance of evil (1 Thessalonians 5:22) while being a friend to sinners wherever they are found (Luke 19:7; Matthew 1:19).

Youth leaders must theologize about this difficult aspect of their ministry. Theology for youth ministers combines deep insights from the world and the Word, from the streets and the sanctuary, from the behavioral sciences and the teaching of the faith. The challenge of relating to human beings in dynamic transition makes one want to understand their changes and to discover with them principles that are appropriate for their world and anchored in eternal truth.

The cries of young people often drive a leader to the Psalms; their pain, to Old Testament stories. Youth's idealistic and apocalyptic frustrations send us deep into the prophets. In all this pain and suffering, Christian theology points to Jesus the Christ, the one who touches hurting people when no other can. God's Servant focused on "broken reeds and smoldering wicks" (Isaiah 42:3). Adults who appreciate broken spirits are desperately needed today, people who can be pillars of justice and morality while being keepers of bent sprouts and flickering candles.

Christ is the fulfillment of an adolescent's often impossibly high ideals. The idealism of keen young minds and the sensitivity of leaders find in Paul's declaration of freedom (Galatians 5:1, 6) and unity (Galatians 3:28) profound keys to many adolescent questionings and rebellions. Neither prophets nor apostles solved the problems of their day. Immersed in the culture of their times, they launched prophetic attacks against critical injustices and planted godly revolutionary seeds to overcome social inequities. They should not be judged for having provided inadequate blueprints for social change. They did what they could, what was possible, and they did it with profound sensitivity and amazing courage. We who face the complexities of modern cultures take heart from their examples.

CONTEXTUALIZATION WITHIN THE SPIRIT OF OUR TIMES

Young people, as all of us, are products of the spirit of the times. Our word to them must appreciate their individual thought processes as well as the ideas that shape their world. That world has been described as post-Christian and postmodern. But what does this mean? Many different explanations are given to this very complex issue. In general, it means that our culture and its media are less influenced by Christian and modern ideals and principles than ever before. Deeper consideration may lead to the conclusion that Christian principles and postmodernism have more chance to get along than Christianity and modernism.

Orthodox Christianity includes these key assumptions:

- a self-revealing God who created all things;
- a world that has rebelled and failed divine intentions;
- personal and social redemption and hope through divine intervention;
- personal and corporate responsibility to divine precepts;
- final personal and corporate accountability to the divine judge.

Modernism includes these critical assumptions:

- the autonomy and essential goodness of human beings;
- the dependability of human reason;
- the human plague of ignorance;
- the authority, trustworthiness, and power of science and education;
- the development of worldwide democracies;
- the success of evolution and the inevitability of human progress.

Note how these assumptions can lead to a sense of Western superiority, to colonialism, and to uncontrolled industrialism and militarism.

The optimism surrounding modernism in Europe and America at the opening of the twentieth century has been sorely tested. World War I, the Great Depression, the human horrors created by totalitarian regimes, the failures of wars to end all wars, the League of Nations, and at times the United Nations, the nuclear age, overpopulation, depletion of the world's resources, the spread of ethnic and religious strife and genocide—all these are evidences that modern authorities and religious institutions have failed to fulfill the common good. This century is closing with little confidence generally and even some extreme cynicism and nihilism.

Postmodernism is not a clear or agreed-upon term. The word roughly describes a loss of confidence in Aristotelian logic and Enlightenment science. The movement questions authorities, resents patriarchy and hierarchies, and resists order and tradition. Postmodernism may be more of a style than a philosophical worldview; it attempts to be free from classical, medieval, or modern epochs and frameworks. The term will be used differently by different writers, and we may expect to be on different ground when it is being used by philosophers, sociologists, artists, and critics of film, television, and music.

A general understanding of postmodernism is important for youth ministers because young people either are strongly influenced by postmodern style and ideas or are reacting strongly against it. Young postmoderns may be untouched by rational apologetics (e.g., the writings of Francis Schaeffer). On the other hand, those reacting against this spirit of the times may be open to and hungry for cognitive explanations of the faith. They will need help in understanding their postmodernist cohorts.

In order to interpret contemporary film, television, or music, one must understand how postmodern art deconstructs traditionally accepted form. There is a conscious effort in postmodern art forms to violate long-held principles of plot, setting, and characterization. If traditional art had a center of focus, postmodern art glories in chaotic collages. A movie or television program may have more than one plot, we may be initially surprised or fooled as to where and when it is taking place, and we may be shocked by certain characterizations or the morals of the story. This is all part of deconstructionism in postmodern art.

Some Christian scholars treat postmodernism as something close to the spirit of the antichrist. Culturally it may mean a closing of rational minds, descent into the indecent, and a fatal addiction for the fast-moving, blurred, emotional, irrational, and entertaining.

It is possible, however, to see Jesus as a precursor of some postmodern elements. He was at odds with many traditions and authorities of his day. He challenged the thinking and customs of many. He was an advocate for new wineskins. Of course, we should see Christ as more interested in reconstruction than deconstruction. Postmodernism is a heresy when it substitutes chaos for God's order. There is truth, however, in all distortions. Narrow theologies tend to see only the dangers; broad theologies are open to discerning positive points in the midst of differing opinions.

Hans Küng[1] takes a grim view of modernity and suggests positive potentials in postmodernity. He draws attention to the fall of authoritarian regimes, the failure of state socialism and neocapitalism, the sense that arms races, world wars, and nuclear holocaust all typified the modern era. Movements away from patriarchal hierarchies and abhorrence of ethnic and religious blood baths are all part of a transition Küng sees as taking the world in a more positive direction.

To minister effectively in current youth culture, the professionally educated youth minister needs to understand the postmodern world. Theology arising from contact with

---

[1] *Global Responsibility: In Search of a New World Ethic* (London: SCM, 1991) 2-24.

young people looks at life from within a youth culture shaped by contemporary thought and mass media. In this post-Christian and postmodern era many have rejected Christian values. For them moral authorities have lost their appeal, reason and science their credibility. Logical systems, theological proofs, and legitimate authority no longer count. Once-powerful apologetics may be seen as merely one individual's or group's desperate attempt to explain a world that is really chaotic and without ultimate order, beauty, and truth. A pluralistic and secular society is either too busy or disinclined to ask: What is the meaning of life? What is truth? What determines right and wrong? Why are we doing what we are doing? Where are we headed? We must find ways to make these questions once again relevant and basic to young people.

OTHER UNIQUE ASPECTS OF THEOLOGIZING WITH YOUTH

Urban societies structure adolescence in ironic ways. On the one hand, they have greatly prolonged the adolescent experience, kept it age-segregated, promised young people too much, and given them too little significant responsibility. While in this holding period, young people are bombarded with double messages: "Do it, but don't do it!" "Be sexy, but don't have sex." "Go ahead and have sex, but have it safely." "Smoke, drink, but don't buy it or get caught." "Be violent, but don't hurt yourself or anyone else."

On the other hand, with less support from extended or nuclear families, children are rushed into quasi-adulthood, a pseudomaturity. Television, their omnipresent nanny and tutor, destroys the "age of innocence" by revealing to them the heaviest burdens and seamiest secrets of adulthood. Lacking protected time and space in which to develop a coherent identity and value system, they learn by imitating contradictory role models in various life situations. As they grow older they encounter differing value systems that they place in separate compartments of their inner lives. The truths of these compartments are not supposed to have mutual coherence.

These young people are described by Neil Howe and Bill Strauss as "particle persons."[2] David Elkind explains how we have produced "patchwork selves" who, as hurried children in a world of value confusion, learn by imitation rather than by integration—forming themselves by substitution rather than by incorporation.[3] They become compartmentalized in their thinking and behavior: what they hear in church has no relevance for their social lives; lessons from home do not apply to school life and thought. The family compartment of these young people has increasingly little to do with the school compartment, which in turn has nothing to do with peer relationships—or one's intensely private life. Lessons they receive from youth ministers or teachers may hold true only in a religious or academic segment of their lives.

It is no small challenge to minister to young people living in the confusion of these mixed messages. We are meeting young people who are continually asked to grow up, yet they consider themselves less than adult. They are constantly encouraged to enjoy sex and violence mentally but to keep it only in their mind. They are supposed to use condoms for what they are not supposed to do. They are legally forbidden to drink but socially allowed to drink. Drugs of adult choice (e.g., tobacco, alcohol) are lauded in movies and commercials while drugs of their choice (e.g., marijuana) are illegal. In this complicated context, they attempt to assume adult roles—and look for adults who are "for real" to be their guides.

They do not necessarily disagree with what we take such pains to teach them—it is, indeed, what they expect from us (as teacher, coach, cop, nurse, parent, youth leader). Of course sex should wait for marriage at church; of course

---

[2] *13th Gen: Abort, Retry, Ignore, Fail?* (New York: Vintage, 1993) 28ff.

[3] *All Grown Up and No Place to Go: Teenagers in Crisis* (Reading, Mass.: Addison-Wesley, 1984) 15ff.

this is the most important subject (or sport) in the world; of course parents expect that whatever you do, you must not get caught and embarrass them. High school students know what their families believe, and they know where this English or social studies teacher is leading them. "We understand that we should try to get along with other races. We know about condoms. Puhleeease. But we've got our particular lives to live in situations that changed just yesterday, and that you can never understand."

A very confused society has made young people feel less able and more to blame. They have been told that as a generation they are stupid, performing at a lower level academically than students in other countries. Somehow they have been made to feel to blame for the stress of family life. They cost families more than ever before. They are in the forefront of violence and crime. It is not surprising that some feel themselves responsible for family tensions, their parents' divorce, or even the decline of the country.

The ironies of our policies toward neglected and restricted inner-city lives are even more pathetic. Young women, hardly more than girls, find themselves with little love and no one to care. To please her boyfriend a young woman may have unprotected sex that results in a baby—and suddenly a little one loves her unconditionally and a new grandmother treats her with more respect. In addition, this new mother may receive an independent income from the government. A young man finds himself in the margins of society with no job and a girlfriend with a baby who may not even need a father in the home. Powerless and without hope in legitimate society, these young men find ways to assert their manhood over what they see as oppressive guardians (police, teachers, social workers, and probation officers) of a closed society. "Juice" provides them with street status when decent (or dominant) society has nothing to offer them. They may steal a jacket or sneakers, not only for status, but for protection. They become bad in order to survive. Our proper objections to their lawless activity and to the excesses of "gangsta rap" may be less relevant because we have neither time nor ability to hear and understand. Instead we merely ask for more police and prisons to protect our privileged lifestyles.

In so many ways we adults leave young people to their own devices, then we scorn the devices. Parents too busy to notice, maybe even to care, let young people become inured to global traumas and personal shame on TV. They are pushed out to day care and school. They often return to empty homes. They mix with friends whose lives are difficult in different ways. Often the best of friends do not share what matters or hurts the most. Sometimes only their music seems to understand and appreciate the suffering and angst they feel.

From childhood, today's youth are bombarded with propaganda. They become partially "ad-and-value-immune"; they are somewhat "message-protected." Mass media desensitizes them and makes them rather callous to meaning and morality. Nevertheless, they are still creatures of God, what theologians call *imago dei* or the image of God is still deep within. Beneath callused, protective layers their souls are still soft and receptive.

This generation has a keen desire for relationships and for practical results. They see through the many failures of previous generations and adult society at large. Somehow they are still ready to try again—in a way that makes sense to them. Their resilience is amazing, and the possibilities of grace are awesome.

Adults who are really there (in the hood, at the mall, around high school, or in detention centers) understand all this. They know the suspicion against intruders and the resistance toward adult teachers. Those who would reach this generation must be sensitive, strong, persistent— and exceedingly vulnerable. This is the cost of contextualization. Into the changing objective and subjective worlds of teenagers, in all the compartments of young lives, in the ambivalence of current culture, youth ministers seek to contextualize the good news and the lordship of Jesus Christ.

Partly to make up for diminishing support from family and home, young people gravitate to friends and the media. Needing a clear self-image and a context to practice how to handle adult complexities, young people cling to cliques and peer groups. Despite this insularity, their worldview longs for unity and universality. Regardless of their own personal exclusivities, they really want to see all people come together. They have little tolerance for institutional discrimination even though they may have their select prejudices and may not be able to mix with those who are different. Out of this longing for grand togetherness come their troubled questions about other religions. They dream of an inclusive church where all might get together.

Now, theology should not be fashioned to fit the moods or predispositions of human beings. A Christian theology should be only as inclusive as the nature and will of God. The mighty works and Word of God demand a certain critical exclusivity. But it is a transcendent exclusivity; exclusivities from cultural or class biases need to be corrected by new theological perspectives.

YOUTH MINISTRY'S MISSIOLOGICAL TASK

The context of adolescence in today's world is not always conducive to young people's growth and welfare. When any group is segregated and slighted by a dominant culture, it tends to stick together for survival. Those in the group develop a subculture or special culture of their own.

Pete Ward has challenged youth workers to enter the various subcultures of youth.[4] He describes several groups of teenagers in his town of Oxford, England, distinct in their dress, music, and interests, and shows how they each must be reached from within their particular culture rather than from without.

As the world's largest and most dynamic unreached peoples group, young people should be the first "foreign"

---

[4] *Youth Culture and the Gospel* (London: Marshall Pickering; Grand Rapids: Zondervan, 1992).

mission of the church. It will take a strong commitment of
any church and a clear calling of its youth leadership team
to reach that mission field at the local campus or hangout.
Any adult who enters the world of youth will learn much,
will be changed, and will find new perspectives about
theology and the gospel.

Youth workers, who are in the trenches of teenage
struggle, are prompted by the nature of their ministry to
search out a world-embracing theology. Just as most young
people reject parochialism and denominational schism, so
youth leaders react against sterile insularity and institutional-
ism. Young folk are very sensitive to hints of arrogance and
dogmatism. Theologies from a certain century or a particular
continent, written for the highly educated, the elect, or the
elite, fail for those whose parish is the campus or the streets.

Youth ministers need a theology informed by the dynamism of young people and by Christ. Youthful theology seeks
to be in touch with the heart of young people and with Jesus.
Youth workers are paying the price demanded by contextualization. That price may be loneliness, low estimation of the
work itself, and misunderstanding about their being salt and
light in the youth culture. Youth workers are called upon to
consider the price paid by Christ in order to reach those
living on the margins of society.

AN INCARNATIONAL STYLE OF THEOLOGY

Classical theology used biblical exegesis and classical
philosophy as its framework. We should not disparage the
contributions of either discipline. But along with the philosophical masters, we must also value the contributions of
those who have studied the deep cries of the young. Here
the behavioral sciences can also help.

Theology is contextualized into the subculture of youth
(or into any unique culture) only through incarnational commitment and experience. It is never enough to study young
people; we must live among them and feel the pulse of their
lives, the beat of their hearts. This principle is articulated by
Paul, who said that one must make the gospel accessible to

various peoples and cultures by becoming "all things to all people" (1 Corinthians 9:22, NRSV). The principle of contextualization sees its highest model in the cross-cultural communication of the Eternal Word: the Creative Principle and Communication (*logos*) "who comes into the world to enlighten everyone . . . the Word became flesh and lived among us" (John 1:9, 14, author's paraphrase).

To follow the life of Christ through the Gospels is to enter the world of the social elite and of the despised—like Nicodemus and the woman at the well. Our Lord was hounded by religious critics as he sought those on the margins of society. The religious authorities of his day condemned him, for one thing, as a rabbinical failure—for eating and sharing table fellowship with those unclean. All the time Christ was revealing to his disciples a model for what they should study and how they should minister.

Considering those for whom Jesus cared should make us extremely interested in their cultures. Jesus leads us into cultures that God also loves (the *kosmos* of John 3:16). We assume at the beginning of our study of youth and popular cultures that diverse and humanly designed cultures are God-ordained. The world or cosmos created by God, entered by the Word, and loved by God *is* our human society. (We are talking about business and the popular culture, MTV, interactive media, music, athletics, and all the rest.) These cultures of the world—created, loved, judged, and being redeemed by God—are indeed worthy of our study.

INCARNATIONAL STYLE OF MINISTRY: THE IMPLICATION OF CONTEXTUALIZATION

Toward the end of his ministry Jesus gave his followers a stunning mandate. If it was not one of his most daunting challenges to them, it should be for us: "As the Father has sent me, so I send you (into the cultures of the world)" (John 20:21, NRSV). A corollary of that commission is also daunting: "Truly . . . the one who believes in me will also do the works that I do and, in fact, will do greater works than these" (John 14:12, NRSV).

It is the challenge of contextualization coming from the commission of Jesus Christ and the complexity of youth cultures that keep youth ministers talking about getting close to young people and their world. Just as God became the Living Word in human culture, so the Word must today be incarnated or translated in cultural terms. Revisions of the Bible attempt to keep the Bible culturally up-to-date. Missionaries translating the Bible into any language realize that their task is more than literal translation. They must understand the culture of the people or tribe if the Bible is to speak truth to that society. Similarly, youth leaders seek new and exciting ways in which to contextualize the Word of God. They will find time to move away from programs, outside the church, to find young people who need to be heard, to be cared for, to find healthy and supportive community. Adventure camping, service learning, and special recovery or support groups are examples of ways we can reach young people where they are and where they hurt.

God, who has treated us from the beginning as stewards and "co-creators" or partners in the work of this world (Genesis 1:28ff.), now asks us to make the Word understandable in all cultures of the earth. This means that the Word must enter the world of skateboarders, surfers, mall rats, rappers, gang members, as well as those around the country club.

Today we need holy youth ministers tested in the waters of contemporary culture. Many young people want to be heard and need to be appreciated. They will open up only to those who have come into their world. They will hear only from those who are present, learn only from those who love them. And the pain they feel! A young man sits blowing his eardrums out with the music of rage. A young women weeps as she watches a movie that shows, all over again, what her stepfather did to her many years ago. Is there any painless and invulnerable path to contextualization?

Youth work collects those who have come out of brokenness to healing, and it calls others who are strong to discover the gift of weakness. Those who serve youth often feel like lightning rods catching and grounding anger—or like Band-

Aids applied to bleeding injuries. Perhaps for this reason youth ministry has its share of powerful "wounded healers." Professional youth ministries must give careful training and adequate attention to all who serve in such risky situations.

In sum, translating the Bible and doing theology are incarnational ministries. Both demand immersion in the culture to which one wishes to speak theologically. Preaching the gospel faithfully and dynamically demands similar involvement in given life situations, in all their fullness and complexity, so that the truth of God can penetrate all the bright spots and dark corners of personal and corporate lives. This is the high privilege of youth ministry: to live and to translate Word and gospel, to be grassroots theologians in today's culture.

QUESTIONS FOR REFLECTION AND DISCUSSION

1. How do you explain contextualization of the Christian faith and the good news?
2. What do you see as the cost of contextualization? What does it mean "to be all things to all people" (1 Corinthians 9:19-23)?
3. With what images besides being salt and light does the Bible encourage our immersion in a particular culture? How does one live *in* the world without being *of* the world? What difficulties do you see for yourself in loving people of another culture and entering into it without being conformed to the world around you?
4. In what ways do you see churches missing the example of Jesus and the spirit of incarnational ministry?
5. How have you tried to translate or contextualize the Word into the culture of those with whom you minister? How do you want to grow in doing so?
6. In what particular ways have you struggled to reach young people of another culture? What particular subculture of youth have you entered? How must your approach be guided by the style of that culture?
7. Give one specific example as to how such reflections as these can keep theology *and* youth ministry honest?
8. Are you willing to work at being a practical theologian?

3 THEOLOGY AND EXEGESIS

Knowing the Word, Your World, and Yourself

> *Ezra . . . was a scribe skilled in the law of Moses that the LORD the God of Israel had given; and the king granted him all that he asked, for the hand of the LORD his God was upon him.*
>
> —*Ezra 7:6,* NRSV

> *Jesus understood people and didn't need to rely on the opinions of others because he understood human nature.*
> —*John 2:24b-25, author's paraphrase*

The work of developing a practical theology is not easy. You have already spent considerable effort understanding its spirit, its unique approach, and the difficulty of true contextualization. To follow the model of Jesus and the apostles requires the further skill of interpretation. Openness to young people and their leaders in different cultures around the world provides further contributions to the field of practical theology—and to the effectiveness of your ministry. Like Ezra, you want to be knowledgeable and efficient in practice. You also strive for the wisdom and grace of Christ.

DEVELOPING A THEOLOGY: A THREEFOLD INTERPRETIVE TASK

Theology begins with an awareness of God and with the *exegesis of Scripture.* But we often overlook the necessity of an *exegesis of the culture* or world in which we were raised and to which we minister, and an *exegesis of self* (biblical scholar or theologian, pastor or youth minister). The word *exegesis* signifies the process of interpreting and explaining. It implies skill and wisdom. To exegete is also to interpret a text for teaching and application.

Theology is a systematic expression of God's Word in a particular time and space; it formulates the good news within a particular culture. Thus theology always involves exegesis or interpretation of the *Word*, of the *world*, and of the *self.* Young people remind us of this point; most will not accept sterile doctrines or partial knowledge. Working with young people will help us interpret the Bible, the world, and ourselves more effectively.

Errors can arise from a failure to analyze the cultures in which the exegete was raised and to which the theologian speaks. Theological disagreements stem from the different starting places and premises of their parties as well as from differences in our personalities and styles. Breakdowns in theological discussion often arise from a failure to be critical of one's own cultural and personal exegesis (errors of ethnocentrism and egocentrism). At some point theologians must agree to disagree on interpretation and doctrine.

Being with all kinds of young people can yield important insights and contributions to the theological endeavor. Just as the theological process among oppressed people has yielded new critiques and emphases, theology among young people pleads for less egocentrism and ethnocentrism, for deeper understandings, and for broader applications.

Change and complexity around us demand a new look at our interpretive skills. They also call for a holistic interpretation wherein our analyses of Word, world, and self are interactive and congruent. Today's world calls for intergenerational approaches to the solution of current crises. Youth leaders can be helpful bridges in this endeavor. They can bridge the gap between parents and children, boomers and busters, conservatives and liberals, secularists and believers.

THE NEED FOR SKILL AND WISDOM

You who serve youth are continually engaging in theological reflection about God's work in young lives, about the nature of the gospel, about the nurturing of faith and the life of the church. Youth leaders receive all kinds of questions from bright, curious, and idealistic young minds. You are confronted by ethical and psychosocial issues not only from eager and confused young people but also from parents and others. Sometimes you are expected to be a family consultant. Schools and other organizations may ask for a presentation or for advice. In many ways, youth ministers have more direct access to the heart of community institutions than other clergy do. Together youth ministers, teachers, parents, and pastors seek a pastoral theology adequate to today's crises.

Such challenges demand a growing body of information and pastoral skill. We are called to a lifelong study of biblical truth, social systems, and human personalities. As a professional servant to young people, whether you are reading a biography, a newspaper, or Scripture, you will want to be the best reader you can be. *How to Read a Book* can make your reading more efficient and effective.[1] This book urges an aggressive rather than passive approach to any literary work. Engage the author in a dialogue like this: "I don't have all the time in the world. What are you really trying to say or prove? Why is it important and what is the purpose of this book? What are your assumptions? What are your main arguments or explanations? And how should this affect the world and our lives?" You can apply what Adler says about effective literary interpretation to the analysis of lives and cultures as well.

These challenges, to be professional, to be informed, to adopt a style of life-long thinking and learning, do not mean that youth ministers must be brilliant or become

---

[1] Mortimer J. Adler and Douglas Van Doren (rev. ed.; New York: Simon & Schuster, 1972).

scholars. Rather, we should want to learn and be thoughtful about our work. Youth leaders who take some minutes each day, a few hours a week, and some days or weeks a year to study will avoid burnout. Because we want to serve young people with professional skill, it is necessary to read well and to think well—"to grow in wisdom and favor with God and people" (1 Samuel 2:26; Luke 2:52). Youth leaders should always be growing personally and professionally, as social workers and as theologians. Such youth leaders give attention to physical and emotional health and to intellectual, social, and spiritual growth.

GENERAL GUIDELINES FOR INTERPRETATION

In coming to Scripture it is important to ask:

- What is God saying in this Scripture?
- What are the unique values and characteristics of my culture and how do they affect the way I read this text?
- Who am I, and what kind of fears and values do I bring to the text?

Like Bible reading, theology involves a threefold exegesis:

- exegesis of the Word,
- exegesis of the world,
- exegesis of the self.

Exegesis should not be a private affair. It is an art as well as a science and demands both individual effort and interaction in community. The theologian (and every Christian is a theologian) needs feedback on the task from the church as the body of Christ and from the world.

Exegesis is often seen as having a single focus—that of getting the meaning out of a text. It may better be seen as having a triple focus: interpreting the Bible, ourselves, and our culture. Ministry may be seen similarly.

1. Approaching the subject matter from praxis or ministry—the mission—

I'm working with runaway and throwaway young people who have so little going for them.

2. Interpreting the subject matter—the analysis—

Eighty-five percent of them have been sexually abused. There is so much pain and denial in them. It's hard for them to trust anyone. Relationships come slowly, but when they do, good things can happen. Some of them have come to trust Christ, and it is changing their lives. Being in this faith community gives opportunity for love and discipline to reshape broken lives.

3. Applying the interpretation back into ministry—the test or application—

We are using what we have discovered to establish a program with sound principles of therapy and Christian community. We will evaluate our results.

This process should be continuous and cyclical. The faith community's need for application urges interpretation. Teaching informs and leads to application. Teaching and living should both encourage and affect further interpretation.

EXEGETICAL STEPS

Our personal story, our cultural story, and God's story all say something about truth. They all have a meaning that needs interpretation. We interpret all three, in simplest form, when we ask:

- What is the story?
- What is its context?
- What does it say?
- What does it mean?
- How does it apply? What difference does it make?
- How can we better hear messages to bring growth and welfare?

These six questions must be asked about the divine Word, about the vast variety of cultural messages, and about ourselves and our impulses. Here, more specifically, are what the six exegetical steps involve.

1. First of all, we are determining premises about the nature of the subject or subject matter. What do we believe about the Word, the world, and the human self? What are the functions and goals of the subject? Exactly how does the Word (or this particular passage), this culture, or this person fit into the scheme of things? What divine importance does this individual, this society or subculture, or this Scripture possess?

2. Then, we consider the context of the subject in terms of:

- background—historical, anthropological and social, political and economic, psychological, and spiritual—
- relationship of the particular to the whole.

3. Using the best linguistic and communications tools available, we go on to analyze the language of the subject and to clarify the message.

4. Analysis of the subject matter prepares us for discussing the meaning of the subject. People fail to see the significance of Scripture, societies, and persons for many reasons. These meanings need to be uncovered.

5. We apply the interpretation of the subject to our lives, to real-life situations around us, and to all the world. How does this Word, this culture, or this person make a difference to the world and in my life?

6. Finally, recognizing the need for a continuous cycle of exegesis.

- Our conclusions drive us back to the first step and the entire process.
- We are never finished because we are always growing and learning.
- Exegesis demands not only skills but also basic humility and an awe of the mystery of God's creation and redemption.
- Mature exegesis does not deny or shirk ambiguity.

These six exegetical steps are now developed more specifically in terms of the Word, world, and self.

BIBLICAL INTERPRETATION

As one who reflects on the situation of young people from God's perspective, you want to do so truthfully and faithfully. If you are going to understand young people, you must interpret their culture. You must also interpret the Bible. This task of interpretation or exegesis is not reserved for scholars; it is a privilege and duty of all who read Scripture. Two seminary professors, Gordon Fee and Douglas Stuart, wrote *How To Read the Bible for All Its Worth* to encourage faithful interpretation:

> We recognize that the first task—exegesis—is often considered to be a matter for the expert. At times that is true. But one does not have to be an expert to learn to do the basic tasks of exegesis well. The secret lies in learning to ask the right questions of the text.[2]

Raymond E. Brown adds a caution with which these professors would agree:

> Because Scripture is inspired and presumably this inspiration was for the good of all, there has arisen the fallacy that everyone should be able to pick up the Bible and read it profitably. If this implies that everyone should be able to find out what the sacred author is saying without preparation or study, it really demands of God in each instance a miraculous dispensation from the limitations imposed by differences of time and circumstance. Of course it is true that considerable portions of Scripture are easily intelligible to all because they voice universal sentiments, e.g., some of the Psalms and some of the simple stories of Jesus. It is also true that spiritual solace and insight may be drawn from the Bible by those who have no technical knowledge and indeed do not understand its literal sense. (Conversely, those who have technical knowledge have at times overlooked the religious depths of the Bible.) Nevertheless, when it is a question of finding out what the human author

---

[2] Grand Rapids: Zondervan, 1982, 13.

is meant to say, and therefore what God inspired, there is no substitute for educated effort.[3]

As practical theologians, youth ministers must study the Bible, and that study should be as educated as possible and should lead them back to biblical scholars and theologians for exegetical help. Collaboration between biblical and practical theologians will be to the advantage of all. Those who are students of people may sense cultural or personal lapses in the work of the biblical scholar, who may in turn save the practical theologian from serious technical mistakes. Gordon Fee admits the need for scholars to be reminded of personal biases:

> The first reason one needs to learn *how* to interpret is that, whether one likes it or not, every reader is at the same time an interpreter . . . We also tend to think that *our understanding* is the same thing as the Holy Spirit's or human author's *intent*. However, we invariably bring *to* the text all that we are, with all of our experiences, culture, and prior understandings of words and ideas. Sometimes what we bring to the text, unintentionally to be sure, leads us astray, or else causes us to read all kinds of foreign ideas into the text.[4]

These reminders and others[5] show us how important it is to understand ourselves and our culture in our interpretation of the biblical text.

All of us have blind spots. The stress of family life, the politics of academia, and the pressures of our professional world work on our personal egos and weaknesses to make us less than objective—and less tolerant of other perspectives.

---

[3] "Hermeneutics," in *The Jerome Biblical Commentary* (ed. Raymond E. Brown, Joseph A. Fitzmyer, and Roland E. Murphy; Englewood Cliffs, N.J.: Prentice-Hall, 1968) 607.

[4] Fee and Stuart, *How to Read the Bible*, 16.

[5] See Samuel Terrien, "History of the Interpretation of the Bible: Modern Period," in *The Interpreter's Bible* (ed. G. A. Buttrick; New York: Abingdon-Cokesbury, 1952) 1.140. In the conclusion of this article Terrien adds a caution regarding covert presuppositions that influence an exegete's interpretation.

Sadly, we do not often have the time or the inclination to listen to those who could do us the most good. Missing vital feedback, we become like someone who observes his face in a mirror and then forgets what he saw as he goes on living. We need to catch our own reflection in the "perfect law of liberty" (James 1:25) and from the hearts of brothers and sisters who represent very different perspectives.

OUTLINE FOR EXEGETING THE WORD OF GOD

Outlines can be attempts to present a rather complex process in simple, workable format. The following suggests an approach to biblical study for youth leaders.

- What does it say?
  - a. What kind of literature (genre) is this? Is it narrative, poetry, prophetic oracle, law, or hymn, etc.?
  - b. What is its content? What is the meaning of its words and phrases?
  - c. What is its scriptural context? What is its immediate context (paragraph, chapter, and book)? What is its context within the entire Bible?
  - d. What was its historical context? What is the culture, date, and situation of the author and readers?

- What does it mean? What is the message?
  - a. What did the human and divine authors intend? What point was the author trying to make?
  - b. How did its original readers understand this passage?
  - c. How has the church read it?
  - d. What does it mean in today's world and in our culture?

- How does it apply? What difference does it make?
  - a. How is my life different and how are our situations changed by the reading and study of this text?
  - b. Remember that application is always the weakest step in exegesis and Bible study.
  - c. The historic discipline of "praying the Bible," which involves moving from meditation on the text to prayer, can help us in this application step.
  - d. Keeping a journal and writing down behavioral goals from the Bible study can help us to live the Word of God.

FURTHER QUESTIONS AND SUGGESTIONS FOR WORKING OUT THIS OUTLINE

1. What kind of literature am I reading in this book or passage? From what kind of societies did this literature arise? In what period of history (of the people of Israel) was this particular book or passage written? What is the relation of this section to the rest of the Bible?

What does this section of the Bible say? What is best understood of its words, grammar, and rhetorical style? Use the reporter's questions:

- *Who* is in this passage?
- *What* is said or takes place here?
- *Where* is it said or does it take place?
- *When* is it said or does it take place?
- *Why* is it said or does it take place?
- *How* is it said or does it take place?

2. What are my premises as to the nature of this book and of God's revelation, and how do I understand the reasons for the various interpretations of Scripture? What were the intention of the author, the needs of the audience, and their understanding of what they were writing or reading?

What does this section of the Bible mean? You are looking primarily for what it meant to the original author and readers. Context and rhetorical principles are important. Secondarily, and very carefully, you may discover additional meaning in the life of Israel and the church—and what God may also want to say through this Scripture to us today. Secondary meanings of Scripture must agree with the truth of Scripture's primary meaning and the teachings of the church.

As you look for the meaning of Scripture, ask:

- What does this teach me about the nature and ways of God?
- How does this help me relate to Jesus Christ as Lord and Savior?
- What do I see here of the working of the Holy Spirit?

- Who is my neighbor, and how am I to love her or him?
- What do I learn here of corporate responsibility, repentance, and restitution?
- What am I taught to avoid?
- What am I encouraged to pursue?

3. How are these lessons to be incorporated into my life in the world and in the church? What is my strategy? What specific goals do I set and what resources and reinforcements do I need for their accomplishment? How do I evaluate growth and progress?

How can you celebrate your efforts at exegesis and its resulting growth and progress? How are you in need of new beginnings and discoveries in your exegesis? At what new level do you now return to the first step?

A BIBLICAL EXAMPLE

The story of Joseph is not to be seen on the same level of importance as, for example, the story of Christ. Still, as part of the scriptural canon, it "is inspired by God and profitable for teaching, for reproof, for correction, for training in righteousness" (2 Timothy 3:16, NASB). A recent newspaper article told of someone working in a residential treatment program for emotionally disturbed children. One boy, who had been abused and rejected, acted out often and was difficult. He wanted to be told only one story in the Bible, about Joseph. He found in Joseph someone with whom he could identify.

We never know what biblical story will touch the heart or pain of a particular person. We do know that Genesis takes just two chapters to tell the story of cosmic creation and thirteen chapters to tell the story of Joseph. And whereas the institution of marriage and family is described in just a few verses of the Genesis account, the reconciliation of a fractured family (Joseph's) covers nine long chapters. Here are immediate lessons (though secondary to the heart of the gospel) for ministry.

In his fine study of British youth, Peter Brierley observes: "Only four people are positively identified in the Scriptures as being in their teenage years—and they all had problems!"[6] Of these biblical teenagers, Joseph's is the fullest story. The drama, which is relevant to young people everywhere, may be seen as unfolding in five acts:

1. Joseph has problems with his family.
2. Joseph is rejected and serves in Potiphar's house.
3. Joseph is tempted.
4. Joseph is sentenced to prison.
5. Joseph is leader of Egypt and his family.

Each of these scenes is filled with rich lessons for young people struggling with immaturity and misunderstanding at home. Joseph's experience will offer inspiration and instruction to those who live with rejection and abuse. Many feel as if they have done their best, only to be let down—by family, friends, society, God. Those lonely and discouraged or tempted and misjudged find much to discuss in the Joseph story.

Without family and friends (and, of course, with no Bible or church), Joseph must have cried out often to a seemingly silent God. The story cuts through all the instant solutions and immediate gratifications of current media to a God who, through our chaos and flux, is good and just and faithful. The savior of the story is clearly God (Genesis 50:20). The salvation provided is not only for individuals; families, tribes, and nations are also delivered.

Exegeting Sexual Affairs

In a sense the temptation of Joseph may be seen as pivotal to the history of redemption. A great deal hinges on

---

[6] *Reaching and Keeping Teenagers* (Turnbridge Wells, England: MARC, 1993) 89. Besides Ishmael, Joseph, and Kings Uzziah and Jehoiachin, Brierley points out those who would today be classed as early adolescents (twelve-year-olds: Manasseh, Jesus, and Jairus's daughter) and others we can only guess to have been in their teenage years (like Isaac, Esther, and Mary, the mother of our Lord).

every sexual temptation—whether it comes to a pastor, a president, or a high school student. No one has fully explained the power of sexual affairs. Some persons enter an affair as a means to the end of fun or feeling better. Others may see their act as an end in itself. They may suddenly feel that nothing else matters, that this spontaneous union will make them feel fulfilled in life. In fact, however, a brief liaison can spell disappointment, permanent scars, even death. Joseph could not have known how much hung on his response to this powerful temptation.

Without a faith community, family, or friends, Joseph was, as far as we know, single, at the prime of sexual urgency, and with seemingly little to lose. He did not yet know the future or God's intentions and providence through his life. We can only imagine a single, hard-working young man who receives little reward, faced by a probably beautiful, available woman. How much was at stake!

> Now Joseph was handsome and good-looking. And after a time his master's wife cast her eyes on Joseph and said, "Lie with me." But he refused and said . . . "my master . . . has put everything that he has in my hand. . . . How then could I do this great wickedness, and sin against God?" (Genesis 39:6-9, NRSV)

Looking for the Larger Context

To get the most out of this incident, we must see it in the context of the entire Joseph story and of the other patriarchal stories of Genesis—as well as its larger context of all Scripture and the history of Jewish and Christian faith. Joseph himself tried to put this powerful moment in the context of God's perspective.

1. How is this like so many stories of our times and of history?

- In what ways is it different in its style and substance?
- Who were the primary readers of this story?
- How might the story of Joseph be divided into dramatic acts or stages?

2. Along with what other stories in the book of Genesis does this one fit?

- What does this story have to do with God's early covenants?
- The main point of this story pertains to the history of Israel. How is it significant to that history and to God's salvation history?

3. Who, What, Where, When, Why, and How are all questions that bring this scene to life and clarify its meaning.

- How old was Joseph when this story began and when he finally was released from prison and stood before Pharaoh? (Genesis 37:2 and 41:46) About how long might he have been a slave? How old was he when he faced the temptation with Potiphar's wife, and how long might he have spent in prison? What difference does all this make?
- About how far did Joseph walk to find his brothers? (Genesis 37:12-17) How far would you say he walked to get to northern Egypt? (Genesis 37:17, 25-28, 36) How can students get involved in determining these distances? What can be gotten from this information?
- What two cultures are meeting in our text?
- What aspects of Egyptian court and social life, architecture, and other customs might enhance our appreciation of this story?
- What factors might explain a powerful attraction of Potiphar's wife and Joseph for each other?
- What word studies and grammatical studies might help to clarify this passage?

4. Why is this story in the Bible? (Expand on what you have seen above.)

- How was it meant to instruct Israel and promote the growth of its people?
- How is it meant to instruct the church as a cross-cultural community?
- How may it promote the growth of readers in all places and times?

- What special impact might this story make on your culture?
- What does this story mean for you?

5. How do you think Israel applied this story?

- How can it to be applied to your culture?
- What are you going to do with this story in your own life?

6. How can this story be celebrated in the church today?

- Who can help us understand and appreciate this story more than we have?
- How has this work of exegesis prepared us to make better use of other passages in the Bible?

Only as you have faithfully asked yourself these hard questions will you be able to field the questions of eager or cynical young people. Why did Joseph taunt his brothers with a dream of his own superiority? Why did God choose Jacob rather than Esau? Why are these stories mostly about men? What about slavery in the Bible? Why is the end of the Joseph story so long and dragged out (Genesis 42-50)? Other questions far from the story of Joseph may come out. These can all lead to profitable discussions with the help of a confident leader.

Biblical exegesis is obviously hard work. Here I have provided only illustrative principles for the youth worker. Those skilled enough to work from the Hebrew and Greek have a great advantage. Fortunately, the works of great exegetes are available for all to read. Biblical study requires rigorous effort, but it can also be fun and satisfying. Above all, skillful interpretation is the necessary foundation for faith, growth, and service.

Being with young people can help one to see interpretation—of the Word, of community, and of self—from the most exciting perspective possible. Many fresh possibilities of analysis and interpretation are suddenly present at adolescence. The urgency of answers is never stronger; idealism and sensitivity to hypocrisy are heightened; and they are listening to you, who have cared enough for them that they trust you. That is why you must take exegesis seriously, whether it is the exegesis of the Bible or the exegesis of culture and self.

EXEGESIS OF CULTURE

The pastoral theologian must interpret culture as well as Scripture. Too many theologians fall back on simplistic and sometimes negative views of society. There are too many one-issue Christians—those whose political agenda is summed up in one repetitious complaint. Whether it is abortion or school text books or a theological subpoint, they tend to ignore pressing problems that need response from the people of God. Overwhelmed by the complexity of a changing world and burdened by personal issues, they have one solution or program that will bring in the kingdom. They have friends who generally agree with them, whose own personal concerns may be vaguely similar, but their interpretations of the world are often a private matter.

We are part of a whole. The whole is greater, and more complicated, than the sum of its parts. One may live alone as an individualist in an urban apartment, but this person's life is entwined in a myriad of social networks. Advertisers know us as clusters, and demographers give each generation a name and classify us according to groups. Our buying and behavior are affected by social realities larger than ourselves and are predictable to experts. Our lifestyles associate us with others in the world. We are not as individualistic as we assume; we are all very much cultural beings.

The church aspires to be a bit of heaven on earth. Working out such a role, Christians find themselves both affirmed and condemned by the world. The problem of living *in this world* (Genesis 1:28; Matthew 5:13, 14) as *heavenly people* (Ephesians 1:3; 2:6) has created tensions for Christians from early times. "How can we be *in* the world but not *of* it?" is a question of every new generation of Christ's followers. There is no easy answer; it is one of the basic paradoxes of faithful living. This paradox demands that we understand our own cultural identities, the benefits of our culture, ways in which our culture is fallen, and how society is being redeemed. A serious task of exegesis stands before us. It is introduced by questions relating to the basic pattern for interpretation already established.

Exegetical Questions of Culture

1. Do I understand that God created the necessity of human culture? Do I see how necessary culture is to socialize a human being? Do I understand that there may be tension between Christ and culture, between the sacred and secular?

2. Can I define "culture" and "subculture"? Do I realize that all cultures must be appreciated for their beauty and truth? Do I recognize the beautiful and ugly, the divine and demonic, in all cultures? Do I realize that culture is fallen and is being redeemed—as in "thy kingdom come"? Do I understand that cultures have a divine mandate to help people grow to their full potential (ultimately in Christ), that any cultural factor that hinders growth is wrong?

3. How can my culture be described? How is it distinguishing, protecting, prospering, and reproducing itself? What is the relationship of this culture to other cultures? How do the systems of this society (family, business, government, media, schools, etc.) interact and affect young people? What is the relationship of individuals to institutions in this society? What are the trends of this society? How does this society hear the Word of God?

4. How are we to study the nature and meaning of our society and popular culture? How can we determine the specific socializing influences of major social systems on young people? What are the relative influences of family, television, school, peers, sports, music, movies, magazines, advertising, and religion as systems that influence the teenagers we serve?

5. What kind of system or specific medium are we considering? What are its relationships to other (e.g., political and economic, or other group) systems? What are the goals and functions of this medium and how does it influence people? Who has power in making the critical decisions regarding the messages of this medium (or system)?

6. What is this medium saying to all those it touches? What are the scientific, artistic, and theological elements needed to understand this message?

7. What is the effect of this message? What are the many different factors that vary the effect this message has on individuals and groups?

8. How does this message affect the culture overall? What should or can be done about enhancing its benefits or ameliorating its evil?

9. How are we now in a better position to receive and evaluate this medium and other media and systems? How can we be more mature and discerning viewers and consumers as well as creators and producers?

Exegeting a Sitcom

Watching a half-hour sitcom can be fun even while you think about its style and message.

1. Why is this program slotted for this time of evening? Who are its intended viewers? How does this program compare with those of five, ten, twenty-five years ago? How does it compare to its current rivals? Who sponsors this and similar shows?

2. Remember that you are watching more than one show: the program and its commercials. Do you know that small children pay more attention to the commercials? What are the story themes of the main program and of the commercials? What kind of human themes are addressed? What kind of human stereotypes are used? How does humor function? What values are upheld and what values scorned? How many times are particular words, themes, or scenes repeated?

3. What are the conclusion and meaning of this story for the various kinds and ages of people watching? What messages are conveyed through its characterizations and humor? What do the commercials imply about the viewer? What solutions do they give to his or her inadequacies, needs, or problems?

4. What impact does this program have on our society? What are its benefits to the producer, advertisers, viewers, and consumers? How is it affecting the socialization of children? What does it do for the family?

5. How does this critique of popular art and entertainment help us to enjoy and appreciate them more, be more discerning in our viewing, and help young viewers to be in control of their own lives?

We can ask similar questions about music and other media. What is positive and what is negative in current rock music or rap? What movies are beyond the limits of good taste? How are we being influenced by magazines and advertisements? Interpreting the culture is such a necessary part of youth ministry that its consideration will fill the greater part of this book. But finally in this chapter we consider the important task of analyzing ourselves.

EXEGESIS OF SELF

Without a knowledge of self we view life as a two-dimensional rather than a three-dimensional drama. We miss much of how we affect others and to what degree we encourage their personal growth. We can be blissfully unaware of the frustration we cause others, and we are perhaps convinced that we have a full picture of truth while we force reality through our two-dimensional grid or filter. Our exegesis is blind to our own egocentric and eccentric methodology. We do not see the influences of childhood fears or youthful crises as they shape our worldviews and theologies.

Some Christian academics do not like each other; many theologians cannot get along with one other. They have invested so much in their theologies and in getting at the truth that the presence of someone who strongly disagrees is threatening, uncomfortable. Often, strangely enough, the closer these professors are in theological position, the greater the antagonism. A Christian and a Buddhist (or even an agnostic) may get along better than any two of the following would: a Jesuit, an Orthodox, a Calvinist, a Lutheran, a Dispensationalist, or a Baptist.

When those who accept our presuppositions interpret Scripture differently from us, we may admit some relativity in our view of truth. Often we either rationalize these differences away or call them minor. Full admission of the effect of personal biases and cultural instincts may seem to threaten orthodox stability or our hermeneutic. But we are responsible for a thorough and honest exegesis. Thus it is better to rest in the truth that holds us than to trust our ability at holding all truth.

We ought to maintain the constancy of what we call orthodox, catholic, or historical Christian truth, as expressed in the creeds. But one can see the truth of Christ and Scripture in different ways. We discover God's Word and we do our theology on the basis of cultural conditioning (language, mores, and style) and personal disposition. The way each one of us looks at God is influenced by our relationships with our fathers, mothers, authority figures, and culture generally. God has not promised to take us out of the world or to exempt us from cultural influence.

Our understanding of the mystery of redemption and the way of salvation must be in harmony with Scripture. But God has not revealed all the details to us in Scripture; God has left us to work out many things cross-culturally, in tribal and technological cultures. The principles of hermeneutics are critical, objective criteria, but they are not absolute. To say a given method of interpretation is final and absolute is the height of spiritual arrogance and denigrating to those in other Christian communions who sincerely interpret differently. We ought to be strong in our own tradition and tolerant of others. This tolerance does not throw us into a slough of uncertainty, by any means; it merely keeps us humble, like the children who enter the kingdom of heaven.

Who Am I?

How can we best take humble assessment of our lives and the way we work with truth? For some, truth is something to know, facts for passing an exam, data to recite. But truth always transcends our comprehension. We learn about it, we study it, we practice it, we discuss its nature; and in all this we are working with the truth and coming to know it better.

A prayerful inquiry before God, asking for honest feedback from those we trust, and self-analysis are all helpful. It is important to realize how our personality, upbringing, family, surrounding culture, crises of faith and doubt, spurts of growth, heroes, and mentors have all influenced us. We should be able to say, "Because of who I am, I tend to lean this way" on issues such as:

- predestination and free will,
- authority and personal freedom,
- evangelization and social action,
- laws of abstinence and separation vs. Christian liberty,
- Christ and culture.

It is good to be able to say, "I am a five-point Calvinist, but I need to be balanced by Arminians." "I am a Catholic, but it is good for me to work with Protestants." "I am a suburban Presbyterian, but I need contact with African-American Baptists." "I am a high church Episcopalian who needs to understand charismatics."

The Greek epigram "know thyself" and the Hebrew injunction "watch over your heart with all diligence" (Proverbs 4:23, NASB) are twins. Both admonitions recognize the danger of ignoring the motivations of our hearts. They imply that brilliant people without self-understanding may hurt themselves and others. Small, central blind spots can create larger errors and trouble. These admonitions also encourage a sense of the great potential we all have for personal growth, which is the basis for enlarged service for kingdom and community.

A theological life determined to see the world in a godly way is one that is self-aware. It takes seriously the preciousness of self, the fallenness of self, and the possibilities of grace in one's self. Good theological method should foster the cardinal virtues of wisdom, tolerance, courage, and fairness—as well as the fruit of the Spirit listed by Paul (Galatians 5:22-23). A life that faithfully interprets self, society, and Scripture will produce the humility, vulnerability, strength, and courage desired in a youth leader.

Four Basic Questions

"What's hap'nin'?" a young junkie would often ask through dazed eyes. When our conversation got a little threatening, "Where you comin' from, man?" Then one of us might ask the other, at a superficial or deeper level, "Where're you headed?" The discussion only really counted if we got realistic, "How're you gonna get there?"

Though obviously dated in wording, these four questions lie at the heart of youth ministry. Youth leaders around the world are using these four basic questions as guides to relational conversations, small group discussions, and curricula. Each subculture of youth words these four basic questions differently. Consider the wording and range of meaning of the following questions.

1. What's going on?
   - How are you doing?
   - Who's important in your life these days?
   - What else has been happening in your world lately?
   - What highs and lows are you experiencing?

2. Can we share our stories?
   - How has our relationship grown? What history do we have?
   - How much of your personal story are you comfortable sharing?

- What are your larger family and ethnic/community stories?
- Do you see the importance of your past?

3. What dreams do you have?
   - Where do you want to go next from here?
   - What in your history can help you fulfill your dreams?
   - How realistic are your short- and long-term dreams?

4. How are you going to get there?
   - How can we help you help yourself to fulfill your dreams?
   - How can your dreams be translated into short- and long-term goals?
   - What obstacles do you see? How can they be managed?
   - How do you need to be supported and held accountable by us, by your friends, or by other resources?

These questions can obviously be taken on various levels, from superficial to very deep. Notice how they move from *present*, to *past*, to *future*, and back to *present*. They offer a basic pattern for helping others.

We should be careful about asking someone, "How can I help you?" To do so is to set the "helpee" up to become dependent and ourselves to become victims. Question four, "How are you going to get there?" does imply our concern and desire to help. But the question should always be, "How can we help you help yourself to get there—to reach your goals?"

Tough love is never overwhelmed by the suffering and needs of others. It never tries to take over another's pain or healing. With compassion it asks those in crisis, "What do you want to do about it?" Jesus taught us this when he asked people what might be seen as too obvious or even ridiculous a question: "Do you really want to be whole?" He was trying to get them to answer two questions from their hearts: "What do you want to do about this?" and "What do you want me to do?"

Our use of these questions can help those we meet with their exegesis or understanding of themselves. "What's hap'nin'?" may be a mere greeting, and "Where you comin' from, man?" can be an irritable rebuke. Or we may take these questions to deeper levels, to what is happening in a life or soul. The spirit of these questions may take us on to a holy ground of human encounter. "I really do care what is happening in your world, and I would hear your story and dreams with sacred intent."

As with any other tool, applying these questions honestly to ourselves before using them with others is important. Many youth workers are trying to help young people before they have helped themselves. Asking these questions honestly is doing exegesis of self and realizing how they relate to biblical and cultural exegesis as well. Done well, the interpretation of self should take us to Scripture and to our cultural roots. Such questions of self are ultimately theological questions. To pursue one's history or future, meaning of life, or ultimate need for guidance and support is to move toward God. Reflection on these questions promotes healthy growth:

1. What's going on in my life?
   - How have I gotten where I am?
   - What do I most want out of life?
   - What am I giving to and getting from this situation?
   - What turns me on?

2. What is my story?
   - What's going on in me?
   - How am I relating to self, others, and God?
   - What's bugging me?
   - What is the significance of my history or personal drama?
   - How am I the product of my family and past?
   - What is my success history and what strengths do I find there?

3. What are my dreams?
   - Where am I going?
   - How is my present situation leading toward those dreams?
   - How have I translated my dreams into long-term goals?
   - Do my short- and mid-range goals match my long-term goals?
   - How do I evaluate and reinforce my progress?

4. How am I helping myself to get there?
  * What obstacles stand in my way?
  * How am I managing this conflict?
  * What reinforcement and support have I built into my progress?
  * How do the Father, the Son, and the Holy Spirit relate to each stage of my life?
  * What part do worship and my faith community play in my present growth?

It is important for us to take times for honest reflection on our present situation, to relive the story of our lives (our personal history), to imagine our dreams for the future, to translate those dreams into goals, and to consider how we can resolve possible conflicts.

PURSUIT OF WHOLENESS

We also need to consider our wholeness. The title of Elizabeth O'Connor's book, *Our Many Selves,* gets right to the point.[7] I am not simply an "I," but a more complicated "we." I need to be conscious of the many parts that go into making me whole.

I am whole only when I know how to *be* as well as how to *do.* I further realize I am not only saint but sinner—and the two are strangely mixed. Honest examination shows evidence of contradictory tendencies. There is in me that which longs to wander and that which wants to settle down, a gypsy and a settler. The child in me creates, spins fantasies, and needs help—he needs to be controlled and nurtured by my internal parent. Too often my critical parent neglects or condemns the child who needs to be loved. I have a Mary part who loves monastic retreats and prays while Martha labors on and gets things done. Fortunately, the disciplined driver in me is slowed down by the goof-off, who suddenly suggests watching a basketball game or taking a nap.

There is in me (and most of us) both a Pharisee and a publican. The Pharisee (like those in the Bible) has some

---

[7] New York: Harper & Row, 1971.

important standards for me (the complex parts of me) to keep. But when he nags and tries to take sole control of my inner life by constant criticism, reminding me in countless ways how imperfect and inept I am at keeping *his* standards, it is time for me to call him to account. The publican may bring impure thoughts into my home or lead me into unhealthy extremes of enjoyment and relaxation. He is wrong to recommend that I cheat a little to relieve the strain of overwork. Both the Pharisee and the publican are parts of my complex being created by God— fallen with the rest of me. It is also true, as in the biblical story, that redemption can come to the publican. Recognizing that he is a sinner, the publican knows more about repentance and brokenness than the Pharisee. Both are needed to bring me to wholeness.

This crazy crowd within me all have their good points and their dangerous extremes. "We" (this family within) need an inner (house or family) meeting to get us all together. Strange things happen in these sessions. My frustrated parent can learn how it has neglected the child within. An angry child may discover how the frightened parent has acted out of fear of rejection and needs our reassurance. Mary comes to appreciate and serve Martha, just as Martha recognizes and appreciates Mary. Salvation may come to our house through the repentance of the publican rather than the righteousness of our Pharisee (though we desperately need his knowledge of the law). This process is all part of the exegesis of self, the pursuit of wholeness.

It takes courage and time to face these tensions and to find balance, harmony, and wholeness. To achieve resolution we need an internal arbitrator—or an outside counselor— to get the inner meeting going. Most of us have waited for crisis or brokenness to find an openness and peace that is both realistic and godly.[8]

---

[8] For help in the task of self-exegesis, see Larry Crabb, *Real Change Is Possible If You're Willing to Start from the Inside Out* (Colorado Springs: NavPress, 1988).

Knowing self and loving self are important in the growth of young people, and vital for youth ministers. Describing a Christian sense of self, Richard Peace asks:

> What does it mean to love ourselves? This is a concept fraught with difficulties. Improper self-love translates into a lifestyle that is hedonistic, selfish, and self-destructive. But we dare not avoid the subject, because failing to love ourselves properly is also self- destructive. With low (or no) self-esteem, people become doormats for others, fail to use their Christ-given gifts, and have difficulty loving others. Jesus calls us to walk the narrow road between selfishness and selflessness. This involves proper self-understanding, a larger dose of humility, and a healthy sense of who we are.[9]

We understand ourselves best when we do so theologically: When we understand our lives (our nature) as messages or sacraments of God's love, we may experience God's grace in new ways. We may hear more clearly what God is saying through us, appreciate the great meaning of that message, accept the limitations of our existence, and rest in our Lord's gracious application of our lives to a grand divine plan. It is exciting theological work when, in partnership with young people (for their visions are fresh and realistic), we discover the grand significance of God's creative and redemptive activity in these complex vessels of clay.

For our theology and our ministry, we need an exegesis of self. When we make the effort to understand and accept our many selves, we will then be much better at tolerating those we have considered unlovable. We can love young people more deeply and effectively as we come to love ourselves in God. Such a love is not self-centered but overflowing—an understanding and healing love.

Criticisms of many current emphases on self should not be taken lightly. There is a dangerous obsession with self that leads to narcissism in self and society. Morbid introspection or pampered selves can spoil marriages or

---

[9] *Learning to Love Ourselves* (Colorado Springs: NavPress, 1994) 7.

lead to serious, even deadly, depression. The antidote for self-centeredness is a balance, urged throughout these pages, a balance modeled in the blessed Trinity, in a whole life, in life for others. It is a balance of self and community, inner prayer and outward service.

If the exegesis of self does not lead to better study of the Bible and of culture, if self-awareness does not yield better relationships in the faith community, if knowing ourselves does not lead us to serve others more effectively, then this study is surely in vain.

QUESTIONS FOR REFLECTION AND DISCUSSION

1. What has most impressed you in this discussion of interpretation?
2. Which do you find most difficult: the exegesis of the Bible, of self, or of culture?
3. Is there anything in this chapter that you cannot understand? How can you most easily get it explained?
4. How are you growing these days and what are your goals for personal growth?
5. Are there any principles here that young people cannot understand? How can you make those principles even simpler as you help young people to grow in understanding and in effective living?
6. How are Christ, the Holy Spirit, and God the Father necessary in all that has been discussed here?
7. What from this chapter can you most immediately use for yourself?
8. What kinds of exegesis could you do with your young people?

TOWARD A THEOLOGY
OF CULTURE

What in the World Is Going On?

You are the salt of the earth.

—*Matthew 5:13,* NRSV

Become all things to all people.

—*1 Corinthians 9:22,* NRSV

Keep (yourself) unspotted from the world.

—*James 1:27,* KJV

Christian scholars and pastors often critique culture, music, or television and make ethical judgments without full recognition of the cultural attitudes and biases hidden in their own subconscious. Thus far we have undertaken a study of our approach to practical theology and our interpretations of significant subjects. We now extend that effort into a consideration of our approach to culture generally and to popular culture in particular.

Youth leaders and seminarians have received a great deal of instruction about the Christian life, missions, and the church. But how are we to live in the world? What do we have in common with neighbors who are not Christians? How do we cooperate with Muslims and Buddhists and agnostics in educating our children? How are we to define the common good in a pluralistic, secular culture?

CULTURAL QUESTIONS IN YOUTH MINISTRY

- What kind of music do I let them listen to in the van? How do I decide?
- Should Christians buy music only from Christian producers?
- Should a youth leader ever see an R-rated movie with young people?
- Should a youth group plan a beach party where bikinis are worn?
- Can a Christian join the military and kill?
- Can teenage Christians look up to leaders who may drink an occasional glass of wine or beer?
- Is there a place for rap or rock music in worship?
- Why do I like to dance, and is it all right to be seen at a dance club?
- Could a couple living together before marriage ever be acceptable leaders in youth ministry?
- How do I assemble my hierarchy of sins? Are some sins more serious than others?
- How much social science is needed to complement Scripture in pastoral ministry?
- What is the difference between black theology and white theology?
- Does preaching the gospel involve issues such as racism and poverty?

There are further questions:

- Are you willing to die for your country?
- How do you, or will you, teach your own children cultural values?
- How do you celebrate those values?
- Do Christians need to celebrate their cultural values just as they need to celebrate their religious values in worship?
- Are ethnicity and culture vital parts of our personhood?
- Can we function as leaders before we come to peace with the aspects of our personhood?
- Must a young person deal with her ethnicity and culture before her identity crisis is resolved?

THE CULTURAL CONTEXT OF YOUTH MINISTRY

Working with young people requires that we observe culture intently and theologically. Consider the many different responses one might hear to the questions above. Honest differences among sincere people of faith demand an acknowledgment of our cultural conditioning and the need for deeper understandings of Scripture and society.

A theology of culture is the way we approach, think about, and interact with culture in view of God and God's mighty works in the world. Some might prefer to say that a theology of culture is the way we think about the world in view of scriptural teaching. They believe there are strictly biblical answers to the above questions. A great rift exists between those who minimize and those who maximize the cultural factor in scriptural interpretation and application.

Christians who struggle in situations of oppression and poverty may stress the political and cultural aspects of biblical hope. They object to the gospel's being restricted to matters of personal salvation and sanctification alone. Such piety, in their view, reduces religion to an opiate of the downtrodden. Seeing Isaiah as gospel along with Matthew, Mark, Luke, and John can lead to a broader and well-balanced view of the good news. Theologies from Catholic, Orthodox, Evangelical, and Liberationist perspectives can all contribute to relevant youth ministry.

Young people feel their own peculiar exclusion and oppression. They desire to be free from adult misunderstandings, unfair restraints, and rejection. Adolescents and their leaders should not try to shape God into their own image. Nor should they demand a gospel and theology that are comfortable. But it is right for them to hear the good news and to understand God's Word in a way that is sensitive to their perspective and applies to their particular life situations. Dynamic expressions of the gospel have always come from the fringes of society—Jesus was there. Honest relationships with all kinds of youth will help make a biblical theology relevant to all of contemporary culture.

THINKING THEOLOGICALLY ABOUT CULTURE

A theology of culture may begin with a theology of family—an understanding that God created man and woman to raise children as the central core of culture. The family is the basic unit of society as we know it. From a theological perspective families reflect the divine Trinity. God created human beings in the divine image: male and female. What is implied in the divine "We" of creation is, orthodox Christians believe, the blessed unity and harmony of the eternal Father, Son, and Holy Spirit. As man was incomplete in the Genesis story, so man and woman are incomplete from an ultimate, divine perspective. We believe every human couple needs a critical third partner, and that third factor is God. This critical "thirdness" is, in fact, needed in all society. All human dialogue needs divine presence and grace.

What Is Culture?

Youth leaders must also reflect on the nature of culture. God "made from one [culture or blood], every nation of mankind to live on all the face of the earth . . . that they should seek God" (Acts 17:26, 27, NASB). From that one culture in the garden (according to biblical faith), cultures spread out across the earth.

A theology of culture must be biblically faithful, but it must also resonate with data from the behavioral sciences. Culture is all learned behavior that is acquired socially. It includes language, values, beliefs, artifacts, technology, mores, norms, and styles. By "culture" then, we mean all that is learned and passed on from generation to generation. Culture is our human environment. Family, education, marketing and economics, entertainment (including recreation and athletics), politics, and religion are its institutions. We will consider how these insitutions are expected to function properly in the socialization of our young. Before helpless infants can take on the complex responsibilities of society, they need instruction from family, school, media, church, and other social systems.

Careful study of cultural differences is a scientific endeavor. Adults usually take culture for granted until they have to raise children. In comparison to animals, human infants have very few instinctual abilities. Babies are very dependent; they have to learn everything. It takes a culture to raise a child. Children raised outside a human environment are feral children. Douglas Candland's fascinating study, *Feral Children and Clever Animals,* looks at wild Peter of Germany, Victor of France, Kaspar Hauser of Nuremberg, along with Amala and Kamala of India. The last two were found living with wolves in a subterranean cave under an abandoned anthill by the Rev. J. A. L. Singh. When he first found them, they could not stand, walk, communicate, or be continent; they were like animals in every way.[1] Raised and taught by wolves, these girls could only display the cultural behavior of animals. Candland, a professor of psychology and animal behavior, uses these cases to test the contemporary understanding of human intelligence. Human culture calls for the socialization of children by social systems including families, towns, schools, and peers. Without family and cultural support a child cannot walk or talk or behave as a human being. Without human models and instruction human babies are unable to think and act in a human fashion.

Culture and Individual Needs

Culture is the way a particular group chooses to balance their universal human needs, their geographical location, the level of their technology, and their belief or value system. Culture arises from basic and universal human needs. Psychologists such as Abraham Maslow, Gordon Allport, and Arthur Glasser have pointed out universal

---

[1] *Feral Children and Clever Animals:Reflections on Human Nature* (New York: Oxford University Press, 1993).

human needs (to which we should add the spiritual need for transcendence):

* to be fed, clothed, and sheltered (survival and security needs);
* to be humanized or socialized—to know how to live and to discover who one is (growth and identity needs);
* to belong, to be affirmed and supported, to love and be loved (affiliation needs);
* to accomplish something significant (achievement needs).

In the passage from infancy to adulthood, human beings need to find their self-identity—the meaning of their lives within a social context. They need to establish clear boundaries between self and others. A mature person has a secure sense of selfhood and the ability to relate generally and intimately with others. Adults are meant to possess an idea of vocation and a sense of personal and fulfilling contribution to the larger community. Thus individuals are both products of and contributors to their surrounding culture.

Arrangements for the fulfillment of human needs, the socialization of the young, and the collective security of a community of human beings are the functions of a culture. Rational responses to social needs in a given geographical and historical situation produce various cultures. As societies develop within a particular environment, they acquire new culture traits. These elements of culture spread from their points of origin and are diffused (as when the Arabic language spreads along the eastern coast of Africa), assimilated (in the creation of a Swahili language using Arabic words and patterns), and rejected (when the whole Arabic language does not take root). Each cultural group consciously or subconsciously chooses some and discards other new foods, fashions, words, and music that come from other societies.

Cultural Conflicts

In this (fallen and being redeemed) world, cultures serve to bring people together, but they also create possibilities for human conflict. Indeed, whenever two cultures meet, they interact in one of three ways:

1. cultural conflict (clash of value systems),
2. cultural assimilation (acceptance of a new value system),
3. cultural accommodation (two different value systems live side by side).

Throughout history many peoples, like the Phoenicians and the modern Lebanese, the Jews, and the Chinese, have settled within other cultures around the world. The collapse of Communism and of colonialism, along with changes in economic situations, have produced many examples of cultural conflicts in today's world. There has been a varying degree of assimilation of immigrants into the culture of the host nation. Finally, to the extent that groups have kept their cultural identities in a foreign land, there has been a spirit of accommodation between their communities and the culture in which they have settled. The African diaspora is a unique and important case, and the intense study of this cultural diffusion is now yielding many important lessons. The richness of African music has created fascinating new types of music in the Caribbean (calypso) and in North America (jazz); the impact of African spirituality is also well known.

Culture and Faith

Christians are likened to sojourners in foreign cultures. They are meant to be leaven, salt, and light in and to their host cultures. What does this mean? How are we to be in the world and not of it? How can we be South African, Australian, British, South American, or North American and Christian at the same time?

There is an overlapping of the cultural and religious dimensions of our lives. All learned behavior is cultural, and culture is passed on from generation to generation. By definition, the spiritual aspects of our souls are what transcend natural laws and phenomena—or at least aspire to the transcendent. Similarly, religion contains both cultural elements and the mysterious and transcendent. We distinguish, for instance, between adolescent interest in spirituality and indifference to institutional religion. This chapter will give even more attention to the tension between our cultural identities and religious identities.

All people of faith experience some tension between cultural and spiritual needs and loyalties. In too many instances the world has watched terrible social dramas played out because of religious and cultural differences. When faced with, or studying, such social tragedies, young people raise theological questions. "If God knows everything and is all-powerful, how could he create such a world?" "How can a good God allow suffering and not intervene?" "How can people kill each other over their different beliefs in God?" Discussions around these questions must reflect an understanding of various cultures and issues involved. Such conversations do not lend themselves to simple anwers or pat solutions. They point to the need for an understanding of grace and a willingness to work at reconciliation.

How desperately we need a theology of reconciliation to deal with cultural conflict today. We must learn new lessons for understanding different perspectives, dogmas, and biases that separate cultures. The world has sadly watched as Christians have killed Christians, or Muslims and Christians have killed each other, without restraint. There is a critical need for transcendent wisdom to release us from ethnic bondage. It must teach us to maintain ethnic pride while finding universal justice. A theology of culture requires adequate doctrines of cultural distinctions, ecclesiastical interventions, creation, evil, incarnation, reconciliation, and eschatology. These theological doctrines must be understood corporately as well as individually.

BALANCING INDIVIDUAL AND CORPORATE THEOLOGICAL CONCERNS

Individualism allows individuals to treat themselves as social ends in themselves at the expense of the common good. Similarly, a state government overides respect for, and the rights of, human beings if it deifies statehood as an end in itself. These are modern and postmodern heresies that undermine hope for universal justice and peace.

A theology of culture helps us realize that, in creating the world, entering the world, and redeeming the world, God is concerned with groups as well as individuals. Both are being judged, both being redeemed. Contrary to individualistic theologies, we were not made alone, lost alone, saved alone, or glorified alone.

From Alexis de Tocqueville to Robert Bellah, observers of US society have admired and been concerned about the American brand of individualism.[2] When we see freedom mainly as a personal matter, we greatly emphasize our private concerns at the expense of the common good, and public welfare may be poorly guarded. American, European, and many other contemporary societies are dangerously lacking a high concept of the common good—a public, moral philosophy.

Moderns also tend to individualize evil. When social systems become pathological, people may seek to identify someone as the cause for terrible times or someone to blame for horrible crimes. To put the blame on an ethnic gang member or young welfare mother short-circuits the process of critical social analysis, which is costly in time and money and difficult to put into simple sound bites. Our society may be more willing to put a long stream of killers away for life than to find out what is causing our social tragedies. Personal responsibility cannot be ignored; criminals should not be given more respect than their victims. Sound public philosophy takes seriously both personal and corporate responsibilities. Society must develop protections against damage done by an emphasis on either individualism or social systems.

Although a large portion of the Bible is concerned with corporate justice and corporate repentance, some

---

[2] de Tocqueville, *Democracy in America* (1840; trans. George Lawrence; New York: Doubleday, 1969); Bellah, et al., *Habits of the Heart: Individualism and Commitment in American Life* (Berkeley: University of California Press, 1985).

theologies and some types of biblical preaching today are almost entirely individualistic. Youth ministry should not follow this tendency. Adult Christians may be content to compartmentalize their politics and religion and let the church speak only to their personal concerns, but the adolescent spirit tends to suspect such truncated theologies and sermons. Young people tend to be more willing to face their own shortcomings than are adults.

Mature teachers of young people need to move freely back and forth between personal relationships with God and relationships with others. They should not be afraid to examine the status quo. Where social systems hinder the growth of young people and oppress the poor, youth ministers should proclaim biblical judgments. For one to have confidence in prophetic teaching, one must gain clarity about cultural realities.

TYPES OF CULTURES

Adults visiting a high school, shopping at the mall, or passing an urban park often fail to recognize the rich variety of cultural groups. Kenneth Roberts outlines types of cultures in this way:

Dominant Culture:
- inherited from traditional ways and beliefs;
- produced by the economically or politically dominant;
- accepted throughout society as common knowledge;
- transmitted in urban societies by mass media.

Subcultures:
- do not challenge but negotiate optional styles;
- youth subculture may disdain adult responsibilities, tastes, beliefs, and restraints;
- working-class subculture may disdain higher education and professionalism.

Contracultures:
- seek not to replace but simply to contest dominant values;
- may exhibit truancy, vandalism, and drugs, etc.

Countercultures:
* go beyond defiance and seek to change values and institutions;
* communes may replace families; play and hustling may replace work; love or protest may replace war;
* radical countercultures may seek revolution.[3]

Youth Culture and Subcultures

Since adult culture has extended the boundaries and neglected the issues of youth, a natural grouping along common interests and sensitivities begins to form among young people. The general subculture of youth (distinct from dominant adult society) may be further divided among its own ethnic, geographical, and class groupings or special (sub-) cultures.

Contemporary youth culture as a subculture is growing worldwide in today's industrialized countries. Through music and advertising, satellites and television, an increasingly global youth culture is emerging. The youth culture functions as a peer culture defined by age. Societies around the world are extending the age of adulthood upward in an arbitrary fashion. Though we are pressing young children toward adulthood in our culture, true adulthood takes much longer to attain. We are forcing children and adolescents to live in the limbo of pseudo-adulthood; true adulthood is more elusive than ever before.

Since traditional rites of passage are being lost in this generational limbo, young people begin to create their own markers or rites of passage (including early and unprotected sex, wild drinking and driving, and other risky behaviors) that are not conducive to their growth and welfare.

Youth culture in the industrialized societies is further characterized by:

* relatively large discretionary income,
* restricted responsibility,
* restricted access to real life and death matters,

[3] *Youth and Leisure* (London: Routledge, 1985).

- strong influence from popular rock culture and celebrities,
- strong global or international character,
- tendencies toward violence.

To define a cohesive identity, youth culture possesses its own values and norms, lingo, fads, and fashions. Furthermore, within youth culture there are special groupings. Teenagers in high schools usually identify with a specific group, and these groupings may form a social hierarchy based on status or popularity. In many areas there are rival gangs or divisions according to ethnic or class distinctions. Within these are even smaller primary peer groups or cliques. As family systems and school systems diminish in effectiveness, these peer systems, along with the media, become stronger influences on young lives.

Anthropology traces a history of cultural change from tribal to traditional to technological societies. Modern technology leads relentlessly to mass society (with mass production, mass market, mass media, and mass organization). The electronic revolution (those who work with children and youth *do* see it as revolutionary) has produced new possibilities for mass communication through music, film, television, and the computer. Technological advances are merging the telephone, computer, television, and stereo into an interactive, multimedia system. Marketing researchers will be using increasingly sophisticated techniques to approach this complex market.

Popular Culture

Pop culture reflects the values (and countervalues) of the masses in a technological or urban culture. The values of any culture must be reinforced and passed on to each emerging generation through cultural celebrations that encourage the internalization of these social values. The customs and festivities in which traditional cultures celebrated their values are no longer effective in urban societies.

Popular culture provides for the celebration of contemporary culture. In contrast to high (cultivated or elite) culture, pop culture stands as the democratic expression of an urban society. Through its mass media—art and architecture, music, movies and videos, radio and TV, newspapers and magazines—it informs, unifies, and entertains.

A crucial question is whether the popular arts primarily *reflect* or *influence* what is going on among young people. Those who are highly critical of music and other media often call for censorship or controls on all that children can see or hear. Popular artists and producers argue that they are merely reflecting what is going on in society. Careful, full, and honest analysis, in my opinion, sees many other factors in society that influence children in negative directions, on the one hand; but I am forced to conclude that the popular arts do exert great influence. Popular art both reflects and influences young people and society generally.

Pop culture and mass communications have a fourfold function in society.

- They survey the culture.
- They bring a certain coherence to the parts of society in response to the environment.
- They collect the social heritage from one generation and pass it on to the next.
- Finally, they entertain society.

John Wiley Nelson also sees popular culture as the celebration of what a society believes.[4] It embraces what it means to be a citizen of Britain, Australia, Kenya, the United States, or any other society. Pop culture provides one view of our cultural identity. It includes what we teach our children (and reinforce for ourselves) about being a part of our country's citizenry. Pop culture, therefore, teaches us what we work for and perhaps what we should be willing to die for. The popular songs of the the 1940s inspired many young people to risk their lives for democracy and for their country. The songs of the 1960s and 1970s did not do the same for many who fought in Vietnam.

---

[4] *Your God Is Alive and Well.*

There are many aspects to one's identity—physical, sexual, familial, ethnic, national, and spiritual. Many youth leaders today are hesitant to declare their national or ethnic identity, to be proud of their citizenship. But it is important for us to be clear about that aspect of our identities if we are to help young people determine who they are in this regard. Being clear about our cultural identities as Christians means we have to sort out and critique the cultural values we encounter daily. In doing so, it is important not to neglect cultural celebrations altogether; we need them when we are tired and in need of social renewal.

CULTURAL AND SPIRITUAL IDENTITIES

Youth leaders work with adolescents within their "tribal culture." By that I mean that their television programs, their music, their fashions, and their slang are meant to distinguish them from adults and adult culture. The elements of this youth culture are as precious to them as the language and rituals, music and dances are to tribal societies. In ministering to those caught in a difficult transition to adulthood, we struggle with the obvious tension between being socially renewed and being spiritually renewed. "Do not be conformed to this world, but be transformed by the renewing of your minds," Paul admonished the Roman Christians (Romans 12:2, NRSV). Yet Paul also encouraged contacts with "the world" when he explained that the Corinthians should indeed associate with the "immoral of this world, or the greedy and robbers, or idolaters" (1 Corinthians 5:10–11, NRSV).

Paul was also conscious of his own cultural identity: "We are Jews by nature" (Galatians 2:15, NASB), and "I too am an Israelite, a descendant of Abraham, of the tribe of Benjamin" (Romans 11:1, NASB). Yet he was willing to become Roman, Greek, or barbarian for the sake of the gospel (1 Corinthians 9:22) without losing his own particular cultural and spiritual identity. All of us must determine our identities socially, economically, ethnically, politically, and spiritually.

This determination of identity is, as we have seen, a critical task of the adolescent life stage. It is in the youth culture generally, and within their cliques or peer groups particularly, that young people work out their identities. So many factors in today's society, such as consumerism's emphasis on style, excessive competition, racism, classism, and sexism, can make this task very difficult.

A person's identity includes cultural and spiritual dimensions. We experience problems and a lack of wholeness when we confuse the personal, sexual, ethnic, class, or vocational aspects of our uniqueness. One may be Asian, adopted, American, bright, ambitious, disadvantaged by poverty and social class, and Christian all at the same time. As a Christian living in a secular society, how does one make whole these aspects of one's cultural and spiritual identities?

As already mentioned, personal and cultural identities and values need to be celebrated. How do people of faith celebrate secular values? Many Americans tend to celebrate their values in athletic contests and music concerts or dances. Such celebrations celebrate values of physical health and strength, courage and endurance, harmony, unity, and intimacy.

How do you celebrate your cultural identity? Hearty religious and cultural celebrations are necessary but lacking for many. Such celebration is part of the attraction of highly emotional worship services or musical concerts. Christians have always struggled with questions regarding participation in celebrations of their cultural identities because many social festivities tend toward debasement of the human spirit.

What exactly does it mean to be Canadian, British, German, Chinese, North American, Mexican, or South African? In what distinctive values of your particular culture do you deeply believe? Would you be willing to die for your culture or nation? How do you want to instruct your children in your social tradition? How are cultural values appropriately celebrated? As parents, teachers, or youth leaders we are helping young folk determine their cultural (and sometimes ethnic) identities. Increasingly, young people are bicultural or even multicultural. They name their cultural identities with a hyphen. Some are called "third culture kids": following their business or ambassador parents, these German, French, or Swiss young people have attended international schools in two or more other countries, and have spent very little time in their own land. In a complex world, the task of clarifying cultural identities is a lifetime process.

Why is the identity crisis so complicated in urban cultures? Many of the developed nations are highly competitive societies. Instead of ascribing status to individuals in their societies, modern urban culture allows the status to be achieved. This ability to achieve status fosters competition for status. Without a sense of worth that comes from seeing oneself as a creature of God in a faith community, citizens of a secular society can measure their position on the ladder of success only by comparing themselves to negative reference groups—those who are younger, less educated, less successful, or inferior in whatever way. Such pressures to compete and to succeed can obviously reinforce racism and sexism. We create a strong need for negative reference groups. In *Why America Needs Racism and Poverty*, James Tillman explains how egos in a secular society need negative reference points to reinforce a self-worth based primarily on upward mobility.[5]

In contrast to the harmony of perfect wholeness for which all strive, human beings experience tensions between nature and grace, body and soul, secular culture and sacred cult. Aiming individually and corporately toward the goals of maturity and unity, we find great differences between the principles of Christ and those of our culture. Until the lordship of Christ is fully realized, these tensions

---

[5] James A. Tillman, with Mary Norman Tillman, *Why America Needs Racism and Poverty: An Examination of the Group Exclusivity Compulsion in America as the Natural Enemy of Rational Social Change in Race and Poverty Relations* (rev. ed.; New York: Four Winds, 1973).

will never be completely resolved. For now we ask ourselves: Do we look upon the world belligerently or amicably? Are those of this world our enemies or potential friends? Do we want to change the world or flee from it? The food we eat, what we drink, the clothes we wear, the toys we buy, the systems that service us and in which we work—are they Christian or are they supposed to be? Every youth leader must ask these questions.

Our theological challenge is to resolve how we are to be in the world but not of it and also to determine the relationship of the church to the state, religion to the world. Moving from individual to corporate issues, we need to review our understanding of how God created and is working in human cultures. All cultures show dramatic evidences of the beauty of the human spirit created by God. Even the subcultures of crime and drugs show remnants of the image of God in flickers of loyalty, generosity, sharing, and community. And all human cultures, even the best of Christian subcultures, display striking instances of destructive tendencies. Each culture is flawed and fragmented by human rebellion against God—antagonism within self and with others. Understanding that culture and its institutions are created by God, fallen, and being redeemed, we see in all societies beauty and ugliness, good and evil, cruelty and grace, the demonic and the divine—at the same time. It is important to realize how much more difficult it is for the collective ego to repent and be redeemed than for an individually fallen ego to do so.[6]

Since the time of Paul, Christians have seen the relationship of Christianity to the world in different ways. Many youth ministers and seminarians have been helped in this matter by a classic description of these various attitudes toward the world held by Christians throughout history: H. Richard Niebuhr's *Christ and Culture*.[7]

---

[6] See Reinhold Niebuhr, *Moral Man and Immoral Society: A Study in Ethics and Politics* (New York: Scribner's, 1932).

[7] New York: Harper & Row, 1951.

CHRIST AND CULTURE

Imagine a dramatic conversion of an alcoholic or a heroin addict, or someone turning to Christ after living a life degraded by extreme debauchery. Such persons, especially in their early Christian life, understandably can consider all they have come from as evil. They may not be in a position to see the beauty and positive elements of the culture they have left. (Some will say worldly culture has no beauty or positive features. I must object; the theology I present here is based on the premise that there is good and evil in all cultures.) Other persons have had little contact with secular culture (the "real world"), and their profession is to warn people about the dangers of worldly thinking. From some theological colleagues I have never sensed any positive excitement about what is going on in the secular world.

All these are examples of those who may have an attitude or approach to the world that Richard Niebuhr has labeled "Christ *against* culture." Such opinions may be prevalent in times of decadence, persecution, or religious revival. Adherents of this position emphasize the opposition between Christ and culture. They cite some of Paul's warnings ("Come out from them and be separate" and "Don't even talk about what the world is doing in the dark," author's paraphrase of 2 Corinthians 6:17 and Ephesians 5:12). They may emphasize a literal spirit in Jesus' hard sayings ("give *all* that you have to the poor," Luke 18:22, paraphrase, or "If your right eye makes you stumble, tear it out," Matthew 5:29, NASB). They may confront others with "either-or" decisions. Niebuhr describes this position as being dynamic, personalistic, or communal and suggests that such ideas may be simplistic.

Some Scriptures seem to favor such a position:

No one can serve two masters. . . . he will be devoted to the one and despise the other. You cannot serve God and mammon. (Matthew 6:24, RSV)

Do not love the world or the things in the world. The love of the Father is not in those who love the world. (1 John 2:15, NRSV)

Come out from among them, and be . . . separate, . . . and touch not the unclean thing. (2 Corinthians 6:17, KJV)

Take no part in the . . . works of darkness. . . . it is shameful even to mention what such people do secretly. (Ephesians 5:11-12, NRSV)

Save some, by snatching them out of the fire, . . . hating even the garment spotted by the flesh. (Jude 23, RSV)

With Niebuhr's help we may think of a long train of those who fit this description: the early martyrs, Ignatius of Antioch, the desert fathers, the Montanists, Tertullian. More recently the Amish, the Anabaptists, and Tolstoy fit some characteristics of this position. The Jesus people of the 1970s were part of a countercultural movement whose communes and simple lifestyle signified their witness to the gospel and rejection of the American way of life. Many conservative Christians accept the economic and political aspects of our culture but are generally against its intellectual and entertainment contributions.

Opposite to the "Christ against culture" position is the "Christ *of* culture" one. This model is extremely positive about the world, emphasizing fundamental agreement between Christ and culture. Niebuhr speaks of those in this camp as seeing Jesus as a cultural hero or role model. For radical liberals, it may be the Christ of secular culture. For Puritans and Dominion theologians it may be the Christ of their subculture. Some Christians seem to be talking about the Christ of civil religion.

A different set of Scriptures may speak for this position:

Wisdom and knowledge are granted you. I will also give you riches, possessions, and honor. (2 Chronicles 1:12, NRSV)

Ask of me, and I will make the nations your heritage, and the ends of the earth your possession. (Psalm 2:8, NRSV)

Nations will come to your light, and kings to the brightness of your dawn. (Isaiah 60:3, NIV)

Niebuhr suggests three additional resolutions of Christ and culture: Christ *above* culture, a centrist position; Christ and culture *in paradox*, standing between Christ against culture and Christ above culture; and finally Christ *transforming* culture, seen between Christ above culture and Christ against culture.

The great gothic cathedrals of Europe, as symbols of the medieval synthesis, pointed skyward to the Christ above culture. For centuries the European world struggled to realize a Holy Roman Empire. An emperor governed an earthly realm checked by the heavenly authority of the pope as vicar of Christ. Here was an attempt to make society a reflection of the heavenly kingdom. The great works of Thomas Aquinas illustrate this worldview.

The rise of a commercial class, the strengthening of princes in cultures with languages and customs other than Latin, and the material wealth of Italian popes were factors that produced a growing sense of national identity in the sixteenth century. Martin Luther's spiritual enlightenment was accompanied by an emerging notion of German autonomy. In some ways Luther's nature, his ideas of church and state, of theology and law, and his very style all contained paradoxical elements. The medieval synthesis, never fully realized, was crumbling. Christ of the church and the law of the land were paradoxically related in Luther's mind; they were separate but interacting realities. This view of these kingdoms with their two swords or jurisdictions is an example of the position called Christ and culture in paradox.

We probably all sense some of the paradox in the mystery of Christ and culture, of our being *in* the world but not *of* it. Growing up involves an acceptance of tensions in both the ideals and the practical realities of world and life. Struggling with this issue, some may see Christ not to be of or equated to any earthly society, yet not against it all. "Christ above" may seem too static and ideal a way of thinking, and "Christ and culture in paradox" may seem too unresolved a view. Is not Christ trying to redeem institutions and societies that are fallen from the divine plan? There are elements of "Christ transforming culture" in the works of Augustine, Wesley, and the Anglican F. D. Maurice. A diagram of what has been explained might look like this:

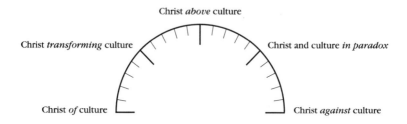

Christ *above* culture

Christ *transforming* culture

Christ and culture *in paradox*

Christ *of* culture

Christ *against* culture

The positions above may be seen as a spectrum or dial on which you may position yourself. They are not meant to be mutually exclusive; you may find yourself having more than one attitude toward the world in different situations. Richard Niebuhr did not mean to settle on any one position as the correct one. But this description of attitudes will help you as you wrestle with your approach to various aspects of the youth and pop cultures. As you consider the alternative approaches described, your dialogue about Christ and culture may be first with yourself, then with friends, and finally with young minds and hearts.

Rather than the Niebuhrian schema, some ethicists and theologians (Stanley Hauerwas and William Willimon, among others) prefer John Howard Yoder's classification of three church styles or stances toward society.[8] What Yoder describes as the *activist* (or theocratic) church is more concerned with the building of a better society than with the reformation of the church. The *conversionist* church (spiritualist reaction) despairs of fixing any society of sinners and concentrates instead on inward change, reforming

---

[8] Hauerwas and Willimon, *Resident Aliens: Life in the Christian Colony* (Nashville: Abingdon, 1989); Yoder, *The Royal Priesthood: Essays Ecclesiological and Ecumenical* (Grand Rapids: Eerdmans, 1994) 71-72.

the church from within. The *confessing* church (the believers' church) is not a synthesis of the two but a radical alternative—true worship produces a new people. The confessing church seeks more to show the world than to change the world—or hopes to change the world by its model.[9] This paradigm is intended to supersede that of Niebuhr and to point to the Pilgrim Anabaptist model as the most desirable. It offers a powerful prophetic challenge that is radical in its faithfulness to Christ and Scripture. Youth workers who seek to develop their own theology of culture would do well to examine these two paradigms of Richard Niebuhr and John Yoder.

THEOLOGIZING IN POP CULTURE

Our theologizing about culture must apply to our present task and ministry. We bring music, TV, movies, American industry, and advertising—all that influences you and young people—into this dialogue. Should I condemn all rap music that is not Christian, all rock music that is not soft and sweet? Do I go to G, PG, or some R-rated movies? Should I quit my job with a company producing offensive weapons of death, or any industry putting profits before human welfare and truth, to live in a simple community? How much should we spend on entertainment, vacations, and so on?

It is not an easy dialogue, is it? At issue are
- Christ and contemporary music, TV, movies;
- Christ and education, fine arts;
- Christ and public school prayer, instruction in Judeo-Christian values;
- Christ and American productivity, commercials;
- Christ and war, terrorism, national security;
- Christ and health, wealth, poverty, unemployment.

---

[9] See also John Howard Yoder, "How H. Richard Niebuhr Reasons: A Critique of *Christ and Culture*," in *Authentic Transformation: A New Vision of Christ and Culture* (Glen Stassen, Diane Yeager, and John H. Yoder; Nashville: Abingdon, 1996).

How can these dualisms be brought into holistic living? What does it mean to be "separate from the world" (2 Corinthians 6:17) and yet be "salt and light" (Matthew 5:13-14) at the same time? How do we see Christ relating to our world, our society, and its institutions? How do we cooperate and communicate with our secular colleagues?

Is Christ happy with it all? How does our Lord view the current trends in pop culture? Is Christ winning? Is he just waiting? Is Christ at work in our culture—and how? What does Christ want us to do? And what are we calling young folk to do? These are the challenges that flow out of this book and a theology of culture.

REMEMBERING THE GOD-ORDAINED FUNCTIONS OF CULTURE

The Bible contains four implicit expectations for all cultures:

1. to nurture children to the full human potential of adulthood;
2. to provide justice for all people and classes of society;
3. to protect, and act responsibly in regard to, the environment;
4. to seek individually and corporately for transcendent meaning in the Creator of all—to "grope after God."

In the foundations for human life set out in the Law, in the conservative and traditional values of the Writings, in the sometimes radical assertions of the Prophets, from the words of our Lord in the Gospels, and among the teachings of the Epistles, there is consensus about the functions and responsibilities of culture. Many Christians do not realize how much of the Bible is written to those outside the covenants—those who did not live under theocratic rule. Substantial sections addressed to Babylon and Egypt, Damascus and Edom, Tyre and Sidon give clear indication of what God expects today from Great Britain and China, Moscow and Lagos, New York and Sao Paulo.

God's special instruction to Israel and the church is meant to complement what general revelation (through nature and culture) teaches all the world. The chosen people are always meant to be a light to the Gentiles, to model God's will for all cultures.

What does God expect from culture? Based on these expectations, how should we of faith judge our cultures?

1. God expects children to be raised to their full human potential, and God judges those who thwart such growth.

   Children are an heritage of the Lord. (Psalm 127:3, KJV)

   Train up a child in the way he should go. (Proverbs 22:6, KJV)

2. God's heart is set on justice especially for the weak and vulnerable. Harsh judgment awaits injustice.

   [God] has showed you . . . [Israel, Moab, and all people of the earth] what is good; and what does the LORD require of you but to do justice, and to love kindness [compassion], and to walk humbly with your God. (Micah 6:8, RSV)

3. God intends divine creatures to treat their environment as the Creator's handiwork.

   The LORD God took the man and put him in the garden of Eden to till it and to keep it. (Genesis 2:15, NRSV)

   You set the earth on its foundations. . . . You make springs gush forth in the valleys, . . . giving drink to every wild animal. . . . By the streams the birds of the air have their habitation. . . . Oh, LORD, how manifold are your works. (Psalm 104:5, 10-12, 24, NRSV; note also how the Lord speaks of creation and describes a personal relationship with all creatures in Job 38 and 39).

   The land is mine; . . . you are but . . . tenants. (Leviticus 25:23, NRSV)

4. God wants all cultures to seek the true and living God, and divine judgment extends to all idolatry and suppression of spiritual life.

   God . . . made the world and everything in it. . . . [God] made from one [common blood] every [culture on earth] . . . that they should seek God, in the hope that

they might feel after [God] and find [God]. [For God] is
not far from each one of us. (Acts 17:24, 26-27, RSV)

Much more could be said regarding these three expectations of all cultures: the significance of children and their
growth, the crucial importance of justice to a society, and
the need of all cultures for divine grace. But these few
explicit references and clear principles are suggested as a
basis for all cultural exegesis, ethics, and pastoral theology.

CONCLUDING REMARKS

If our study of culture and its relationship to Christ is
not to be resolved until the final day, should we then give it
up as too complicated or useless? Or is this difficult dialogue a way of growth and maturity in Christ our Lord? An
honest and thorough effort in doing our theology of culture
ought to make us more effective in our incarnational presence and ministry, that is, in our relating, listening, and
talking with young folk, in communicating the gospel, and
in discipling young Christians.

No one can live without culture. Living in any particular culture, Christians are under a mandate to follow principles that provide for human growth and welfare—and
ultimately bring glory to God the Creator of all. We are all
human, yet we all have the divine breath of life in us and
divine aspirations. We are individuals with corporate bonds.
We are fallen yet redeemed. We live in that which we must
leave. Our lives have complicated dimensions, but we share
in God's intention for our common good.

None of us will ever solve all the problems of interpreting faith and culture. There are no neat answers to
these complex issues. But we can arrive at some partial
answers by humbly accepting help from those working
from different perspectives. Individually we can be faithful
in our attempt by "keeping our hearts with all diligence"
(Proverbs 4:23).

Christ is the key to our interpretation of culture. The divine nature permanently identifies with human culture. The eternal Son takes on a physical body in a particular culture. While retaining his divine identity, Christ relinquishes so many prerogatives! This mystery of the incarnation offers us a grand and useful model for all youth ministry. The God who left glorious security to become a vulnerable servant is the basis for life in the church and for outreach to the world.

The paradoxes of incarnation and spiritual life remain. The Word becomes flesh that we may find spirit. The self-denial and crucifixion of Christ and many of his followers lead to life and self-realization (Philippians 2:5-12). Culture is the transient stage of an eternal drama. Culture is judged that it might be redeemed. We are to be very much in the world without being of it. As salt we are an irritant to any culture—with a sense of humor and hope that preserves and enlivens whatever social situation we attend.

A heart that has integrity and is humble, open to the Word and to the world, seems to be the best secret for faithful integrity: "Where your treasure is, there will your heart be also." "Unless you are converted and become like children, you shall not enter the kingdom of heaven" (Matthew 6:21; 18:3, NASB). Children accept life's deepest mysteries with trustful hearts. That is why Jesus told us older ones to copy them. Clear focus, humility, and a tolerance of differing opinions will do us well.

QUESTIONS FOR REFLECTION AND DISCUSSION

1. Do you see cultures as socially constructed and part of a divine plan?
2. Discuss this statement: All cultures are beautiful because of their creative origin and are to some degree destructive because of human rebellion. Are all societies under judgment and grace?
3. Do you see yourself called to be a blessing to cultures as well as to individuals?

4. What impresses you most and what is most difficult for you to understand in this chapter? What might help you get a clearer picture of Christ and culture?
5. Where do you see yourself in Niebuhr's five positions? Is it possible to see yourself in more than one position?
6. Do you see this theological discussion as relevant to youth ministry and to your personal growth?
7. In what specific ways might you use these insights with young people? How might your understanding of this material enable you to train volunteer leaders more effectively?

THEOLOGY OF GROWTH AND DEVELOPMENT

The Universal Goals of Growth and Development

I'll tell you something: If you're not growing, you're dying; and most adults seem to have stopped growing.
> —*Voices of youth*

You spend your time thinking about making money and the meaning of your life, but for us and most of the world, the issues are survival and development.
> —*Voices from the third world*

The boy Samuel and the boy Jesus grew in wisdom and stature and favor with God and people.
> —*See 1 Samuel 2:26; Luke 2:52, paraphrase*

We must no longer be children . . . we must grow up . . . to maturity . . . to . . . the full stature of Christ.
> —*Ephesians 4:14, 15, 13,* NRSV

GROWTH IN THE BIBLE

And the child [Isaac] grew and was weaned, and Abraham made a great feast on the day that Isaac was weaned.
> —*Genesis 21:8,* NASB

Because youth ministers are so involved with growth, they need a strong theology of growth. The Bible strongly emphasizes growth, from the growth of herbs and trees in the garden of Eden, the growing up of children throughout Scripture, the growth of Israel, of the temple and of the walls of Jerusalem, to the growth of the church and individuals and the final appearance of the new city as described in the Apocalypse. God grows plants (Genesis 2:8; Jeremiah 2:21; 11:16-17; John 15:1) and nurtures sheep (Psalm 95:7; Ezekiel 34:11-16). Jesus tells powerful stories describing lilies growing (Matthew 6:28), seeds sprouting, wheat and tares, and a mustard seed's remarkable growth (as found in Matthew 13:4ff., 24ff., 31ff.). Our Lord lays hands on children and blesses their growth (Mark 10:13-16). In anger Christ curses those who hinder the growth of young ones (Matthew 18:1-6). Paul is driven by twin passions for individual and church growth (2 Timothy 1:3-6; Acts 15:41; 19:8-10; Romans 16:25-27). The significance and urgency of growth should impress all who read Scripture.

GROWTH AS A THEOLOGICAL ISSUE

Various European and American theologies have been built around concepts such as divine decrees, covenants, dispensations, conversion, healing process, semantics, and liberation. These are all topics that we should not dismiss. Amazingly, however, the indexes of some theological texts do not contain crucial concepts such as growth, poverty, and suffering. Theology may certainly begin with a consideration of the nature of God and God's mighty works in creation and history. God's salvific works in the conversion of nations and individuals are indeed central, but they must always be interpreted in the light of the key issues of each culture and its individuals.

Theology does not hear enough from the poor and the young. Those who suffer deeply turn to the Bible for its promises of healing. When the oppressed read Scripture, they find affirmation regarding their special closeness to the heart of God—the special promises of liberation. Black theology finds inspiration from the central redemptive action of the Old Testament: the exodus. Those dedicated to ministry with the young find strong affirmation of growth in all God's creatures. Similarly, those who suffer from all kinds of disadvantages, whose life struggle is to provide opportunity for self and family as God intended, need a theological basis for community development. And liberation naturally precedes development.

Without losing crucial emphases on the cross, conversion, healing, and liberation, we who seek God's intentions for young people must deal with personal growth *and* community development. Such considerations will affect the way we present the good news to young people in various cultural situations.

Theologies are formed under the authority of Scripture, with the guidance and teaching of the church, in the context of personal and communal experience illumined by the Holy Spirit. Any theology that is true to Scripture and the historic creeds, that is Christ-centered and focuses on the atoning work of the cross, that dedicates itself to the strengthening of the church and serving of the world, should, by the integrity of this process, be kept from heresy and false emphases. Heresies distort the central doctrines of God, of Christ, creation, fall, incarnation, atonement, salvation, church, and eschatology. False emphases allow minor issues to usurp core truths and distort a balanced perspective.

A biblical consideration of culture is expressed in Paul's Athenian address (Acts 17:24ff.). God's cultural mandates to our human ancestors were to reproduce (Genesis 1:28) and to rule the earth (Genesis 1:26, 28-29). Biblical language seems to imply our being invited to become like partners with God in building a human society of compassionate justice (note the sense of our loving others as God loves us in John 15:9ff.; 1 John 4:7-12, 19; and throughout Scripture). Reproduction involves bringing new human life to full maturity, and ruling the earth implies orderly development. The divine-human covenants of the Bible explain a divine sanction of human cultures and direct us toward divinely intended goals for human societies. A significant

function for all cultures is to foster growth and development. This godly mandate becomes an ethical criterion that
we should apply in all societies.

Tired ministries may be the result of tired theologies.
Theologies are renewed as the cries of the world provoke
fresh insights into God's Word. New networks of professors
and trainers of youth ministers are gathering around the
United States and in Oxford to read papers and engage in
theological discussions.

Youth ministers of all denominations of the church
hunger for theological insight and encouragement. These
leaders at the grass roots of global youth ministries are
particularly interested in theology that offers instruction
and inspiration for the effective nurture of human and
spiritual growth.

SECULAR AND THEOLOGICAL UNDERSTANDINGS OF GROWTH

Does a theology of growth have important theological
implications beyond youth ministry? The quest of youth
ministers for universal understanding regarding human
growth may provide us with a key to a most difficult issue
of our times. How are Christians to collaborate with secularists? How are we to cooperate in great civil endeavors
such as the rearing of children? Is there any possibility for
consensus and tentative coalitions?

Many societies are paralyzed by polarization between
religious fundamentalists and liberal secularists, between
moral concern on the right and concern for freedom
(which the right sees as moral drift) on the left. Remorse
for lost values and fear of chaotic change drives those on
the right; anger over the inhibiting and regressive tendencies of conservatives and reactionaries, along with hope for
a new era, energizes those on the left.

Our postmodern, post-Christian society often loses
sight of goals long considered basic to personal growth and
to the common good. Life is dominated by profits and
consumption at one end and self-realization and instant,

superficial relationships on the other. Children, who have been increasingly neglected by parents, are manipulated by media and seen as an audience that can be programmed to buy toys of violence and dolls with sexual allure. Things are no longer used to help people; people are used for profit. Having lost God, we have lost our true purpose, the twin goals of individual maturity and a just society; our technological means have become tyrannical ends in themselves. We struggle to exist without the satisfaction of a fulfilled life.

Failures of human development are redressed in the incarnation.

> He [Christ] is the image of the invisible God, the first-born of all creation. . . . In Him [Christ] all the fulness of Deity dwells in bodily form, and in Him you have been made complete. (Colossians 1:15; 2:9–10, NASB)

> It was he who gave some . . . so that the body of Christ may be built up until we all reach unity in the faith . . . and become mature, attaining to the whole measure of the fullness of Christ. (Ephesians 4:11–13, NIV)

The incarnation affirms creation and culture. This doctrine teaches that God has not yet given up on us. God still wants us to do a good job filling the earth with a rich variety of cultures.

How a culture socializes its young, how it helps them achieve maturity, full manhood and womanhood, is of crucial importance to all. As youth workers we are for healthy growth, and we must think well about what such growth involves. The growth of Jesus himself is described in *physical, psychic* (intellectual and emotional), *social,* and *spiritual* terms (Luke 2:40, 52). God's intentions for the growth of children and youth are also given classic expression in the story of Samuel (1 Samuel 2:21, 26; 3:19).

Because they have been given a divine responsibility to nurture the proper growth of the young, parents, educators, and youth leaders should be deeply interested in the theories of developmentalists. The following are considered experts on child and youth development:

- physical development, Jeanne Brooks-Gunn and Daniel Offer;
- cognitive development, Jean Piaget and Daniel P. Keating;
- emotional development, Erik Erikson and Stuart T. Hauser;
- social development, Erik Erikson and David Elkind;
- moral development, Lawrence Kohlberg and Carol Gilligan;
- faith development, James Fowler and Kenneth Hyde.

As Carol Gilligan has challenged some of the male biases in developmental theory, so writers like Diane T. Slaughter and Jawanza Kunjufu provide insights regarding the growth of African-American children.[1] More studies are needed among other ethnic groups. Developmental theories have not always given adequate attention to the crucial influence of primary systems around young people (family, community, school, peers, and media). We are conscious today of the dramatic ways in which the growth of children can be stunted and twisted.

The ultimate end of growth is full human maturity—God's full intention for human beings. The goal of each boy or girl to reach total manhood or womanhood should be shared by every youth worker and adult. It is a terrible crime before God to keep (or treat) men as boys—or women as girls—and either as objects. This goal of maturity is a criterion on which people of various faiths and goodwill ought to agree in a secular society. This is the glue that should hold contemporary secular cultures together.

Jesus damned systems and individuals who thwart the divine mandate of growth when he declared:

---

[1] Gilligan, *In a Different Voice: Psychological Theory and Woman's Development* (Cambridge: Harvard University Press, 1982); Slaughter, *Black Children and Poverty: A Developmental Perspective* (San Francisco: Jossay-Bass, 1988); Kunjufu, *Developing Positive Self-Images and Discipline in Black Children* (Chicago: African-American Images, 1984).

Woe to him through whom [stumbling blocks] come. It would be better for him if a millstone were hung around his neck and he were thrown into the sea, than that he should cause one of these little ones to stumble. (Luke 17:1-2, NASB)

Among the prominent images of God in Scripture are those of parent (mother-father), shepherd, and farmer. Parents, shepherds, and farmers are all concerned with growth. Their hearts are bent on seeing children, sheep, and plants fulfill their destiny in maturity or harvest. Young parents find an increasing commitment to the welfare and continued growth of their children.

Similarly, the hearts of teachers, counselors, and youth ministers are bent on seeing growth in young lives. Human growth is God's business; we are called to assist various aspects of that growth. As Christian youth workers understand it, growth is facilitated by:

- proper role models (begins with parents, early teachers, etc.),
- a relationship that facilitates full and deep communication,
- a grounding in norms and values and information,
- the development of skills necessary for life and study,
- a commitment to Christ as the key to full growth,
- counseling to rectify improper parenting,
- and learning.

As parents, teachers, coaches, youth evangelists, and counselors, we should be united in a common task. We realize that society's role models and the systemic instructors—especially in media—play a powerful part in the healthy or pathological growth of young people.

Around the world youth leaders are dealing with young people in cultural transition. As ideological immigrants they may be moving (to the great consternation of their parents) from values of a conservative culture to those of a wide open society. In many countries, especially developing ones, leaders in large cities are ministering to youth who have just left a rural farm. These urban immigrants find in the city a technological world that is a much more complex and difficult place to grow up than the tribal or traditional environments from which they have come.

Today's world is not merely fallen from God's intention—it is self-consciously secular. Rapid change and the demand for economic survival overwhelm attempts to reevaluate our cultural beliefs and values. We hardly notice our loss of rich traditional treasures. Europe and America are losing not only their Judeo-Christian heritage but also their Greek ideals of purpose and harmony.

Aristotle and those who followed him were convinced that all things in creation were growing toward an ideal form or purpose. From the acorn to the human fetus, all had a potential, a *telos* (end or purpose). The mighty oak or the fully mature (and godlike, as the Greeks would say) man and woman were that which all by nature strained to become. Anything that hindered that growth or marred the ideal was wrong.

The Greeks also taught us lessons of *harmonia* or balance. This wisdom warns us against imbalance and extremes of all kinds in personal and public life. Balance in our theology, ministry, and personal lives is guided by concepts of justice, unity, and peace. *Harmonia* encourages our pursuit of individual and social wholeness.

A DISTURBING PICTURE

Not only has the modern world lost important lessons and values of Western civilization but it also has scorned important ideas from other cultures, such as the East (ideas like the high value of silence and respect for the environment). We might have been spared some of our current woes if we had paid more attention to the Native American's and African's respect for elders and ancestors, reverence for nature, and communal solidarity. Soulless and sterile, modern urban culture turns too much to chemical mood conditioners and media sensations for pacification and arousal. Lacking anchors and compasses, we often seem to be drifting without clear direction or ultimate purpose.

When cultural agnosticism and relativism are put together with unrestrained greed for national power and private control, the result is a narcissistic and addictive society. Family, schools, and churches are greatly weakened. Children pushed to achieve in such an acquisitive society will become what Erikson called *pseudomature in pseudospecies,* Sebald identified as *multi-personae,* Elkind described as a *patchwork selves,* and Howe and Strauss referred to as *particle man.*[2] My own studies have made me conscious of the tendency in today's young people to compartmentalize their lives into separate "value fields" or worlds to an extent that is confusing, stressful, and often self-destructive.

The further a society moves from positive commitment to growth and development, the closer it comes to destruction and death. Thomas French, a newspaper reporter, spent an amazing year with students inside Largo High School in Florida. Students initially resented his intrusion into their school and private lives. Soon, however, these young people opened up remarkably to this adult who seemed genuinely concerned with their lives and stories. The absence of fathers, the sincere struggles of mothers, the pressures of peers, and the apparent meaninglessness of life to youthful idealistic hearts are themes of this report.[3]

This high school has a special alternative program named GOALS for those who would have dropped out or been suspended from school. In the pod, as the alternative program is often called, French hears spontaneous and often disheartening discussions. In one of these a teacher tries to discover more of Eric and where he is at by asking why he burned his Ouija board. "It told me I was going to die," he replied. The class was immediately alert. As French observes:

---

[2] Erikson, *Identity, Youth, and Crisis,* 41–42, 138; Hans Sebald, *Adolescence:A Social Psychological Analysis* (4th ed.; New York: Prentice-Hall, 1992) 84; Elkind, *All Grown Up,* 17; Howe and Strauss, *13th Gen.*

[3] *South of Heaven: Welcome to High School at the End of the Twentieth Century* (New York: Doubleday, 1993).

Death is always in the Top 40 here in the pod. It surfaces constantly in the kids' conversations, floating through so many of their favorite songs, swirling silently in the overwhelming grimness of their wardrobes. Black is the color du jour every jour. They wear black shoes, black shirts, black jeans, black dresses, black jackets, black hats, even black motorcycle helmets. If it comes in black, they want it.

No one has carried this infatuation further than the Smurf Killer. He's not in GOALS any more. . . . [But] by now the stories about this boy have taken on an almost mythic air. It wasn't just the Smurf allegedly dangling from a noose in his locker, . . . [the boy] showed signs of deep psychological disturbance. As best as they could tell, he was actively worshipping the devil. . . . A possum skull adorned with a candle was also found in his locker. In class he was obsessed with death and despair, constantly writing on those themes in English. At one point, he even wrote obituaries for himself and other members of his family, inventing horribly violent ways for all of them to exit this world.[4]

This is an extreme example from what some may see as an extreme group of young people. But from such samplings we gain insight into the illness of a society. Today's urban cultures bring young people emptiness, then fill the void with media messages and merchandise to suit their disillusioned moods. French continues:

Many teenagers—and indeed, many adults—are interested in death, but not to the pervasive degree found with so many GOALS kids. It's not just the gruesome songs and the black clothes, either. They wear necklaces and rings and earrings adorned with skulls and skeletons. They draw ghouls and monsters on their folders. They carve pentagrams and other satanic symbols on the tops and bottoms . . . of the wooden tables in their classes. When they're bored they've been known to sketch portraits of the Grim Reaper.

Maybe it has something to do with their feelings of powerlessness. Or maybe they're just young and especially eager to

---

[4] Ibid., 125.

shock their teachers and parents. But they are especially fascinated when they hear something macabre that hits close to home.[5]

Studying these high school students empathetically gives us greater insights as to how families, schools, media, and peer groups often thwart the development of teenagers. We sense how neglect, value confusion, stereotyping, insults, racism, classism, and sexism can undermine their life task of growing up. They become unusual heralds of our society's unnatural disinterest in healthy growth. A society that is not growing is dying, and people whose growth is stunted may be obsessed with destruction and death.

David St. Clair's *Say You Love Satan* is a fuller study of a young man like the "Smurf Killer," but in this case the teenage boy actually killed his friend.[6] In *Satanism and Occult-Related Violence,* and *Recovery from Cults: Help for Victims of Psychological and Spiritual Abuse,* Michael D. Langone has studied ritual abuse, the occult, and the morbid preoccupation described by Thomas French above.[7] From these studies come a greater appreciation for the vulnerability of young people today and the seductive attraction of cults that promise the security and sense of belonging they crave.

Stories of other troubled youth illustrate how vulnerable youth are. The anonymous diary, *Go Ask Alice,* and Betsy Israel's autobiographical *Grown-Up Fast* poignantly describe self-destructive attempts to find self-identity, acceptance, and love in drugs and sex (in the late 1960s and 1970s, respectively).[8] In *Troubled Youth, Troubled Families,* James Garbarino studies abuse among runaways in the

---

[5] Ibid., 125–26.

[6] New York: Dell, 1987.

[7] Langone, *Satanism and Occult-Related Violence* (Bonita Springs, Fla.: American Family Foundation, 1990); idem, *Recovery from Cults: Help for Victims of Psychological and Spiritual Abuse* (New York: Norton, 1993).

[8] *Go Ask Alice* (Englewood Cliffs, N.J.: Prentice-Hall, 1971); *Grown-Up Fast* (New York: Poseidon, 1988).

context of generational abuse, families, and other social systems surrounding delinquent youth.[9] His studies help us understand the cycle of abuse that can spiral out of control through generations.

In the powerful and disturbing *Best Intentions: The Education and Killing of Edmund Perry*, Sam Anson describes the development and destruction of a young African-American student from Harlem who gains entrance to and honors from Phillips Exeter Academy.[10] Edmund Perry's unusual human and intellectual potential do not find the necessary guidance in an American society tainted by racism. Superficially accepted, he becomes successful on the surface, but he is not helped to grow holistically. He is shot dead on a New York City street before he can take advantage of a full scholarship to Stanford University. His closest male mentor concluded that the burden of living between two conflicting environments and maintaining defense mechanisms drove him to risky street behavior on that fateful night.

These narratives and studies reveal troublesome trends, but they need not fill us with despair or cynicism. Although corrective attempts are hindered by the polarization of extremists, there is still hope for consensus among moderates of goodwill and positive intentions in our society. Parents and youth leaders can find allies among those willing to face the times and help young people to grow.

POSSIBLE CONSENSUS

Society instinctively senses a responsibility for raising its next generation of leaders. As clearly as parents of all species recognize an urge to reproduce, cultures are bent toward socializing their young. At some point and time any culture

---

[9] James Garbarino, et al., *Troubled Youth, Troubled Families: Understanding Families At-Risk for Adolescent Maltreatment* (New York: Aldine, 1986).
[10] New York: Vintage, 1987.

should say: "Don't harm our children or prevent their growth into well-functioning adults." It is evidently difficult for societies to recognize the point where such thwarting of growth occurs. Boundaries against media abuse or harmful manipulation are hindered by our values of freedom and a tolerant legal system. It is difficult to protect both the common good and individual welfare at the same time. Wild claims are made for personal or commercial freedoms of expression. Although many shy away from strong and objective moral guidelines, society in general still retains a strong protective sense for childhood growth and welfare. Deborah Prothrow-Stith has given us a model for curbing media license (and forging a sane coalition of Christians and secularists) by making the issue of violence a public health issue. Her point needs to be studied.

> The more I learned [from the criminal justice system, the mental health profession, and the biological sciences] the more I was convinced that a new inter-disciplinary approach to violence, one beginning with the perception that violence is an assault on the public health, was required to save the endangered lives of our young. . . .

> As individuals we do not have the power to protect all the children. We do have the power to ban the sale of handguns, end the sale of illicit drugs, or require that violence be portrayed realistically in the mass media. . . . As individuals we only have a little power, but the power that we have is profound nevertheless. It is the power to care.[11]

For Christians, Christ is the model of growth and of its goal, maturity. This Christian model of maturity shares a common goal of growth with the secular ideal of fulfilled humanity. We hope that leaders of goodwill may unite around such an ideal. Youth leaders want every boy and girl to grow into full manhood and womanhood.

---

[11] *Deadly Consequences: How Violence Is Destroying Our Teenage Population and a Plan to Begin Solving the Problem* (New York: Harper-Collins, 1991) 10, 202.

Scripture describes the heart of God as set on growth and development in unity, justice, and peace. All that stifles growth, hinders natural development, produces inequity, and fosters animosity is contrary to God's will. Efforts to ameliorate injustice and evil, endeavors that contribute to healing and growth, are pleasing to God.

In a complex world and for people desensitized by millions of images of real and fictional affronts to dignity, purity, and peace, it is important for our secular culture to agree on this ideal as a working criterion: That which hinders and hurts is wrong; that which heals and fosters growth is right.

THE GROWTH PRINCIPLE IN YOUTH MINISTRY

The youth minister of the gospel must face a question something like this: "Besides introducing all those I can to Jesus Christ, do I have a responsibility under God to help those not willing to commit themselves to Christian faith?" Pondering this question takes us back to the example of Jesus. Did our Lord help only those who made adequate profession of faith, or did he touch people because they had need? Students of mine have sometimes responded: "No, my limited time and energy must be reserved only for those who respond to the message of Christ." Then I ask them to consider themselves as parents of a son or daughter who turns away from Christ. "Are you still going to help them get through college and help their general development?" If we agree that we should help young people unconditionally (regardless of their present faith commitment), the question is, How are we to do that?

We need to share a message of growth and development, a message that all can hear. At first, and in certain situations, we may not use the name of Christ. But this work is all done, and all messages are given, in the name that is above all names and values and goals. Indeed, this name offers the only goal, purpose, and means by which the world can develop in a just manner and individuals can attain full growth. Ultimate growth (according to the Christian gospel) will be centered in Christ and the victory of the cross—though much can and must be done without immediate, explicit reference to this glorious reality. In a world that is fallen and being redeemed, Christians and Christian theology are aware of the paradoxical nature of growth and development. We talk about health and growth, development and prosperity, in a fallen world. Although the goal is life, it comes through death. Although we want to be whole, we must be broken first. Egotism or self-centeredness must give way to being Christ-centered for Christians; to life for others and the common good for secularists. Sometimes only brokenness removes defense mechanisms that prevent fuller growth.

Joseph and Moses had God-given dreams of growth and leadership. But Egypt's prison and the school of the desert came first for both. Paul wanted to know "the power of Christ's resurrection," but he could reach it only through "the fellowship of His sufferings, being conformed to His death" (Philippians 3:10, NASB). Paul's life of paradox was further expressed: "I am crucified with Christ; nevertheless I live; yet not I, but Christ liveth in me" (Galatians 2:20, KJV).

COMMUNITY DEVELOPMENT

Listen to our emphasis here on personal growth. Imagine how Western and middle class—hence irrelevant—it sounds to those struggling for survival in urban ghettos, in Haiti, Ethiopia, and so many countries of the world. But God's will for the world is for community development as well as personal growth.

By now some may wonder whether the need for personal faith and salvation has been lost. No—any full analysis of the world, with recognition of our failed human attempts at reform and renewal, points to faith as crucial for growth and to ongoing conversion as crucial for the renewal and development of human communities and society.

Others will feel overwhelmed by the complexity of the needs in our communities. Such anxiety can turn us into protective isolationists or can bring humble vulnerability, opening us to the mysteries of God and to help from all sorts of neighbors. It is easy to retreat to the ghetto of Christian subcultures, to work inside parochial walls, to become so involved with our institutional problems and affairs that we never venture into the mainstream of life where salt and light are desperately needed.

The paradox of real life and growth is difficult enough for us as leaders. Young people being conditioned to become self-centered and compartmentalized consumers can attain true growth and maturity only when they have accessible role models. These role models must tell their stories and those of Jesus Christ as stories of service and worship in Christian community.

Most young people will come to faith and maturity only as they share, grow, and serve in positive and supportive peer groups—as countercultural brands enlightening the darkness of contemporary society. Whole persons with visions of global community—this is the necessary vision for our times. This is the challenge of youth ministry today.

QUESTIONS FOR REFLECTION AND DISCUSSION

1. Do you see growth as a central theme and aim of youth leaders? Does it provide a good base for counseling and instruction?
2. Is growth an important ethical criterion? Can a secular society agree that all which hinders growth in a society is wrong and that all which promotes true and healthy growth is good?
3. How would you explain that a person is either growing or dying?
4. Is growth fundamental to biblical or gospel concerns?
5. Should you be primarily concerned that those young folk among whom you minister show evidence of long-term growth?
6. Do you find yourself thinking and praying about growth goals for young people you know?
7. Would you describe your pattern of counseling young people as a "growth model"? How might the "four basic questions," given in chapter 3, be used in such counseling?

6

THEOLOGY OF FAMILY AND PEERS

Strong Influences

Then God said, "Let us make humankind in our image . . . male and female."
—*Genesis 1:26-27*, NRSV

Jesus said, . . . "From the beginning of creation, 'God made them male and female.' 'For this reason a man shall leave his father and mother and be joined to his wife.' "
—*Mark 10:5-7*, NRSV

No one has greater love than this—that a man lay down his life for his friends.
—*John 15:13, Weymouth*

Without counsel, plans go wrong, but with many advisers they succeed.
—*Proverbs 15:22*, NRSV

GROWING UP IN TWO IMPORTANT SYSTEMS

As youth leaders attend to young people, it is important to see each individual as a product of several systems: family, community, schools, media, peers—and for some, church. Beyond these immediate systems, economic and governmental institutions produce an environment of overlapping systems in which the life and growth of a person take place.

A young man grew up in a strong, urban family. Both his older brother and his father were policemen, but he became caught up in the wrong crowd and ended up involved in a murder. He had moved from the influence of his family system to that of a competing system. Weeping, he called his uncle, also an officer, living in another state. The uncle convinced his nephew to turn himself in, and this young man now faces a lifetime of confinement.

In another scene, a suburban family is shocked to find out that their daughter has drifted into a group involved with drugs and sex. Suddenly, this family feels as if it has lost a member; she has traded family ties for high-risk behavior. A Christian family discovers that their second son is already deep in the drug scene. He denies having any problem and says he is just having fun partying with others who occasionally drink and experiment with drugs. Heartbroken, the family tries everything to get him to stop using drugs, to no avail.

These accounts, all too common, illustrate a relationship between two of the most important systems in a teenager's life: family and peers. To these stories should be added countless scenes of young people following the difficult right path with *supportive families* and with *good friends*.

In chapter 4 I asserted that a child cannot become human apart from culture. The Creator has established a pattern by which individuals begin life in the cultural institution called family. What weakens family life threatens children—and society itself. On the principle that whatever hinders the growth of a person to full human potential is wrong, the religious and secular teachers of our society ought to agree and collaborate. Without cooperation among the primary systems surrounding young people, today's urban societies have little hope.

Adolescents wrestle with critical issues of *identity, new relationships,* and *leaving home.* After growing up in a family, a person must establish his or her own life and home. Theological reflection on adolescence requires consideration of the nature of family of origin, transition, and, finally, a new, adult family or single living.

Most youth ministers are still in this growing-up process themselves. This should not lead to any lack of confidence in their work. Young people are looking for honest young guides who are themselves not quite fully adult. The young adult leader is an important complement to parents as they provide models and instructions about the nature of identity and relationships.

DEFINITION OF FAMILY

Two competing definitions of "family" illustrate the cultural debate of our times. The *American Heritage Dictionary,* 2d ed., calls *family* "The most instinctive, fundamental social or mating group in man and animal, especially the union of man and woman through marriage and their offspring; parents and their children." A fifth definition in the same dictionary gives an alternative notion: "All the members of a household; those who share one's domestic home." *Webster's New Twentieth-Century Dictionary, Unabridged,* 2d ed., however, has a reverse emphasis and gives as a first definition, "the collective body of persons who live in one house," and second, "a father, mother, and their children." The order of *Webster's* illustrates the emphasis in family theory as it is taught and written about today.

UNDERSTANDING THE FAMILY TODAY

Most social scientists have recognized the importance of the family. According to Hans Sebald:

> Of the various groups to which we belong, the family has the most far-reaching impact on personality development. Quality of family interaction, and its bearing on the way the young grow into adulthood, is significantly affected by the structure of the family.
>
> Family dynamics penetrate into the individual's personality and have a decisive influence on how he or she weathers the crisis of adolescence.[1]

---

[1] *Adolescence,* 178.

The family is a social system undergoing rapid transition.

1. The family system is affected by its larger social context; sometimes the transition is from a more traditional or conservative culture to a more urban society.

- Value systems are in flux, and there is less social support for the family.

2. Family structure is changing from extended families, including grandparents, uncles, or aunts, to more isolated nuclear families.

- Children have fewer role models and less available time and interaction with them.

3. Between 1960 and 1980 the family often changed from a home with a single breadwinner and single home-maker to a situation in which both parents were (or the single parent was) forced to work.

- Latchkey children learned to care for themselves at a much earlier age. Television or stereo welcomed them home. Friends of either sex might be invited in.

4. Divorce rates have greatly increased. David Elkind's chapter on "Family Permutations" describes the effects of a single decade (the 1970s) in which the number of children affected by separation and divorce doubled.[2] Studies gradually convinced experts of the immediate and long-term difficulties divorce inflicts on children and young adults.

- Children now fear the divorce of their parents more than the death of their parents. They grow up with less family security.

5. The family is losing what is called its "primary-group quality": there is less cooperative interaction among its members as a group. As the family gives up some of its traditional functions, these are taken up by other institu-

---

[2] *All Grown Up,* 115–35.

tions, which tend both to complement and to compete with the family.

- Children may lose a safe place and clear mentors at an age when they should be forming an integrated sense of self. They depend increasingly on media for support and instruction.

6. Many experts have noted a lack of parental skill; some have even called for a "child license" before parenthood.

- Adolescents may sometimes feel the burden of instructing their parents in social skills.

7. Members of the family have been treated socially and legally more as individuals than as part of a family group. Legislation has stressed the rights of children as individuals, and some children may remind their parents of limits to their control. This can further erode family unity.

- Many young people sense that they must rely on themselves and on an array of social systems outside the home while they are growing up.

Advertiser James Patterson and researcher Peter Kim report:

> We [Americans] have lost faith in the institution of marriage. A third of all married men and women confessed to us that they've had at least one affair. Twenty-nine percent aren't really sure that they still love their spouses. . . . More than half of all Americans genuinely believe that there is no good reason for anyone to get married.[3]

This may be an extreme picture of the American attitude toward the family at the beginning of the 1990s. But it is based on some research, and it calls for a new commitment to society's basic building block.

---

[3] *The Day America Told the Truth: What People Really Believe about Everything That Really Matters* (New York: Prentice-Hall, 1991) 236-37.

THE BLESSED TRINITY AS THE MODEL FOR HUMAN LIFE

As we search for the theological beginning of families, it is hard to miss a remarkable pronoun in the creation story. The Bible's opening chapter provides a key for all human interaction: "Let *us* make human beings in *our* image." The "us" of the Godhead created male and female to be with each other and with God. From early centuries the Trinity has been held up as a holy model for all of life's relationships and communities. We need each other—and God.

It is important to see how the dynamic relationship of Father, Son, and Holy Spirit is meant to be mirrored in each individual (whether we see ourselves in biblical terms of body, soul, and spirit, or in functional terms). The ultimate support for each marriage, each community of neighbors, and every organization of human effort is the cooperation of opposites with God's support. God is the necessary third partner in every human relationship. Without divine partnership, any human relationship is as unstable as a two-legged stool. Adolescents and young marriages will need to build on such fundamental principles more than ever before as we approach and enter the twenty-first century.

THE REALITY OF FAMILY LIFE

As the first social system, families are specially meant to reflect the harmony and support of the divine nature. This is not to say that all families follow a particular traditional pattern. Biblical principles must always be worked out in unique situations and cultural contexts. Even if there were one established scriptural model (e.g., one working spouse, one at-home spouse, and no single parents), youth leaders would still have to deal with great numbers of young folk living in divergent and difficult situations.

Pastoral theology seeks enlightenment from the biblical and traditional ideals to discover sources that will support and nurture single parents, blended families, and other kinds of households. Youth workers are not called primarily for "model families" but for those—the majority—who need something extra. The dramatic rise in divorces, blended families, single-parent families, and the extra stress on the family generally means that youth ministry, more than ever before, must support and strengthen whatever kind of family exists around a given young person.

Pastoral theology will always stand between the ideals of dogmatics and the urgent needs of the sometimes wayward church members that pastors must shepherd. Divorce and remarriage, infidelities, premarital cohabitation, are all situations that must be taken seriously, but pastoral theology does not provide absolute solutions to these matters. Some pastors may hold ideals so rigidly that their ministry to those who need them most is hindered. Others may lose the power of the gospel because they have succumbed to popular theories that condone aberrations from God's will. We must guard against all tendencies that pull practical theology off course. To stay on course we need a realistic view of the family, such as Thomas Moore proposes:

> According to the Bible, Adam was formed out of the mud of the earth. . . . Starting with Adam, at our very root, we are not fashioned out of light or fire; we are children of mud. Scholars say that "Adam" means red earth. Our own families recapitulate this mythic origin of our humanity by being close to the earth, a veritable weed patch of human foibles. . . . If we don't grasp this mystery, the soulfulness that family has to offer each of us will be spirited away in hygienic notions of what a family *should* be. The sentimental image of family that we present publicly is a defense against the pain of proclaiming the family for what it is—a sometimes comforting, sometimes devastating house of life and memory.[4]

Moore, a psychotherapist, goes on to caution us against superficial acceptance of our family life on the one hand and overly psychological interpretations on the other. He would

---

[4] *Care of the Soul: A Guide for Cultivating Depth and Sacredness in Everyday Life* (New York: HarperCollins, 1992) 27, see also 26-29.

have us recount the stories and myths of our families rather than subjecting them to sterile scientific analysis. He encourages our acceptance of dark family shadows rather than the denial and twisting of reality.

> We may be tempted at times to imagine the family as full of innocence and good will, but actual family life resists such romanticism. Usually it presents the full range of human potential, including evil, hatred, violence, sexual confusion, and insanity. In other words, the dynamics of actual family life reveal the soul's complexity and unpredictability, and any attempts to place a veil of simplistic sentimentality over the family image will break down. . . .
>
> In my practice I've worked with many men and women whose families were intolerably violent and abusive, and yet all that pain has been redeemable, able to become the source of much wisdom and transformation. . . .
>
> To care for the soul of the family, it is necessary to shift from casual thinking [and scientific analysis] to an appreciation for story and character, to allow grandparents and uncles to be transformed into figures of myth and to watch certain familiar family stories become canonical through repeated tellings.[5]

Moore helps parents and youth pastors keep a balanced approach by describing a tendency in family counseling:

> Often I will ask a patient about the family, and the answer I get is pure social psychology. "My father drank, and as a child of an alcoholic I am prone to. . . . " Instead of stories, one hears analysis. The family has been "etherized upon a table." Even worse is the social worker or psychologist who begins talking about a patient with a singsong list of social influences: "The subject is male who was raised in Judeo-Christian family, with a narcissistic mother and codependent father." The soul of the family evaporates in the thin air of this kind of reduction. It takes extreme diligence and concentration to think differently about the family: to appreciate its shadow as well as its virtue and simply to allow the stories

---

[5] Ibid., 26, 27, 29.

to be told without slipping into interpretations, analysis, and conclusions.[6]

Understanding and accepting the full reality of family life, we will be able to help youth grow as the people they are, as members of a particular family heritage they can never change. We are called on to affirm inadequate parents, to listen to alcoholics, to encourage those who are weak in discipline. Youth leaders minister not only to troubled young people but also to lost parents. Martin Luther King Jr., once observed that we can change only those we love. Without affirmation, neither families nor individuals can be encouraged to discard harmful attitudes and behaviors and to pursue proper growth. Youth ministers are always building on the positive—and that positive is often discovered only through time and creative relationships.

THE INFLUENCE OF FAMILY ON TEENAGERS

The 1980s were a tremendous watershed for children in many ways. Up to 1960 three-quarters of mothers with children were at home and one-quarter in the work force; as divorce rates soared between 1960 and 1980, this proportion was reversed. In the 1980s children, often in empty homes, had cable television, MTV, and VCRs available to them. They were early witnesses of a new ascendancy of the electronic media in our lives. Few of us can admit the power media has over us. More than the rest of us, adolescents consider themselves invulnerable to injurious consequences of commercials and excessive violence and sex in programs and music. Yet, they may be influenced more and in different ways than they or we imagine.

In the 1960s a majority of teenagers were citing their parents as the most important influence in their lives. And they were probably echoing the opinion of children throughout

---

[6] Ibid., 29.

most of human history. By 1980 a majority of teenagers named their friends as the chief influence in their lives. Parents had slipped to second, and the media showed a remarkable rise.[7] It is easy to see how children turn to television and friends to fill the empty places in their lives. The power of various influences in the lives of young people is a significant issue that will not be debated here. Family, peers or friends, community or "the street," media, and school are primary influences for most. The order of these influences varies, depending on whether one is a wealthy student at a boarding school, a young man or woman in a low-income housing project, an international student, or one whose parents are immigrants. For many teenagers, if not most, family will have the greatest lifetime influence and peers the most immediate power.

LEAVING FAMILY AND HOME

Jesus quoted the Old Testament about a man leaving his father and mother to be united with his wife (Mark 10:7; see Genesis 2:24). This process of leaving home is often difficult because the family is instrumental in shaping a person, and neglectful or overprotective parents may make the transition harder; but the move from family of origin to a world of creativity need not be a dramatic or painful departure.

Youth leaders understand the difficulties involved in this departure, and one of their functions is to help teenagers leave home gracefully. There are many ways this can be done. First of all, we need to provide young people with a Christian rite of passage that includes separation, instructions, solitude and reflection, integration back into adult and church society with a celebration of the event. Exciting ideas about family-based youth ministry need to be incorporated. Teenagers can profit from doing things with their parents in new settings. Contact or mentoring with other

---

[7] See Jim Burns, *The Youth Builder: Today's Resource for Relational Youth Ministry* (Eugene, Ore.: Harvest, 1988) 33.

adults is an important aid in moving from home into the adult world.

A young adult is ready to go out into the world when she or he has developed internal mechanisms for love and approval, responsibility and discipline, along with playfulness and creativity. That is, we are ready to go out on our own when we have developed our own internal parent, child, and adult. The small childhood triangle of "Mommy, Daddy, and Me" must become a mature relationship among God, self (including one's internal parent, child, and adult), and others. For some the basic family triangle never existed; for all it must come apart. That is one reason divine linkage is crucial.

GROWING UP TO ADULTHOOD

One difficulty of contemporary adolescence is the absence of markers or rites of passage.[8] When and how do we become adults? Postindustrial societies have no clear way to mark the attainment of adulthood. But Western psychologists define maturity in terms of identity, autonomy, and intimacy. Thus, the reaching of adulthood could be described in the following way.

1. Adulthood is achieving one's identity—
   • Who in the world am I (in distinction from others),
   • What do I want to do vocationally?

2. Adulthood is being independent from parents and family—
   • financially,
   • emotionally.

3. Adulthood is becoming ready for lifetime intimacy and parenting—
   • able to share one's vulnerability,
   • willing to be mutually responsible in raising children.

---

[8] See Elkind, *All Grown Up*, 93-114, and Sebald, *Adolescence*, 7, 115-17.

From "Mommy, Daddy, and Me," an adolescent must find an autonomous or independent "I." It is not easy, and we adults continually make it more difficult for young people to accomplish. One must be able to see oneself with integrity and clear boundaries, as a real person, as having a set of values and opinions, and ready to make decisions. To be a healthy and mature man or woman, one must be able to parent oneself (to give self the nurture that once came from parents). Too many never achieve a state of self-assurance and self-nurture. They are unable to say:

> I give myself unconditional love and realistic approval while holding myself responsible for the lives of others in obedience to God. God, self, and neighbor form my triangle of love and affirmation. If I cannot give myself love and affirmation, I will probably have difficulty in prayer and in receiving love from God. Others will feel limitations of acceptance and love if I cannot love myself. If I am still dependent on Mom and Dad, I can neither receive nor give the kind of intimate love and realistic affirmation needed by me and others.

As adolescents we work out our personal identity in contrast to our parents' identity. We push away from that which conceived and nurtured us (Mark 10:7). The necessity of gradually dissociating from parental identity is seen in the yearning of the adopted teen to know the birth parent. "I am partly the product of my adoptive parents, but isn't there a further missing clue to my adult identity? How can I 'push away' from a ghost?" The process of defining self is by no means impossible for adopted children, but it may be more difficult than for children who live with their birth parent(s).

It is God's intention that human beings grow up in a protective and instructive environment. Leaving that environment is a difficult task. Today's society, with its hurried childhood, pressure on families, confused value messages, and complex adult society, make this task more rather than less difficult, providing youth ministry with special challenges.

PEER GROUPS

One important answer to the question of how adolescents make successful passage to adulthood is through the help and encouragement of the peer group. This answer strikes many people as strange. Isn't peer pressure a prime enemy of family and religion? It may be, but remember that all cultural institutions have the potential to be useful or harmful. Social systems like peer groups are beneficial when they promote human growth and welfare. It is when institutions hinder growth or hurt the welfare of people that they should be condemned and countered.

As already noted, in much of the world peer groups have become the most significant influence in young people's lives. To the extent that peer groups encourage growth toward responsibility, maturity, healthy marriage, and successful career, they are a necessary and cherished aspect of youth culture. To the degree that they manipulate and impede responsible womanhood and manhood, they are to be criticized and, one hopes, modified.

Peer groups are important for adolescents today for several reasons:

1. The prolongation of the adolescent period in urban societies tends to separate them from adult society and heightens their need for peer group support and immediate friends.
2. The increasing complexities of today's societies lead to postponing adult responsibilities and extending time in the youth culture with peers.
3. The busyness of parents and their increased absence from the home pushes teenagers more deeply into their peer groups.
4. As the youth culture becomes increasingly alienated from the dominant culture, teenagers feel that only other teenagers really understand their predicaments and pressures.
5. With friends, young people practice skills needed in later life. They hope their friends and the youth culture will be more forgiving of their mistakes and failures than parents and adult society seem to be.

To expand on this last point: Adolescent peer groups are, in a sense, practice sessions. Children play adult life; teenagers practice adult life. Just as children should have a safe time and space to *play* adult life, adolescents need the same to *practice* adult life. They do so with their peers in a subculture of youth. We do well to cheer (and pray) for healthy peer groups because they indicate the health of tomorrow's families and organizations.

If peer groups are units of the special culture of the young, there is more to this phenomenon than transition—as important as that is. Peer groups become the families of teenagers. A locus of authority passes to these groups. High schoolers usually need permission from their peer groups (as children do from their parents) to attend a youth group or go to a camp. If friends consider something weird, better not go. Adults usually can't understand how difficult it is for teenagers to go against the social norms of their peers and do what is considered "uncool."

Regarding the positive function of peer groups, Sebald explains:

> Excepting certain destructive by-products, the peer culture serves a valuable function. . . . A major function of modern adolescence is renunciation of dependence on the family and substitution of peer groups for the family group. This substitution includes fulfillment of emotional needs essential for individual growth, such as stimulation, empathy, loyalty, the opportunity for role playing, identification, and sharing of guilt and anxiety.

> It can be said, then, that the peer group facilitates the young individual's autonomy process and emancipation from the family.[9]

Still some Christian educators and church leaders fail to give adequate attention and respect to peer groups and the youth culture. We should remember how much adolescent growth goes on outside the family and the church.

---

[9] *Adolescence,* 162-63.

Significant development of self-image takes place among friends; we need to understand peer groups as a very influential social system.

Dawn's mother describes her as a special education student of "below average" intellect. As a fifteen-year-old ninth grader, Dawn wanted to be a nurse. Drug use and selling were widespread in her vocational high school, she said. She resisted a boy's repeated attempts to sell her marijuana. After a friend of hers went to the administration to complain, the authorities decided to use Dawn in the difficult job of apprehending a seller. Feeling coerced, she finally agreed. The aftermath has been ugly. Over the past two years Dawn's life has been threatened and her sister's car vandalized by stone throwers. A knife was passed around her in class and students made finger-across-the-throat gestures. Dawn has been ostracized by her peers and fears for her life.[10]

In a television docudrama, a mother of a girl with leukemia sobs when she relates how her daughter's playmates taunted her as they pulled out her loose hair in clumps while singing sarcastic mockeries. Children and teenagers can be cruel in subtle or blatant ways. Family abuse is becoming well documented and is receiving more attention now than ever before, but too little attention has been paid to the damage inflicted by vicious or thoughtless peers.

Dr. Barbara Staggers, an African-American physician honored by a Lewis Hine Award in New York (1994), serves teenagers in clinics at Fremont High School and Children's Hospital in Oakland, California. Constantly treating young people suffering from self-destructive behavior, she laments negligent families and peer groups engaged in risky behavior. Staggers gives this advice to parents:

> We don't get very far by just telling teenagers not to take risks because it scares us. When we demand to know why they've screwed up, the kid says, "I had to. Everybody else

[10] Joseph P. Kahn, "The Reluctant Narc," *The Boston Globe*, March 17, 1994.

was doing it." The adult replies, "If everybody else jumped off the cliff, would you, too?"

The honest answer to that question is *yes*. It's really, really important that we understand this. For the teen at that moment, being down at the bottom together feels better than being on the edge of the cliff alone.

What we need to engage our teens in discussing is the question: What else can you do to be part of a group and still survive, while taking reasonable risks? If you've got to jump off the cliff, can't you choose one that's not 50 feet high? Can you jump off the cliff that's 2 feet high instead?[11]

The Bible does not give us a theology of peer groups, though it does contain principles applicable to and needed in all human groups and subcultures. From those principles, our experience, and the social sciences, we can construct a theological way of thinking about and ministering to young people in groups. We must be sure we are aware of the vital function of peer groups and the positive ways they support young people.

When fifth-grader Ian O'Gorman's cancer-treating chemotherapy caused his hair to fall out, his friends closed ranks around him with a wonderful gesture of positive peer support: they decided to shave off their hair. Soon the class was full of bald heads; even the teacher shaved his head. Ian's father exclaimed, "It's very emotional to think about kids like that who would come together . . . to do such a thing to support Ian."[12]

Many other unheralded stories of positive peer pressure could be told—street kids who would die for one another; suburban and rural youth who find creative ways

---

[11] See Douglas Foster, "If the Symptoms Are Rapid Increases in Teen Deaths from Murder, Suicide, and Car Crashes, Alcohol and Drugs . . . the Disease Is Adolescence," *Rolling Stone,* December 9, 1993, 55. Reprinted in *Utne Reader* (July/August, 1994) 50, under the title, "The Disease Is Adolescence: And the Symptoms Are Violence, Suicide, Drugs, Alcohol, Car Wrecks, and Poverty."

[12] Gary Warth, "Classmates Clip Hair in Support of Friend," *Blade-Citizen,* March 10, 1994.

to encourage friends in desperate need. It is the task of youth ministry to diminish the negative and to promote the positive features of peer groups. Those who care about young people become students of all kinds of friendships and groups in youth culture. It is a dynamic and fascinating culture, and we are privileged to enter it. God is at work within youth culture, as in any other culture, and it is exciting to meet God there. Those who minister are always the learners. It is important that what we learn finds its way into our strategy for ministry— that is the aim of this book.

MISSIONARY METHODS

We should always model our ministry or missionary methods after the life and incarnational ministry of Jesus Christ. Because Christ spent so much time with families and with what might be considered a peer group (diverse as the disciples were), we can learn much by following the steps of Jesus. To this model should be added good missiological principles.

As already mentioned, we would expect a child to ask for parents' permission before coming to one of our activities, and we can anticipate that young people will need permission from their friends to participate in any activity. Those in youth work have not always understood the implications of this dynamic for youth ministry. Groups rather than individuals are the building blocks of youth work. Missiology knows it is better to reach people in groups than as individuals apart from their culture.

As missionaries need anthropological insights, so those who are called to the subculture of youth must use insights and techniques from the behavioral sciences. Sociograms, for instance, can diagram the relationships of cliques or friendship groups in the cafeteria, at dances, and at ball games. It is important to understand status and leadership within youthful subcultures.

Understanding group dynamics in their culture will help us in our goals of evangelization, building community, and nurturing. We must understand that teenagers learn best within a positive peer group. Young people discover and learn primarily for themselves. There seems to be little significant learning and growing apart from a supportive peer group where concepts can be tested.

Theological and behavioral reflection within youth ministry, therefore, leads its practitioners to appreciate the desirability of:

- reaching young people in their groups, as a group;
- seeing bonding as the first step for any youth group;
- using groups to share, to foster growth, and to serve.

Youth ministers find ways of affirming peer groups as well as cautioning against holding them up as an ultimate value or authority. Young people finding little support at home (and feeling even less from self) may cling desperately to a peer group. Our method will be to build up self-esteem and life's possibilities rather than to berate their friends or relationships.

Holistic Youth Ministry

We want our ministry to be as holistic as possible. As we seek to overcome the fragmenting and isolating tendencies of our society, we have much to learn from other cultures. For instance, traditional "counseling" in African cultures is much more familial and community-oriented than are Western therapies (although the African scene is changing and there are attempts to make Western counseling more holistic). In many traditional cultures people with emotional problems are helped back to health and responsibility in the context of their immediate groups.

It is hard to comprehend all that a family can provide for its members—especially for a growing child. Still, other social systems must complement the family. Brendtro, Brokenleg, and Van Bockern refer to an observation of Martin Marty that "as crucial as the family is to preserving civilization, it has always been the 'tribe' rather than the nuclear family that ultimately ensures cultural survival."[13] Much of the literature on youth ministry today assumes strong families in nice communities and good churches. The fact is, and has always been, that many parents are unprepared, unskilled, and irresponsible. Children need the support of the larger "tribe" and especially of people in the community who care.

In traditional life a variety of complementary supports— the extended family, neighbors, clan, and community—aided the family in raising its children. Life in our urban technological societies has seen an erosion of such supports. Financial and logistic pressures isolate and inundate the nuclear family. Increasingly harried parents have turned to day care, schools, malls, churches, and the media to help them babysit, entertain, and instruct their children. The burden of socialization is being shared by many social systems.

We should be concerned that there is so little agreement on how our children are to be raised. As various social systems are money-driven, they seek profit more than the common good of young people. The messages, values, and goals of the social systems cooperating in raising children these days may be at odds. Francis Ianni's important study describes the way youth at risk receive incongruent messages from *parents, school, and community.*[14] Confused by conflicting messages and values, teenagers are understandably driven back to their peers, who alone in all the world understand their predicament from immediate, firsthand experience.

Being In the World

We see Jesus accepting the diversity and roughness of the disciples as his primary group. From there and with

---

[13] Larry K. Brendto, Martin Brokenleg, and Steve Van Bockern, *Reclaiming Youth at Risk: Our Hope for the Future* (Bloomington, Ind.: National Educational Service, 1990) 10.

[14] *The Search for Structure: A Report on American Youth Today* (New York: Free Press, 1989) 4-7.

them, Christ moved out to enter the subcultures of social outcasts and disreputable folks. Part of the scandal of his life for the "religious" of his time—and it still offends many pious—was that he spent time eating and drinking wine in the homes of sinners—this in contrast to John and more ascetic religious leaders (Luke 7:33-35). We can imagine Jesus at parties in the house of Zacchaeus or with the friends of Levi (Luke 19:5-7; Mark 2:15-16). In such places it seems Jesus was welcomed, was able to relate naturally, could enjoy himself, and above all, was able to make a significant impact in the name of his Father and the kingdom he was announcing.

The ministry of Jesus seems to say that the church must do more than invite sinners into its fellowship. There is a mandate to go out into the world, to enter its subcultures and social systems, and there be salt and light. Spiritually mature leaders have always been able to bring a ministry of presence to dysfunctional families and rough peer groups. Such a ministry challenges us to be "in the world but not of it." This interpretation of incarnational ministry within teenage peer groups implies that we should be reaching teenagers as groups before winning them as individuals. Leaders who are sure of their own personal and spiritual identities, who appreciate the role and power of youthful peer groups, can serve as leaven in today's youth culture.

QUESTIONS FOR REFLECTION AND DISCUSSION

1. How does the life of Jesus challenge the way you think about and do youth ministry?
2. Do any of your own family and school peer group experiences confirm, question, or contradict the principles above? Do you consider yourself fully adult?
3. How does the discussion in this chapter compare with what you observe of adolescents from junior high through college today?
4. With what part of this chapter do you most agree, and with what part most disagree? What questions or suggestions do you have regarding this discussion?

5. As a result of this reading, do you now have a better sense of how God wants the family, peer groups, and youth leaders to encourage the growth of each young person?
6. In what ways can your present ministry with young people be more holistic, relevant, or professional in terms of the reflections here?
7. In what specific ways can you do more to affirm parents? How can you integrate family ministry with youth ministry?
8. If you are married or thinking of marriage, how can you best balance the home and ministerial demands and needs in your life? If you are single, how can you best affirm and support yourself in a life that is whole and rewarding? What group of friends is family for you?

7 THEOLOGY OF POP CULTURE AND ITS ART

Compelling Images

Listen, I am sending my messenger.
> —*Malachi 3:1; Matthew 11:10; Mark 1:2; Luke 7:27,*
> *author's paraphrase*

They were amazed at his teaching, for his message was with authority.
> —*Luke 4:32, author's paraphrase*

And with many such parables [stories] Jesus was speaking the word to them.
> —*Mark 4:33, author's paraphrase*

Let no one deceive you with empty words.
> —*Ephesians 5:6,* NRSV

POP ART AND OTHER ART

As a critical audience, we must understand and appreciate the artistic, as well as the commercial, aspects of pop culture. For example, many Christian critiques of rock music or television are too narrowly focused and negative. They lack important cultural and artistic sensitivity—thus losing the right of a hearing and dialogue with musicians and fans who could benefit from some critique. It is therefore important for Christians interested in or concerned about media influence to understand the basics of pop art.

Popular art must be distinguished from classical, high, or avant-garde art, on the one hand, and folk art, on the other.

Classical and avant-garde art demands historic understanding and specialized training; it tends to be elitist. Folk art is of the common people, the expression of a particular culture or subculture. It is restricted, not to the the well-educated, but to those who are really part of a particular culture. Think how many kinds of pop music were "folk" before they became "pop." They were first part of an exclusive subculture; then they became commercially popular with a broad audience—and lost their ability to be the voice of a particular folk, the unique expression of that folk or subculture. Reactions to mainstream art or music often bring attempts to produce a new folk art—music that is not money driven and tries to restrict itself to a given subculture. As it becomes more popular and enters the mainstream, its power of critical rebellion diminishes. Powerful alternative music tends to become mainstream and to lose its distinction by its own success.

YOUNG PEOPLE AND POP ART

The interaction of young people with their popular arts and music is a complex and dynamic affair. Imagine Wayne, a high school junior, listening to an album of his favorite rock group. He is attracted to its beat and guitar riffs. He has come home from school feeling intensely trapped, put down, and jittery. He feels pressured by his father, smothered by his mother, teased by a more successful sibling, and unfairly judged by teachers and school administration. The music that he and his close friends are into seems to relieve him of an urge to strike a family member or put his fist through the wall. As he listens to a condemnation of authoritarian oppression and sterile suburban life, he is struck with the possibilities of a better world and becoming an instrument of reconciliation and betterment.

The idea of doing something intrigues him and simmers on the back burners of his mind. Hearing about a service trip to Haiti from friends in a youth group he sometimes attends, he decides to commit part of his summer to this project. Several times he begins to lose interest or doubt his own power to contribute. At such times he returns to his music.

Pop art must be understood from a psychological and social perspective. For adolescents pop art, whether it be television, film, music, or whatever, may provide:

- a rite of passage (a means of transition toward adult autonomy),
- religion (when church seems to have nothing to say to them),
- idols (heroes, fantasy love objects, or role models),
- tribal affiliation (a means of identifying themselves as a special and segregated age group or subculture—a vital, cohesive peer force),
- an escape (with the possibility of becoming an addiction),
- a social elixir (in the tradition of work and war songs, energizing them out of debilitating lethargy),
- an expression (freeing them from social neglect and silence),
- a lament (in the tradition of biblical psalms and the blues),
- a protest against personal or social discrimination or oppression,
- just plain fun.

All these factors explain the power of media and entertainment in the lives of young people. Let us take just one of the above. The biblical tradition and Hebrew society gave people great opportunities to lament. Today young people feel more need to lament than ever before, but churches generally fail to provide real opportunities for young people to express their sorrow and rage. Funerals give families opportunities to grieve and celebrate their loss. Within the youth culture there is an evident need to actively, almost aggressively, express and celebrate deep feelings of loss and hurt. Mosh pits, some dance floors, and rock concerts do that. Many of us adults have lost our natural bent toward physical and emotional catharsis and celebration.

We can learn a great deal about pop art in the youth culture. Various groups on campus or on the streets, and each individual, may explain what a magazine or television show, a song or movie, means to them. Pop art shows itself to those who understand modern media as commercial, political, artistic, and social phenomena. Opinions based on any single perspective are incomplete.

ART AND THE HUMAN NEED FOR DRAMA

Drama is usually defined as a special use of story (generally of human conflict to be acted on a stage). The dramatic impulse grows out of deep human needs. Life's complexity, paradoxes, frustrations, and boredom demand means of reflection and celebration. Humor, stories, art, and drama all fulfill this need. Good art, drama, and stories perform three social functions.

1. They relieve and please.
2. They enlighten.
3. They ennoble and inspire.

It is important to bear these functions in mind as we come to interpret pop culture and pop art. Particularly, now, we consider the critical importance of stories.

In his essay "The Artist and Society," James Baldwin provides his own viewpoint as to the purpose of drama and art. Educated in the European tradition but speaking from the viewpoint of an African-American, Baldwin calls on the artist, in prophetic style, "to illuminate [the] darkness, blaze roads through that vast forest, so that we will not, in all our doing, lose sight of its purpose, which is, after all, to make the world a more human dwelling place."[1] If we look for it and are honest, we will find a striving for these goals in much of pop art.

Christians have spent too little time and effort considering the cultural purpose of art. Such reflections would suggest that art contributes the following to the common good:

---

[1] *Literary Cavalcade,* February 1994 (first published as "The Creative Process," in *Creative America,* 1962).

- attraction and pleasure through the beauty of its forms,
- relief of the boredom of life,
- a greater breadth of understanding by vicarious experience,
- encouragement through vision and noble portrayals,
- unification of the human community,
- instruction and redirection of our personal and corporate lives.

When drama, a novel, or music moves us out of discouragement or apathy, makes us feel bonded to fellow human beings, encourages us to follow a collective vision that will relieve suffering and restore human dignity, and when, perhaps, it also gives us some idea as to how this may be accomplished, it is fulfilling the important function of art.

John Wiley Nelson explains how Americans, like every other people, share a belief system that holds them together.[2] The weakening, or lack, of any apparent belief system in many societies today only strengthens the contention that a society or culture is, by definition, held together by certain common beliefs. Diversified and polarized as we may be, there must be a common belief that drives our buying, our entertainment, our voting, and our legal system. That something can take us to war—though wars can be fought for more trivial reasons or for special interests.

Uncelebrated beliefs, cultural or religious, can get stuck in the head alone. In "patchwork selves" or compartmentalized lives, they remain unintegrated with the whole of a person's soul. Social ideals will gradually erode if they are not celebrated. Without celebration of values there will be no vision, and without a vision a society, organization, or individual will die.

Writing in the 1970s, Nelson saw the Western as a celebration of traditional American values.[3] Its themes were a challenging frontier, open spaces far from urban blight, hard work, family and community life, and savior figures. The closing of the Western frontier, growing ur-

---

[2] *Your God Is Alive and Well,* 15-29.
[3] Ibid., 30ff.

banization, the loss of a social challenge after World War II, and changing work and family patterns had been eroding confidence in the American dream—and in traditional values worldwide. The Western motif did not die, but the anti-Western challenged the primacy of the older values. Heroes in the anti-Western were not spotless and they did not always win. Bad might even look good. Movies that glorify urban crime are examples of anti-Western films. Parodies also appear when traditional values and visions begin to fade. *Batman,* for instance, may parody obsolete American moralities and styles at the same time it attempts to celebrate the triumph of good over evil. A society that witnesses space trips and walking on the moon may need more than a victory of good settlers over scheming cattlemen; the *Star Wars* trilogy celebrates the moral struggles in fantastic and futuristic settings. Urban societies must find dramatic ways to celebrate their cultural identities, struggles and values.

John Wiley Nelson attempted to show Christians the significance of popular culture. He likened the celebration of cultural beliefs and values to the way many churches celebrate religious beliefs and values. He described the function of movies as society's worship or revival services; television as family devotions; magazines as personal devotions, and music (especially country) as our culture's hymnody. The arts not only reflect the life of a society but also guide its destiny. Their power over young lives must be considered by those who care about young people.

THE ORIGIN AND POWER OF STORIES

For millennia many human beings have finished out the day sitting around the flickering flame of a campfire listening to stories. Imagine how storytellers would share age-worn tales for the enjoyment and instruction of their audience. Outside a cave or tent or village hut, lights and shadows would play across the weathered face of a skilled storyteller. In medieval castles and colonial homes, stories were passed on from generation to generation. These stories contained the heritage and values of the culture. Good youth ministry is a safe place where young people can tell their stories and hear God's story.

With its flickering blue flame, television now brings us our stories. We have moved from the telling and hearing of a few choice stories per day to a society flooded with story lines. For the young person going to bed after watching television, the program and the commercials just watched are her bedtime stories.

How are we to think theologically about the stories of our society? Can you imagine a culture without means of communication and stories? Language and the techniques that carry messages are the glue holding a society together. To be encouraged in the struggles of life, people need not only to converse but also to sense some kind of meaning.

Stories can certainly be for sheer entertainment. But they also provide inspiration, information, unity, and meaning. The elderly need to reflect on the significance of their lives, and stories give them opportunity to do so. Those who are burned out from overwork need a good story's renewing power. Children and youth are forever curious about what faces them and why things are as they are.

Stories have a capacity to provide for each person what is needed at the time. When we are bored, stories can transport us to exciting adventures. When we are rejected or depressed, we may be relieved vicariously through the same or greater pain in an appropriate drama. Our love can be affirmed, or loneliness assuaged, in great romance. Tired of caring for others, our souls may find nurture through narrative. Feelings of insignificance may be replaced by a sense of new challenge. In all of this we are being culturally instructed as well as relieved and uplifted.

Every society has its own stories. The history and values of a society are communicated through cultural stories and songs. Those who tell the stories and pipe the tunes may be those who control the future of a society. Music and drama help express the soul of a culture. A culture rich in stories is deep in soul power. Didn't God use stories to give to his people the power to survive?

People of all cultures crave drama, and this craving suggests that God has made us storytelling (and story-hearing) creatures. Whether gathered around a campfire or sitting before the television set, we human beings are hungry for new stories—or to hear a good, old story one more time. Consider, then, the power of those who tell stories—how those who tell stories can shape a society. It may be that storytellers and musicians are more powerful than politicians, in that they have a more immediate and longer-lasting influence on more people.

Jewish tradition is filled with stories. William J. Bausch tells one: Long ago a revered rabbi, in times of great misfortune, went to a particular place in the woods, lit a fire in a certain way, and offered a special prayer for the Jews. Over time subsequent rabbis forgot, first how to light the fire, then the special prayer, and finally even the place where the old rabbi prayed. So when great trouble came to the people in a much later time, a rabbi finally prayed to God in desperation: "I am unable to light the fire, and I do not know the prayer, and I cannot even find the place in the forest. All I can do is to tell the story, and this must be sufficient." According to the tradition, it *was* sufficient because God made us and God loves stories.[4] We are storytelling people; we feel especially human—and close to humanity—when we are telling or hearing a great story.

The Bible is *the* great story, made up of many stories. We might say that stories were first, and then came a theological perspective—that narrative theology precedes propositional theology. God gave a story, and we have created systematic theology. Acceptance of the primacy of story today might bring therapeutic relevance to some sterile theologies. Recovering the drama and mystery of story, of God's dynamic

---

[4] *Storytelling: Imagination and Faith* (Mystic, Conn.: Twenty-Third Publications, 1989) 16.

work among the faithful, might bring us to a theological posture more humble, open, and relevant.

THE CRITIQUE OF ELECTRONIC STORIES

If we are created by a storytelling God, if we need stories for the preservation of our human heritage, if we find ourselves bonded to one another by stories, then it is a terrible crime to pervert stories. Stories that undermine the divine intention for human growth and society are an offense to the Creator. The corruption or manipulation of human beings, by media or any other means, is of great theological concern. It is also of paramount social concern.

Michael Warren has asked some critical questions regarding contemporary electronic communication. "Who tells the stories?" "Who imagines the world for us and by what procedures?" "What stories do they tell?"[5] I hope all those who work with young people will ask the following questions in their exegesis of the media.

- Who is telling the stories of our society?
- Who is imagining the world of these stories?
- Who is allowed to listen?
- What drives the telling of these stories?
- What values are being transmitted?
- What kind of stories do loving parents and caring adults tell?
- What kind of stories does Jesus tell?
- How can we reimagine stories for our day?
- How must youth ministry critique and focus on the telling of stories?

Although storytellers have always played a powerful role in society, storytelling in the latter twentieth century differs from that in all previous history. First, the number of stories received by each member of society has greatly

---

[5] "The Electronically Imagined World and Religious Education," in *Media and Culture* (ed. Reynolds R. Ekstrom; New Rochelle, N.Y.: Don Bosco Multimedia, 1992) 33-50.

increased. A one-hour evening television show may have a main story and three or four subplots developed at the same time. Commercial breaks every ten minutes or so may present the viewer with seven to nine thirty-, twenty-, or even fifteen-second advertisements—and each commercial is a story. Sitting down to relax, a viewer may have been told more than fifty stories in an hour. No one has the energy to process that many messages after a full day. Listeners used to hear a few stories from a face-to-face speaker. They could relate to this narrator and size up his or her message, style, and intent. Electronic images manipulated at great speed do not allow for such scrutiny. Images, music, words, and special effects combine to rouse feelings, elicit associations, and sow seeds of self-doubt with suggested needs for commercial products more quickly than our conscious mind can process. This technique, this massive onslaught of stories, is new in human history.

COMMERCIAL STORIES

The power of electronic communication neither derives from a single social system nor is the conspiracy of a sinister inner group. Certain social cliques of authors and producers may prevail for a time, but outside innovators and public opinion come along to challenge the thinking of these narrow elites. Thorough study of the entertainment media reveals interlocking channels of influence. Hollywood producers, New York authors, advertisers, and programmers interact with family, religious, educational, and political systems. Industrial interests, market analysts, and media masters combine their sophisticated resources to produce an evening of television viewing or a big summer movie. A particular movie venture may feature T-shirts, toys, and sound tracks that generate several times the profit of the film itself. Economic, artistic, information, and technical systems combine to make indelible impressions on media receivers.

More than ever before, storytelling is driven by money. One week of television and movies may involve more money than some countries' annual gross national product (GNP). The GNP of the United States is supported by consumption, which is promoted by advertising. Since the US GNP guarantees its world leadership, which most US citizens and all US politicians are committed to maintaining, politics, advertising, and media are vitally connected.

Meanwhile, studies show that television viewers are remembering less of what they see while the number and cost of commercials increase. It becomes more and more difficult to maintain the wealth and power of such a consumptive society. We place a great responsibility for our wealth and power on the ad people who stimulate consumption. Criticisms of the media need to consider all these and further dimensions of the issue.

Television is present in 99 percent of US homes, and in many remote global villages. Television is apparently a contemporary necessity. After the purchase of the set, and excepting cable and the small cost of electricity, viewing seems to be free. But this service is successful only as long as there is a unspoken partnership between producers and spectators; the former must sell, sell, sell, and the latter, buy, buy, buy.

THE PROFIT MOTIVE

We must understand the commercial aspects of pop culture as a driving force of much in our society. While the media is supposed to educate and inform, the bottom line for television, commercials, and all aspects of pop culture is profit. The target of advertising is a mass market or clusters within a mass market, and a primary intention is efficiency. Producers of mass media must ask, "How can we reach the greatest audience with greatest efficiency for the greatest profit?" Few of us have a strong, alternative social (economic and political) model to replace the bottom line model of our current society.

Thus children grow up being told hundreds of thousands of times that they are inadequate without a certain product or service. They get these messages from billboards, television, movies, newspapers, and magazines.

Boys probably read magazines that tell them more about things; girls may be more interested in those that tell about appearance and relationships.

Girls suffer in a special way at the self-conscious age of puberty. Suddenly, they are leaving girlhood and entering what seems like a new social arena. An onslaught of media messages is comparing them to unrealistic airbrushed images of super models, is telling them to become sexier, more attractive, and more acceptable. As if this electronic barrage were not unfair and cruel enough, there are voices from boys, other girls, and siblings that may produce deep feelings of inadequacy. They are asked to adapt to cultural norms often antithetical to their freedom and growth.[6]

In the land of commercial stories, there is a pill for every pain and a chemical stimulus for every special occasion. If everything in commercials saves someone work, then hard work must not be a positive value. If pain must be treated immediately, then all painful aspects of life and growth are to be avoided. As the children of an electronic age return to the television program, they find life's most difficult problems are solved in half-hour segments—and often by violent means. This, too, is a lesson not missed by children of this generation.

To understand the commercial aspects of pop culture and its art, we must question each medium (of television, film, magazines, music).

- How much profit is being made from and around this medium?
- Who is making the profit?
- Who is purchasing this medium (age, sex, etc.)?
- What tends to sell this medium (what needs, interests, drives are being appealed to or exploited)?
- What messages are being sent?
- What images and values are involved in the sell?

---

[6] Mary Pipher, *Reviving Ophelia: Saving the Selves of Adolescent Girls* (New York: Ballentine, 1994). See also Peggy Orenstein, *SchoolGirls: Young Women, Self-Esteem, and the Confidence Gap* (New York: Doubleday, 1994).

- What restraints or regulations control harmful excesses of this commercial endeavor?
- What benefits or ill effects come to our society from this commercial activity?

THE QUEST FOR OBJECTIVE CRITERIA

In our effort to critique the electronic media, we judge art on the basis of its *form* (how it is structured and presented), its *content* (its substance, appearance, and message), and its *function* (what it does for the observer or listener and society in general). Judging art involves both a subjective exercise (something in the eye of the beholder) and an objective discipline (judgment on the basis of generally accepted criteria). Art must be judged in terms of its social function as well as its artistic merits. It is inevitable that the results of our critiques will vary from person to person.

Whether highbrow or popular, art is art. We should not judge the artists of pop culture (music, movies, or whatever) by the criteria of elitist art or folk art. Good artists—whether performing in rock or opera—succeed in fulfilling the basic functions of art. Artists should be judged as to whether they have these basic characteristics:

- skill, an unusual ability to convey beauty and truth through a given medium;
- insight, providing unusual reflections on our life condition, its meaning, and the human drama;
- integrity, a faithful linking together of skill and insight into genuine personal and social experience.

EMPOWERING YOUNG PEOPLE FOR ARTISTIC CRITIQUE

Our goal as youth ministers is not to show young people how much we know. They will quickly humble us if we try to impress them with any such knowledge. Rather, we want to study with them and learn *their* ideas about drama and music. We are interested in their empowerment to discern and protect themselves from the manipulation of electronic communication.

If you would critique modern pop art with them you must do the following.

- Be wary of simplistic critiques that reject all that is different and not Christian.
- Gain an appreciation of human drama in every age and culture.
- Remember that God's image remains in every human heart and culture, and that common grace is bestowed on the righteous and unrighteous alike (Psalm 19:1-4; Matthew 5:45).
- Look for that which
  —relieves, comforts, and heals;
  —encourages and instructs, fostering growth;
  —unites, promoting cooperation and interdependence.
- Be aware of all that
  —demeans persons and groups;
  —aggravates the pain and sickness of society;
  —hinders growth and promotes unrealistic dreams;
  —puts things before persons and people against people.

Simply put, art should please, relieve hurt, inspire hope, and foster growth. It is grounded in reality while it aspires to beautiful ideals. Art that glorifies filth and ugliness is poor art—though it may issue an important wake-up call to an uncaring and oppressive culture. As leaders of youth we must identify with the hurts expressed in their music and urge them to rise above its obscenities. We must also admit to their parents the degraded nature of some of this pop art while positively posing prophetic questions regarding their adult responsibilities for the social systems that hinder youthful growth and welfare. Rock and rap music have spoken out on many issues that have been overlooked by churches—environmental pollution, racism and discrimination, and matters of personal irresponsibility.

We need to critique stories or songs that delight in hurt and discourage growth toward wholeness and nobility. Whether we overlook such unworthiness or directly confront that which is especially injurious depends on our situation. Of course, we cannot claim any consensus in applying these standards. As "bold fools" we must still declare: "There is a nobler way." We cling to a belief in the resilience of the human spirit. No matter how battered or misshapen, the youthful heart still longs for beauty, love, and truth. These qualities must be encouraged by music and drama. Good art, as good therapy and effective youth work, brings the ideas and personifications of beauty, love, and truth to people in need of healing and growth.

Such an understanding of social aesthetics requires much of the artist and of the consumer. Those who reject all objective artistic norms must be confronted "for kids' sake." The secular world seems to lack art critics willing to label something as wrong. But if art degrades, if it contributes to rape and violence, then it is against the common and individual good and should be treated as a public health issue.[7] Public health must be moral, and morality must be expressed publicly. Feeding violent and sexually irresponsible tendencies of human nature is as harmful as putting lead in paint children may chew. If children's smoking can be seen as a public health issue, so can the contamination of their minds. Of course, the application of moral standards in society is a complicated issue. This is not an argument for simplistic censorship. It is rather an encouragement to talk about the influences on children and young people in terms of the common good and the health of our society.

The health of a society requires pop art to raise prophetic objections to cultural affairs on the one hand and to enhance noble aspirations on the other. It has been stated earlier (in chapter 4) that art both reflects and affects a culture. Since the mid-1930s research such as the Payne Studies and the Cressey Report have demonstrated that the media do influence people, especially the young, but that they do so in conjunction with other social and psychological factors. Specifically these studies have shown that two young people can be influenced in different directions by the same movie.

---

[7] Deborah Prothrow-Stith treats violence as a public health issue in her book, *Deadly Consequences.* See above, pp. 97–98, for an excerpt.

Furthermore, there need to be some generally accepted norms to determine the wholesomeness of art. This is a much more difficult matter in today's society especially in regard to taste and ethical matters. We have argued for an understanding of wholesome art in terms of what promotes growth to full manhood and womanhood and contributes to a fair community and the common good. This does not solve particulars, but it does at least point us in the right direction and encourage significant dialogue. Without wholesome art a society cannot be healthy, and unwholesome art is a symptom of an unhealthy society. Christians should be a stimulant for social justice and artistic accomplishment. We need to have more of a say into what is considered wholesome. Without a wholesome vision for the arts and society, our young people will perish (see Proverbs 29:18).

This task must reach into the youth culture. When asked why they listen to a particular kind of music (or watch music videos), teenagers may respond: "It's great to dance to"; "I like the beat"; "I just love those guys (the artist or group)"; "It makes me feel good"; "I like the words and message"; or "My friends like it." Further questions may bring out remarkable insights regarding the technical aspects of the music, the message of the song, or even the feelings, hurts, or longings of the individual. Only in free and open conversations with the consumers of art can we and they begin to reach adequate judgments. Young people learn only when they discover something themselves and articulate it to their friends.

Critiquing Film

How does our judgment of art work out, for instance, in the movies that young people watch? One hundred years ago, they were not watching any; fifty years ago, they might have seen two or three a month; today, many teenagers see three to five movies a week. A video store clerk is not surprised by teenagers who pick up six to twelve videos for a weekend.

Is this consumption of movies artistic longing? prurient passion? mere escapism? an addiction? Let's try to get inside the teenage moviegoer and home-video viewer and ask, What are the needs and longings that bring you to this pop art? The honest answers we get might be translated into our words in the following summary:

- to be with my friends;
- to be relieved of pressure and pain through humor and vicarious experience;
- to escape boredom and be excited through violent or suspenseful action and adventure;
- to exchange my drab life for the strange, bizarre, or occult;
- to see how much (horror, violence, etc.) I can take;
- to be instructed relationally and romantically;
- to be aroused sexually or to arouse my partner;
- to live out good and evil, right and wrong, through social dramas and science fiction.

1. *The Movie Industry:* The film industry is even more aware than we are of the needs and wishes that influence young viewers to see movies. We should keep in mind several things about the movie business:

- It exists to make money.
- It has the least tolerance for failure among the arts (the financial risks are greatest here).
- It has experienced the highest rise in costs among the arts.
- It competes with other art forms on which it also depends—written fiction, music, plays, and TV.
- The industry's strategy becomes attracting the broadest audience possible, particularly their main audience of twelve- to thirty-five-year-olds, focusing in on the nineteen-year-old-male as key, and offering the lowest common denominator of appeal. Secondary, lower-cost films to particular audiences may also be profitable.

Admission to the movies in the 1930s was as low as five cents and as high as two dollars at high-class theaters. Hollywood's control of film production, distribution, and exhibition was ruled contrary to anti-trust regulations in the late 1940s. They were forced to sell their domestic theater chains; still they controlled distribution, forcing cinemas to take a package of "A" films with stars and high costs along with "B" and "C" low cost films produced at low-cost with less popular and unknown actors. "A" pictures needed to be directed at the broad audiences, while "B" films could be directed toward the interests of narrower groups.

Because film is both art and business, it is important to realize how costs have risen. In the 1930s movies could be made for twenty-five to seventy-five thousand dollars. In the 1950s small-budget movies were still made for a few hundred thousand dollars. By the 1970s average film costs were more than a million. Films cost ten to twenty million in the 1980s—thirty something million by the 1990s.

Blockbusters are "A" films with extra-large budget, super-star cast, extraordinary effects, and huge hype; they are "event" films. Here are some sample costs and gross incomes for such extravaganzas (you will notice that not all of these films made money):[8]

Film	Date	Estimated Cost (millions)	Estimated Domestic Gross (millions)
Quo Vadis	(1951)	7	12
The Robe	(1953)	4	18
Around the World in Eighty Days	(1954)	6	22
Ten Commandments	(1956)	13	43
Ben Hur	(1959)	15	38
Lawrence of Arabia	(1962)	12	19
Cleopatra	(1963)	44	26
The Sound of Music	(1964)	10	80
Greatest Story Ever Told	(1965)	20	7
Hello Dolly	(1969)	24	15
Molly Maguire	(1970)	11	1
Patton	(1970)	13	28
Star Wars	(1977)	10	193
Return of the Jedi	(1983)	32.5	169.2
Four Weddings and a Funeral	(1994)	5	250
Pulp Fiction	(1994)	8.2	100
Waterworld	(1995)	170	90

[8] William D. Romanowski, *Pop Cultural Wars* (Downers Grove, Ill.: InterVarsity, 1996) 192; *Variety Magazine* (Nov. 13, 1995) 8.

As in any business, profit is crucial in the film industry. It was during the 1970s that Hollywood realized that its most dependable movie goers were young people. The 1980s produced a spate of "teen flicks" such as *Risky Business* (1983), *All the Right Moves* (1983), *Ferris Bueller's Day Off* (1983), and *Pump Up the Volume* (1990), along with the John Hughes/Molly Ringwald trilogy of *Sixteen Candles* (1984), *The Breakfast Club* (1985), and *Pretty in Pink* (1986). This decade also saw the proliferation of sexploitation films directed at teenagers: *Fast Times at Ridgemont High* (1982), *Porky's* (1982, plus sequels), and many more. Demographic statistics showed peak movie attendance of teenagers in the 1980s, and marketers had discovered the amazing total of their disposable income. These films also drew adults fascinated by adolescent experiences.

2. *Discussing Films:* It helps, in talking about films with young people, to keep in mind the various genres of films they are watching: comedy, action adventure, relational or romantic drama, social awareness, science fiction and fantasy, sexploitation, gothic, horror and occult, war, slasher films (combinations of explicit sex and gore) and films that become cult movies like *The Rocky Horror Picture Show* and *Heathers*. Four girls in Largo High School, Florida, "the Fearsome Foursome," make up the most exclusive clique on campus—bright, multi-talented, intense, fun-loving. They have watched *Heathers* (1989) so many times, it has become for them a "cult film."[9] This morbid depiction of peer pressure and high school cliques must be interpreted to an adult who could, in turn, bring real understanding to the film. Young people who don outrageous costumes for a midnight showing of *Rocky Horror* (1975), a spoof on horror films, with its sex, transvestitism, and rock and roll, are part of its long-term cult following. Only by spending time in earnest inquiry can we know what we should about the effect of film on young people and where

---

[9] French, *South of Heaven,* 18ff., 75, 299, 360.

they are today. And we can get closer to them in the process.

There are great opportunities for discussions based on questions like: What is the message of this film—what is it trying to say? What is its appeal, or to what instincts in us is it appealing? Is it just trying to get our money, or is it also attempting to give us something positive? How do you think it is affecting the various ages and types of people in its audience—particularly the kinds of people (e.g., gender) it may stereotype? How does its theme compare to the message of Jesus? As young people discuss, interpret, and evaluate what they or their friends watch, the characteristics of good art, the casting and stereotyping of characters, the values, the messages, and the effect of such art on small children may all be part of your fruitful conversations.

Critiquing Television

In order to empower youthful minds to become responsible, critically-thinking viewers of television, we must have a general understanding of the following:

- television as technology or technique (how it works),
- television as an industry (how it is produced),
- television as advertising (how it is sponsored/funded),
- television as audience (how it is viewed and rated),
- television as programs (what is shown).

Some television critics (as described in the next few pages) see television as an unmitigated social disaster. They are respectable social commentators, and much of what they are saying is true. But we will seek a more balanced evaluation. Some of us who have observed childhood and adolescence over several decades have noticed the extent to which kids are bonded to the television set. For some children the bonding to TV comes just after the bonding to mommy. Instead of a present and caring daddy, it is Mr. Rogers or Big Bird that takes them by the hand as they move out from mother's arms to the outside world. In many interactions with children and young adults, we sense that television has become a family member to them.

Positive television programs do provide children with beneficial instruction and adventure, but gradually kids begin to watch more than children's television. Childhood was once described as the age of innocence, but no longer are children protected from the heavy burdens and seamy secrets of adulthood. There is no adult responsibility or perversion absent from the small screen, and kids are watching it all intently. In many ways they are stripped of their innocence and any single value system. From home to day care to school to television, they are forced to adjust to many differing value systems. They miss the opportunity to develop a clear self-image, a personal value system, a long-term attention span, and tools for literary analysis. These electronic children tend to lose an appreciation of their past and their futures.

The conspiracy to rob kids of their childhood goes beyond television. Experts point out how, in so many ways, parents and adults are all pushing "hurried children" toward what might be described as pseudosophistication.[10] They know all about life, but not really. Without adequate time with nurturers and mentors, they learn by imitation rather than by integration. Instead of internalizing one consistent set of values, they develop within themselves compartments with differing value systems from home, school, friends, and the media.

The irony of society's rushing children into adolescence (and pseudo-adulthood) is that it has at the same time postponed entry into adulthood. Adolescence begins earlier and lasts longer than it ever has before. In the 1990s we have seen early adolescents clinging to childish toys and activities—something they lost too soon. The appropriate time for marriage is later than it used to be. It takes longer to become self-sufficient—free financially and emotionally

---

[10] David Elkind, *The Hurried Child: Growing Up Too Fast Too Soon* (Reading, Mass.: Addison-Wesley, 1981); Neil Postman, *The Disappearance of Childhood* (New York: Delacorte, 1982); Marie Winn, *Children Without Childhood* (New York: Penguin, 1983).

from parents. Contemporary society has wiped out clear markers for the transition to adulthood. Adolescents have had to invent their own markers: getting a driver's license, getting drunk, losing one's virginity, graduating from high school, graduating from college. Many teenagers don't look forward to adult life. Our culture has not made it easy to grow up these days. What many of them have seen of adult stress and divorce in real life and on TV has made them reluctant to leave the security of the youth culture. No other medium influences children at the young age that television does, and therefore its effect is quite profound. That is why analysis of television is so important.

Social critics Jerry Mander, Neil Postman, and Allan Bloom see television as an unmitigated social disaster.[11] The logic of their polemics may be summarized as follows:

- Television replaces reality with images—it begins to shape the viewer into conformity with an artificial, commercial environment. We begin to mistake illusion for reality and to substitute style for substance.
- Television replaces active, logical analysis with passive, sensual entertainment. It is show business, says Postman; it cannot truly inform since it is entertainment and is commercially driven. We are "amusing ourselves to death." Postman brilliantly describes how we have lost the power to hear long and persuasive arguments (style has replaced substance in political debate) and to reason logically as people did in an earlier, typographical era.
- Televsion poses as our culture's instructor, but it is actually its entertainer. The mass audience that television has produced would rather be entertained than instructed, and these viewers determine ratings that determine profit and cost. Since the profit motive drives and controls the industry, the industry cannot be reformed.

---

[11] Mander, *Four Reasons for the Elimination of Television* (New York: Quill, 1978); Postman, *Amusing Ourselves to Death* (New York: Penguin, 1985); Bloom, *The Closing of the American Mind* (New York: Simon & Schuster, 1987).

- By substituting sound bites for disciplined analysis, shifting and juxtaposed images for typographical and linear logic, style for substance, and entertainment for instruction, television is destroying the kind of discourse and decision-making necessary for sound democracy. Television is destroying our very ability to discriminate and act.

On how to achieve the elimination of television, Mander concludes: "I certainly cannot answer the question. It is obvious, however, that the first step is for all of us to purge from our minds the idea that because television exists, we cannot get rid of it."[12]

The above critiques may go too far and miss the main point. They seem to imagine past ages more golden than they actually were and place too high a trust in human cognitive powers. This rosy picture of the past may lead to oversimplifications regarding today's social pathologies. Vast changes in our economic, political, and social systems are more responsible than any one medium for the ills listed above. We are at a point where some would rather attack symptoms than deal with the full causes of our moral dilemmas. Such analysis would call for discussion of the undermining of the free market by greed, the effects of special interests and contributions to politics, the persistence of discrimination fostered by classism and racism, the protection of inadequate teachers by unionism, ego-fed politics in grass-roots community organizations, the weakness of many families—all of which go beyond our intention here.

A balanced evaluation of television is needed. Television would seem to be beneficial for our society when it:

- brings company into the life of a homebound, lonely person;
- allows harried persons to relax;
- brings a family together in laughter;

---

[12] *Four Reasons,* 357.

- helps a family discuss a serious contemporary problem like racism, suicide, rape, homosexuality, or sexual abuse;
- gets a whole nation talking about "Roots" or "The Holocaust";
- lifts a city's spirits with a bowl victory or a nation's with a moon landing;
- instructs us through honest dialogue or well-done documentaries;
- provides young people with good role models (like straight, community-serving athletes), allows them to study friendship, assess their values, test their ethics, and consider self-sacrifice;
- performs the functions of good drama (see earlier discussion in this chapter).

Television undoubtedly provides a way to meet the above social needs. Although there may be other, better ways to meet these needs, they are not always available. For instance, shut-ins may not have supportive communities or churches; television may be their only contact with other people. Some parents may need the break that they get when their toddler watches *Sesame Street.* Thus, in some situations, television does provide an answer to people's needs. In other situations, however, there are preferable alternatives to the television habit. In these instances people, young and old, will need to examine with discipline and discrimination their approach to television. Some people will get rid of television in their homes; others will pull out the plug from time to time. The important thing is that people begin the process of evaluating their use of television.

Television is a technology passing into a new multimedia age of massive, interactive information and virtual reality. Not only will television remain with us, but television, telephones, and computers will all merge into one home center for learning, business, and entertainment. The approach and skills encouraged in this book are meant as a preparation for an electronic revolution greater than the coming of television in the 1950s or the proliferation of walkmans, cable, and VCRs in the 1980s. We can prepare ourselves and the next generation to be able to read and interpret media, great books, and the Bible.

The blame for bad pop art and consumer tastes has been directed too long at a sole cause, whether young people, parents, artists, or the entertainment industry. No single enemy causes violence, drug abuse, or teen pregnancy. Pop art is a reflection of us all. It may miss much of what is normal and healthy in our society; it may delight in the extremes. But it is largely determined by consumers.

Whether concerned parents and adults (particularly from school, church, or youth organizations), young people, and the entertainment industry could agree on some common standards for the pop art being devoured by young people today is a huge question. It must continue to be addressed—though this discussion of social policy needs to be broader and more civil. Cultures at the end of the twentieth century are facing a great moral crisis. We must come together with mutual consideration and with respect for honest theological discussion.

Youth ministry has significant contributions to make in this civil discussion. Creative youth programs will have young people involved in the media, perhaps conducting a television log or monitoring violence, critiquing commercials, and discussing rating systems. Two high school honor students (one of them my daughter) took a senior semester to create an excellent multimedia computer presentation on the influence of media on teenagers. Their presentation is an example of young people's interest in and ability to critique the media torrent, whose overwhelming effects most of us are not even aware of.

Those who care about young people must face the challenge of being with young people in their popular arts and knowing some art theory, relevant theological principles, and the social implications of art. Theologizing is bringing God into our concerns and discussions. To theologize about difficult issues such as those considered in this chapter is not to produce easy or dogmatic answers. But it provides hope and direction in confusing times. The gospel works for the liberation and empowerment of young people threatened by oppressive stereotypes and compromising values. It provides a necessary moral foundation for life in a complex world. In a changing world we must offset the enticement of ignoble paths by encouraging the needs and desires of young people in noble directions.

QUESTIONS FOR REFLECTION AND DISCUSSION

1. How have art and drama influenced your life? How have your viewing and reception of the electronic media changed since you were younger? How do you want it to change at this point?
2. Would you argue for the elimination of television?
3. Is your life enriched by watching good stories? Do you remember the last time you found a new bonding with another person through the sharing of personal stories (or histories)?
4. What questions do you have about this discussion of electronic media and pop art? How do you want to further this study?
5. How is Christ to be found in contemporary art? Do you think Christians should be involved in all the media and pop culture? If so, how might they express themselves and their convictions in these fields?
6. Consider several specific ways you can take the theological and artistic principles discussed here and use them with young people.

TOWARD A THEOLOGY OF HUMOR

What's So Funny and Why?

[Humanity is] distinguished from all other creatures by the faculty of laughter.

—*Joseph Addison*

So I commend enjoyment, for there is nothing better for people under the sun than to eat, and drink, and enjoy themselves, for this will go with them in their toil through the days of life that God gives them under the sun.

—*Ecclesiastes 8:15,* NRSV

A little nonsense now and then
Is relished by the wisest men.

—*Anonymous*

THE SIGNIFICANCE OF HUMOR

Everybody likes to laugh, but it's not always easy to explain what is funny. Surprisingly we often take humor lightly, but humor helps us survive the hardships of life. Youth leaders (parents, teachers, and others) need to think seriously about humor and the vital role it plays in the lives of young people. Youth ministry needs a theology of humor.

To see their children laughing delights all parents. Youth leaders beam when young people let down their defenses, let tension go, and laugh. We all enjoy good humor. Research has shown the physical benefits of mirth

and fun.[1] In one version of the Bible four verses link
laughter with joy (though the second two are from a
negative standpoint):

> [God] will yet fill your mouth with laughter, and your lips
> with shouts of joy. (Job 8:21, NRSV)

> Then our mouth was filled with laughter, and our tongue
> with shouts of joy. (Psalm 126:2, NRSV)

> Even in laughter the heart is sad, and the end of joy is grief.
> (Proverbs 14:13, NRSV)

> Lament and mourn and weep. Let your laughter be turned
> into mourning and your joy into dejection. (James 4:9, NRSV)

A high view of our Lord Jesus Christ and the holy
mysteries creates a setting where healthy humor can flour-
ish; we need not take our lives and ministries quite so
seriously. Young people are often longing—sometimes even
crying—for adults and the adult church to "lighten up."
Youth ministry couldn't get along without humor. Leaders
need it for their own proper perspective. More importantly,
humor is a staple of the youth culture, and any successful
ministry must allow opportunity for laughter—spontaneous
and planned, individual and group.

The youth culture has its own sense of humor, as do all
cultures. It is an important, distinctive, and changing aspect
of the social life and culture of youth. Like many aspects of
adolescent life, youthful humor tries to be funny in a way
that will shock and confuse adult society. Sometimes humor
has a terrible potentiality for injury. We are aware of how
easily humor can cross a line from good fun to hurtful "fun."
Humor may be violent and can injure adolescents, just as it

---

[1] Lee Berk and Stanley Tan, et al. "Neuroendrocrine and Stress Hor-
mone Changes During Mirthful Laughter," *American Journal of Medical
Sciences* 298, no. 6 (1989) 390-96. Berk has even developed a software
program for doctors, hospitals, clinics, and rehabilitation centers for cus-
tomized laughter prescriptions allowing doctors to create individualized
humor reports for patients. These Christian doctors from Loma Linda
University Medical Center, Department of Pathology, base their work on
Proverbs 17:22.

can hurt anyone: women, men, ethnic groups, the disabled, and various classes of people. It can take some real time and effort to heal what a moment's thoughtlessness has caused.

Recognizing how prevalent and powerful the use and misuse of laughter are—how very healthy it is for families or youth groups to have a good laugh together—we want to know more about it, to better understand its ability to shape our view of our world and ourselves. Admittedly we cannot even precisely define humor. We are not really clear as to why something is funny. Still, we must ask, What *is* humor, and when does it cross the line of human decency and Christian appropriateness? These are difficult questions and subject to culture and taste, but much can be gained from careful reflection on the subject.

Among youth ministers, Phil McDonald of Minneapolis is one of the masters of humor. He remembers being impressed in the 1950s when he heard of a survey asking high school students what they considered to be the most important criteria for a good teacher. Their number one criterion was mastery of the subject; their second, a good sense of humor. As important as humor is, Phil also understands how risky intentional humor before audiences can be. He is struck by how forgiving people can be of speakers or singers, yet how unforgiving they are when it comes to humor. Night club audiences, for instance, can become mean when a comedian fails to deliver. And failed humor is a terrible introduction to speeches before young people.

Though humor can divide us, it also has a universal quality that can bind us together. In the early 1960s Phil was asked to do program at a camp up the river in Peru. A two-engined Catalina seaplane was flying people into the site. Fascinated, local Indians sat watching on the bank. A crewman stood on the wing to throw out a securing rope when the nose of the plane hit a bank and he plunged into the water. The natives rolled with laughter, and Phil marveled at the universality of humor.

Not all humor is universal, however. When I taught at Cuttington College in Liberia, years ago, I was impressed with how differently humor is expressed in different cultures. What is funny to people in one society may not be to those in another. Similarly, what people find funny in a given situation may not be in another. Americans standing on the bank of the river in Peru might or might not find the incident funny. Some might be sorry for the soaked crewman or too embarrassed to laugh. Those same people might chuckle, however, to see the scene on a funny videos program.

Michael Ashburn, whose "backwoods" humor has made so many laugh, finds it easy to be funny. The challenge for him is to be godly and funny. High standards for humor get compromised when one is unprepared; nervousness can produce inappropriate jokes. Humor is the great mixer, according to Ashburn, and he often thinks of its effect in terms of being as "good and pleasant" as the precious oil running down Aaron's beard (Psalm 133:1-2). But, if humor makes one person feel put down then it has strayed off the mark. Humor can either lift up and confirm or tear down.

The stress of technological cultures has led to psychological studies of humor and its possibilities in therapy. Interestingly, a literary leader was one of the early promoters of laughter for its medicinal properties. It was in illness that Norman Cousins discovered the power of laughter.

> In *Anatomy of an Illness*, first published in 1976, I had reported my discovery that ten minutes of solid belly laughter would give me two hours of pain-free sleep. . . . Of all the gifts bestowed by nature on human beings, hearty laughter must be close to the top.[2]

After his book was published, a study in the *Journal of the American Medical Association* provided scientific evidence that he was right about laughter's ability to combat serious illness.[3]

---

[2] *Head First: The Biology of Hope* (New York: E. P. Dutton, 1989) 126-27.

[3] *JAMA* 261 (1989) 558.

Many books have since been written concerning the medical and the therapeutic value of humor.[4] Loretta LaRouche, from Plymouth, Massachusetts, is a combination of stand-up comic, storyteller, clown, psychotherapist, and business consultant. She works in Boston's Beth Israel Deaconess Medical Center as well as for businesses concerned about stress among their employees. She calls herself a "jollyologist" or an "M.D.—a mirth doctor." "Feeling stressed?" she asks. "Keep a mirror handy, look at yourself and periodically ask, 'How serious is this?' Everyone is a joke on some level."[5]

The authors of *The Laughing Classroom* offer some important insights on humor based on their study of humor and its application to education.

> Humor is a mysterious phenomenon. Ask most teachers if they have a good sense of humor, and 99 percent will respond affirmatively. Moore Colby wrote, "Men will confess to treason, murder, arson, false teeth or a wig, but how many will own up to a lack of humor?" . . . Steven Allen wrote, "We will accept almost any allegation of our deficiencies— cosmetic, intellectual, virtuous—save one, the charge that we have no sense of humor." To do so would cause great embarrassment . . . which, if discovered, could lead to social ostracism.

> It's important to remember that what is funny to one person isn't necessarily funny to another. One person may find the slapstick comedy of the Three Stooges outrageously funny, while another enjoys Victor Borge's dry wit. Each generation, each gender, and each culture also differs in what it considers humorous or funny. Although there are

---

[4] Allen Klein, *The Healing Power of Humor: Techniques for Getting Through Loss, Setbacks, Upsets, Disappointments, Difficulties, Trials, Tribulations, and All That Not-So-Funny Stuff* (Los Angeles: J. P. Tarcher, 1989). Francis A. McGuire, Roseangela K. Boyd, and Ann James, *Therapeutic Humor with the Elderly* (New York: Hawthorne, 1992). Herbert S. Strean, ed. *The Use of Humor in Psychotherapy* (Northvale, N.J.: J. Aronson, 1994).

[5] Judith Gaines, "Stressing Laughter: Therapist Uses Humor as Antidote for Anxiety," *The Boston Globe,* December 8, 1996.

differences, humor is universal and exists in some form within all cultures and, hopefully, within the learning environment.

There are many "hues" of humor, running across the spectrum from playful, witty, and affectionate to satirical, degrading, and biting. . . . There are two very distinct sides to the humor coin: the comic and the tragic. Humor can act as a social lubricant or a social retardant . . . it can educate or denigrate, heal or harm, embrace or deface. It's a powerful communication tool, no matter which side is chosen.[6]

Recognizing how powerfully humor affects us—for good or ill—and how healthy it is for families and youth groups to have a good laugh together, we want to know more about it. How do we define humor? How should we use humor? When does it cross the line of human decency or Christian appropriateness?

THE NATURE OF HUMOR

Webster's doesn't help much when it defines humor as "the quality that makes something seem funny, amusing, or ludicrous"; or "the ability to perceive, appreciate, or express what is funny, amusing, or ludicrous."[7] On this subject, dictionary definitions seem circuitous: Humor is something that is humorous or funny. But what makes it funny? And why do we have a need to be funny or be around funny people? Why was it such a good party *because* we all laughed so much? How can we understand the nature of humor?

Historically the word "humor" comes from the ancient understanding of human physiology and well-being. The

---

[6] Diane Loomans and Karen Kolberg, *The Laughing Classroom: Everyone's Guide to Teaching with Humor and Play* (Tiburon, Calif.: H. J. Kramer, 1993) 13-14.

[7] *Webster's New Twentieth-Century Dictionary, Unabridged,* 2d ed., s.v. "humor."

Greeks assessed mental health in terms of a balance between four humors or bodily fluids. Hippocrates applied
the understanding of human nature from philosophers
to his theory of medicine. A disproportion of one humor
over the others resulted in mental illness. So humor's therapeutic function, underplayed until recently, was recognized
back in the time of the ancient Greek philosophers.

> The body, says Hippocrates, is compounded of blood, phlegm,
> yellow bile, and black bile; that man enjoys the most perfect
> health in whom these elements are duly proportioned and
> mingled; pain is the defect or excess of one "humor," or its
> isolation from the rest.[8]

The Greeks saw laughter as a corrective to any excessive
or ridiculous behavioral tendency. A person with a ludicrous
extreme was considered a humorist—someone who was the
object of laughter and needed to laugh. From there it was only
a step to speak of the humorist as one who was amusing or
who was able to provoke amusement in writing, acting, or
speaking.

As little as we may agree with ancient explanations of
what is funny, we find it difficult to come up with our own
theory of humor. We know when something strikes us as
funny, and some things may seem laughable to every one in
a large group—or perhaps funny to all except one or two.
We may become accomplished at making people laugh and
still not have a satisfactory theory of humor. Discussions to
solve this problem may themselves be a funny experience—
or a frustrating exercise in futility.

Theories of Humor

Theories of comedy or humor have centered in no-
tions of *power, incongruity,* or *relief.* Philosophers who
choose the notion of power describe humor in terms
of those in a dominant position laughing at those in a

---

[8] Will Durant, *The Life of Greece* (The Story of Civilization, II; New
York: Simon & Schuster, 1939) 344.

weaker or degraded situation. "Laughter is never far removed from derision," says Quintilian, an ancient Roman rhetorician.[9] Do you think there might have been jokes about lepers, beggars, and prostitutes in the time of Christ? If so, can you imagine rabbis, prophets, and Jesus objecting to the negative impact of such callous amusement?

Dissatisfaction with the derisive and negative connotations of a theory stressing power led to a second and somewhat later theory emphasizing incongruity. People laugh when what they *see* differs significantly from what they *expect*. Feelings associated with one action jostle feelings connected with another very different action, and people are amused. The philosopher Schopenhauer illustrates this principle of incongruity with a classic joke. Prison guards invite a prisoner to play cards with them, and when they find him cheating they kick him out of the jail.[10]

A third theory sees humor as a release of tension or inhibition. John Dewey described a smile as a "termination of effort" and laughter as "a sigh of relief."[11] Along similar lines, Sigmund Freud added the notion of humor as "outwitting the censor." Freud believed that civilization and education have developed a strong tendency to repress what society sees as primitive and dangerous sexuality.

> The repressive activity of civilization brings it about that primary possibilities of enjoyment, which have now, however, been repudiated by the censorship in us, are lost to us. But to the human psyche all renunciation is exceedingly difficult, and so we find that tendentious jokes provide a means of undoing the renunciation and retrieving what was lost. . . . The task of dream-formation is above all to overcome the inhibition from the censorship . . . the conclusion

---

[9] *The Encyclopedia Americana,* International Ed., s.v. "humor" (older editions of this encyclopedia have a more extensive article on "humor").
[10] Ibid.
[11] Ibid.

that joke-work and dream-work must, at least in some essential respect, be identical.[12]

Freud considered some kinds of humor as forbidden thoughts slipping past our internal censor, our prohibitions and inhibitions. We may sometimes disguise insults as compliments, sneak desires into double meanings, or give vent to suppressed wishes or malice that are not allowed as part of our normal thinking and behavior. Humor works when it highlights a contradiction between our conscious logic and our subconscious sense or between our cognitive processes and our emotional disposition. A building of tension in the joke or situation builds up to a sudden and unexpected release of tension in a tickle—instead of an attack.

Types of Humor

From wit, puns, and sarcasm, through fuller and more elaborate forms of comedy to dramatic irony, society needs humor. Many comics come from an oppressed class or race; a comic's life has often been touched with some special form of pain. We all know of battlefield humor, mortuary humor, and the jokes of the operating room; such humor is needed to take us through extraordinarily difficult human situations. Dogs are funny to us when they act human; children are funny when they come out with profound adult statements. We can make others and ourselves laugh

---

[12] Sigmund Freud, *Jokes and their Relation to the Unconscious* (The Standard Edition of the Complete Psychological Works of Sigmund Freud; trans. James Strachey with Anna Freud, vol. VIII [1905]; London: Hogarth, 1960, 1986) 101, 165. Obviously, no one theory of humor is adequate. Each theory is able to explain some types of humor, and all three theories overlap. Youth ministers should develop the ideas of this chapter into a working theory of their own—a practical theology of humor. Along with this chapter, take some time to read encyclopedic entries on humor and then some of the references they cite. Besides the article in *Encyclopedia Americana*, see W. F. Stinespring's essay on humor in *The Interpreter's Dictionary of the Bible* and Linton's article in the *International Standard Bible Encyclopedia*, rev. ed. Following that with Henri Cormier's *The Humor of Jesus* (New York: Alba, 1977) may change the way you read and teach the Bible.

when we "lose it," do something entirely out of character or inappropriate. These examples point to a key to the nature of humor.

Norman Cousins further considers the nature of humor in the following:

> The response to incongruities is one of the highest manifestations of the cerebral process. We smile broadly or even break out into open laugher when we come across Eugene Field's remark about a friend "who was so mean he wouldn't let his son have more than one measle at a time." Or Leo Rosten's reply to a question asking whether he trusted a certain person: "I'd rather trust a rabbit to deliver a head of lettuce." Or as Rosten also said, "Let's go somewhere where I can be alone." These examples of word play illustrate the ability of the human mind to jump across gaps in logic and find delight in the process.
>
> Surprise is certainly a major ingredient of humor. Babies will laugh at sudden movements or changes in expression, indicating that breaks in the sequences of behavior can tickle the risibilities. During the days of silent films, Hollywood built an empire out of the surprise antics of its voiceless comedians—Harold Lloyd swinging from the hands of a giant clock, Charlie Chaplin caught up in the bowels of an assembly belt, or Buster Keaton chasing a zebra.
>
> It has always seemed to me that laughter is the human mind's way of dealing with the incongruous. Our train of thought will be running in one direction and then is derailed suddenly by running into absurdity. The sudden wreckage of logical flow demands release. Hence the physical reaction known as laughter.[13]

This is a very apt description of laughter, and yet we still have not actually defined humor. Like sex and music, art and beauty, humor seems to defy easy definition. Yet, we do need clearer understanding of this important part of young people's lives and culture. Humor surrounds them—in television and movies, in their music, and sprinkled throughout their

---

[13] *Head First,* 127-28.

conversations. Our ability to analyze humor and comedy will enable us to equip young people to determine how humor is affecting them and whether it helps or hinders their growth. Unless we possess some skills of comic analysis and a theology of humor, we will be of little help to them.

Jokes about zits and bodily parts and functions all point to the human insecurity felt supremely in adolescent years. Idealistic young people may feel and see the powerlessness, the incongruity of life, and the need for comic relief, much more than adults do. No one feels more intensely the twin passions of desire to be a superstar and fear of being a loser than does a teenager. Humor may relieve what is felt in adolescence—the awful fear of failure, terrible embarrassment, and ultimate rejection. Humor can also unite the members of a group when they all laugh in friendly relief at their many anxieties.

We are coming closer to a working definition of humor. We might say humor is the human ability to contrast a specific word, action, or characteristic to an expected standard in a way that catches the mind off guard and allows for the release of tension and for human bonding. Humor provides us with a quick, psychological break and the release of nervous excitement or dangerous emotions. Drama, humor, and music all have this in common: they seek to relieve the human predicament and suggest hope for something better.

Laughter is medicine for body and soul—a relief from various tyrannies of the mind. But there are some occasions when we do not want to forget or be relieved. For example, humor should be only selectively and carefully used at funerals. Youth workers must acquire the necessary skill in comic analysis so as to be able to determine when drama and humor are an aid and when they cross the line of decency.

Some seem to possess an almost masochistic willingness to be mocked. Consider those who pay to enter a nightclub or comedy club and are then humiliated by a comic who objectifies women and emotionally attacks the privacy and vulnerability of those in the audience. Superficial smiles try to prove they are "cool with it"—even though their manhood or womanhood has been impugned or their sexual privacy has been violated. In our society it is very difficult to restrain (with government censorship) those who exploit humor for personal gain at the expense of personal injury and social pollution. It makes more sense (since economics is the most immediate restraint) for us to refuse to patronize such humor.

TOWARD A THEOLOGY OF HUMOR

How did humor enter the world anyway? Is humor a divine gift, or does it express our insubordinate discontent in being mere creatures? No matter how you understand the human situation, there is a tension between the spirit and the flesh, between heavenly aspirations and human struggles. This tension was for the Greeks and Elizabethans the stuff of tragedy. Taken less seriously, the incongruity of the mortal life is comic. Our human condition calls for humorous relief.

A Christian psychologist once came to help in a training program for urban youth leaders. He took the dogmatic position that humor was a result of the fall and human sin—that there would be no humor in heaven nor is there much need for laughter in the spiritual life. He tended to depreciate humor and encouraged alternatives to making people laugh. I'm not sure why he singled out humor. Money, games, and recreation, gender and sexuality, and perhaps music are all gifts from God that will pass away or be radically altered in our heavenly state. That does not take away from their value for us in our earthly lives.

Scripture ought to inform our theology of humor. Although the Bible is generally a serious text, it also has lighter elements. The Bible contains humor, particularly in the form of wordplays. Unfortunately these are usually apparent only to those who study Hebrew or Greek or who know about ancient Middle Eastern cultures. Some scholars have noted the harsh nature of ancient humor. "In the Old Testament there are 29 references to laughter, out of which

13 instances are linked with scorn, derision, mocking, and contempt and only two are born of joy."[14]

Stinespring points to the didactic or moralistic purpose of humor in his essay on the subject. "One of the most common kinds of humor (or rather wit) in Bible . . . is the pun, a form of wordplay or paronomasia. Paronomasia . . . goes far beyond humor in the Bible, because of the oriental fondness for this sort of thing."[15] Casanowicz and Russell count seven hundred instances of wordplay in the Bible.[16] Scripture reflects many instances in which serious matters are sprinkled with puns and wit. The Gospels invite us to smile at Jesus' picture of children failing to keep to the rules of their cute little game of weddings and funerals in the marketplace (Luke 7:32).[17] Jesus' words about "specks" and "beams in an eye" (Matthew 7:3-5) and "straining out a gnat and swallowing a camel" (Matthew 23:24) use levity to deal with serious issues. The Bible also has its share of irony.[18] The Bible views laughter as a good thing:

> Then our mouth was filled with laughter, and our tongue with shouts of joy. (Psalm 126:2, NRSV)

> A time to weep, and a time to laugh . . . (Ecclesiastes 3:4, NRSV)

> Blessed are you who weep now, for you will laugh. (Luke 6:21b, NRSV)

On the other hand, humor may sometimes be inadequate to cure human heaviness of heart, and it may even be hurtful,

---

[14] *The New Encyclopedia Britannica: Macropaedia, Knowledge in Depth,* 16th ed., s.v. "humor."

[15] *Intepreter's Dictionary,* s.v. "humor."

[16] I. M. Casanowicz, *Paronomasia in the Old Testament* (Boston, Mass.: J. S. Cushing, 1894) and E. Russell, *Paronomasia and Kindred Phenomena in the New Testament* (Leipzig: W. Drugulin, 1920), cited by Stinespring above.

[17] See S. MacLean Gilmour and John Knox, "The Gospel According to St. Luke," in *The Interpreter's Bible,* vol. VIII (ed. G. A. Buttrick; New York: Abingdon-Cokesbury, 1952) 140.

[18] Jesus' words in Matthew 23:32 and Paul's in 1 Corinthians 4:8 are examples of irony.

as is implied in the wise saying: "Even in laughter the heart is sad, and the end of joy is grief" (Proverbs 14:13, NRSV).

Do we ever seem funny to God? Does God have a sense of humor? If God doesn't, how did we get this universal sense of humor? If God does have a sense of humor, may it be that the Lord has chosen to participate with us in the tension between good and evil, perfection and imperfection, while remaining perfect and unchanging? Isn't relief a basic function of humor? Like the question discussed by the systematic theologians, "Does the divine nature possess emotions or feelings?" this matter is not easily resolved. We cannot say that God needs relief, nor can we be dogmatic about what God can or cannot feel. Here we enter into mystery and our need for thinking about God in human terms.

Jean Leclercq wrote about new theological thinking on humor in the late 1970s.

> Today, both exegetes and theologians have begun to speak not only of the humor of the sacred writers, but also of the humor of God and that of Christ. . . . In the sort of book in which the message of Jesus is made available to the contemporary world in a language which it can easily understand, one religious writer has noted that "humor is never wanting in the Gospel. It arises less frequently from the words themselves than from the context in which they are spoken."[19]

Henri Cormier introduces *The Humor of Jesus* in this way:

> It is easy to speak of Christian humor, of humor in the Gospel, or in the Bible. But we hesitate to say explicitly that "God has a sense of humor," or "Jesus has a sense of humor."
>
> Why do we hesitate to speak of the humor of Jesus? (For Christians) . . . to say that Jesus laughed, that he had a sense of humor, would be a lack of respect to the Son of God. . . . The ultimate reason behind our repugnance to

---

[19] Prologue to *The Humor of Jesus,* by Cormier.

speak, and especially to write, about the humor of Jesus
seems to be our lack of realism with respect to the humanity
of Jesus who became "like unto us in all things, excepting
for sin."[20]

Some translations of the Bible speak of God's *laughing*
from heaven's throne (at the folly of human rebellion in
Psalm 2:4, KJV). We have mentioned Jesus telling a funny
story in the Gospels. Even though Scripture describes the
Anointed One predominately as a man of sorrows, not as
funny, there is much more humor in the life of Christ than
we could probably imagine. Don't you think there were
times when Jesus laughed as he partied with sinners (e.g.,
Zacchaeus or Levi) or enjoyed the hospitality at Bethany?
Still, among all the portraits of Jesus I have seen, only one
was of a laughing Christ.

Elton Trueblood was having family devotions with his
family one evening. Their oldest son was only four years old
at the time. In the midst of a solemn reading of Matthew 7,
the boy began to laugh out loud. His parents at first were
perturbed and asked him what was the matter. He continued laughing at the thought of a human eye with a beam in
it! The boy caught the original point we usually miss.[21] The
Bible is a much funnier book than we realize, and we miss
many lessons without such an appreciation of oriental humor. Jesus found himself in many very difficult situations
and with some very slow learners. He used humor in
masterful ways that we need to study.

Some might never have listened to a sermon had the
preacher not had a good laugh with them first. Jesus
reached such people in a way few would expect from God.
When we think about all the incongruities of God becoming human, our imagination cannot refrain from picturing
Jesus smiling over the whole idea of what he was doing.
I can conceive of Christ laughing with those who needed

---

[20] Pages vii, x.
[21] Elton Trueblood, *The Humor of Christ* (New York: Harper & Row,
1964) 9.

to laugh, just as he wept with those who wept (Luke 19:40; John 11:33–35; and Romans 12:15).

THE SPIRITUALITY OF HUMOR

Jack Carpenter is a much loved and respected youth minister. He is one of that select group that spends an entire lifetime serving young people. Literally thousands have been touched by his personal concern for them and just as many have laughed themselves silly at his outrageous performances. Along with his sense of humor, Jack is a deeply spiritual person. His personal journal reveals some precious insights into humor.

> God, we believe, accepts us all, unconditionally, warts and all. Laughter is a pure form of response to God. . . . When I laugh with other people in genuine mirth, I accept them. So in laughing at myself I accept myself. Laughter is opposite to self-satisfaction in pride. For in laughter I accept myself not because I'm some sort of super-person, but precisely because I'm not. There is nothing funny *in* a super-person. There is everything funny *about* a super-person—seeing a person who thinks he or she has reached such a state. In laughing at my own claims to importance, I receive myself in a sort of loving forgiveness which is an echo of God's forgiveness of me. Selfishness and pride can be found in much conventional contrition; it can scarcely be hidden. In our desperate self-concern, we blame ourselves. But in laughter we sit lightly on ourselves. That is why laughter is a very pure response to God.

> In this regard I further pictured myself in a yoke with Jesus ("Come to me all you who are weary and over-burdened. . . . Put on my yoke and learn from me. . . ." Matthew 11:29 PME). At one point Jesus looked at me with a smiling, knowing wink. As I continued to reflect on this image, a new picture came to me. Jesus and I had gone from exchanging smiles to grimaces from the exceptionally heavy load, then broke out in hysterical laughter (as when a bunch of guys on a tough and seemingly impossible project look

so ridiculous to each other that all break into uncontrolled laughter).[22]

If you are going to communicate with young people, you must be willing to see yourself and your life as funny. We seek a humor that heals individuals, that binds people together, that frees people to look for brighter hopes. We seek humor, like good drama, that unifies and inspires. Our world cannot be preserved without comedy. Let us hope there will be more good comedians than greedy comics for young folk who need to laugh. May we not take ourselves too seriously! Let swelling laughter begin with us and spread to the tense fringes of our ministries.

THE USE OF HUMOR

All ministry demands knowing ourselves. To love others we must first love ourselves. Full communication to others means that we are able to communicate within ourselves. Laughing at our own complexity and incongruities allows us to make others laugh in a healthy way. It is helpful to understand your own style of humor, which is tied to your personality. Diane Loomans and Karen Kolberg provide four categories to help us identify our "humor style." They class one style as mostly positive, two other styles as positive and negative, and a final category as mostly negative.

> *Joy Masters* rise above the doom and gloom projected by others. They laugh for the sheer joy of laughing and have . . . learned to transform the pain and disappointment of life into positive learning experiences.

> *Fun Meisters* know how to have a rollicking good time, and want to include you in it. They see the potential for fun in almost every situation, but would never be socially inappropriate just to get a laugh. They are bold with their humor and

---

[22] Private journal of John B. Carpenter, Founder and Director of Youth Forum Maine.

laugh loudly and unselfconsciously. . . . They are usually the life of a party. They never laugh "at" people but "with" them. Fun Meisters engage in playful, slapstick antics and may take up clowning as a profession or a hobby. When Fun Meisters adopt the negative qualities of a Life Mocker, their fun turns against people and becomes degrading.

Joke Makers remember punchlines and know how to weave funny tales . . . their comic timing is impeccable. They have an uncanny ability to use their voice in strange and humorous ways and are good imitators. Joke Makers like to create funny stories based on their own experiences and pride themselves as being able to see the humor in even their most difficult lessons. When Joke Makers combine their characteristics with the qualities of a Life Mocker, their jokes turn ugly, self-depreciating, and bitingly satiric and can hurt others.

Life Mockers take humor to its lowest form and use it to ridicule, shame, and dehumanize others. They sneer rather than smile. They consider themselves superior to everyone on the planet using their humor as a weapon to destroy feelings of charity and contentment. They live mostly in their intellect and are constantly commenting on what is wrong with the world around them. Life mockers . . . are cynical and sarcastic and treat life itself as a joke and dismiss joy and fun as frivolous and childish.[23]

Youth workers, as well as teachers, will do well to study *The Laughing Classroom* for its many specific ideas in teaching and discussions. The book also offers general encouragement for a more joyful and pleasant style of life and positive communication.

Something Freud said about smutty jokes may help us realize the negative potential in humor. He noted that there are three people involved in smut: the first is the teller of the joke; the second is the object of the joke's hostile or sexual aggressiveness, and the third is the listener, who is supposed to receive some kind of pleasure in hearing and laughing.

---

[23] *The Laughing Classroom,* 14–19.

It is not the person who makes the joke who laughs at it and who therefore enjoys its pleasurable effect, but the inactive listener. . . . When the first person finds his libidinal impulse inhibited by the woman, he develops a hostile trend against that second person and calls on the originally interfering third person as his ally. Through the first person's smutty speech the woman is exposed before the third, who, as listener has now been bribed by the effortless satisfaction of his own libido. It is remarkable how universally popular a smutty interchange of this kind is.[24]

Reflecting on Freud's idea can challenge all of us who use humor. Is there a way we are bribing a captive audience to laugh at another gender, race, or social class, or at those with any kind of physical differences? The easiest way to sell a car or get a laugh is by misusing images or references to sexuality. As ministers of the gospel, we must guard ourselves against misusing humor.

Used positively, humor can benefit and enhance youth ministry at many levels: in informal conversations, announcements, discussions, teaching sessions, speeches, and comic skits. As with many areas of ministry, there are those specially gifted with comic talent, but it is the responsibility of all to develop and use the capacity to make people smile and laugh. We grow as we seek feedback from young people and our colleagues as to our sensitivity and spontaneity.

Seek a humor that relieves and uplifts young people, that glorifies Jesus Christ and brings us all together. To love young people is to want to see them laugh. But we never want a laugh at the expense of any individual or group. As we all seek to grow in this regard, may our serving be fun and our communication be sprinkled with laughs.

QUESTIONS FOR REFLECTION AND DISCUSSION

1. What, more than anything else, makes you really laugh these days? How can a better sense of humor be developed and the therapeutic effects of laughing be increased?

---

[24] *Jokes*, 100.

2. Have you ever imagined yourself laughing with God? How would Jesus respond to your humor?
3. What in this chapter has helped you think more constructively about humor?
4. About what do you currently hear teenagers laughing?
5. How do you see classes of people and individuals being hurt by humor? How can hurtful humor be reduced?
6. What is the best use of humor you have seen in ministry? What is the poorest you have noted? What standards would you suggest for humor?
7. What are some of the best current sources of humor and how can we be more creative in our use of humor?

TOWARD A THEOLOGY
OF MUSIC

Appreciating the Music of Young People

> *The man that hath no music in himself,*
> *Nor is not mov'd with concord of sweet sounds,*
> *Is fit for treasons, stratagems, and spoils;*
> *The motions of his spirit are dull as night,*
> *And his affections dark as Erebus:*
> *Let no such man be trusted.*
>
> —*Shakespeare,* Merchant of Venice

> *Music, the greatest good that mortals know,*
> *And all of heaven we have below.*
>
> —*Addison, "Song for St. Celia's Day"*

> *Then the* LORD *answered Job: ". . . Where were you when I*
> *laid the foundation of the earth . . . when the morning stars*
> *sang together?"*
>
> —*Job 38:1a, 4a, 7a,* NRSV

> *With trumpet sound . . . lute and harp . . . tambourine and*
> *dance . . . strings and pipe . . . loud clashing cymbals . . . Let*
> *everything that breathes praise the* LORD!
>
> —*Psalm 150:3-6,* NRSV

KEEPING UP WITH MUSIC

Young people are into music, and youth leaders need
to be too. Keith Thompson, professor of music education at
Pennsylvania State University, found that US teenagers listen

to music for 2–5 hours a day (urban youth: 4.43 hrs. per day; rural youth: 3.54 hours per day; suburban youth: 1.98 hours per day).[1] Some have found some teenagers spend more time listening to their music than to their teachers.

Bruce Springsteen once sang: "We busted out of class / had to get away from those fools / We learned more from a three-minute record / than we ever learned in school."[2] How many teenagers have felt that listening to their music for a little while gave them more than a whole day's schoolwork or a long church service?

Because teenagers are listening to so much music, and because it is evidently so important a part of their lives, leaders ought to take notice of it. We should be asking:

- How does it sound to them?
- What does it mean to them?
- How is it helping them to get through the day, to deal with their world?
- How can this role of music be expressed in terms of good and harm to their lives?
- How can we help them sort out the difference?

Music is communication. How can our attention to young people and their music teach us more about what communicates effectively to them today? Music is also cultural (and subcultural). How can we better understand their friends and groups through attention to their special music? And how can music be used to keep our ministry relevant? These questions point to reasons for studying the music of our times and suggest that we formulate theological guidelines for the appreciation and use of music.

None of us can keep up with all the music. Young listeners and fans must be our constant instructors; we can learn much from them. Our study of music currently popular with young people begins with listening to some of the music, reading reviews, and hearing the opinions and

---

[1] *USA Today,* April 1993, vol. 121, p. 4.
[2] From "No Surrender"; reproduced by permission. © Bruce Springsteen 1985. All rights reserved.

comments of young friends who listen to particular groups or genres. It is helpful if we can bring to this consideration some general knowledge about music; young people will fill in particulars with admirable skill. Obviously, they not only know more about their favorite music than we do—they are the experts on how it makes them feel and why they listen.

GENERAL KNOWLEDGE OF MUSIC

Music is defined as "the art and science of combining vocal or instrumental sounds or tones in varying melody, harmony, rhythm, and timbre."[3] The creative mixture of these elements in harmonically complete and emotionally expressive compositions is what we most often mean when we speak of music. Music also refers to the satisfying sounds of wind, water, and birds in nature. We may speak of a person's ability or inability to respond to, or take pleasure in, music when we say something like, "He has no *music* in his soul."

As to the origin of music, Anthony Storr writes:

> Music can certainly be regarded as a form of communication between people; but what it communicates is not obvious. . . .
>
> The origins of music may be lost in obscurity but, from its earliest beginnings, it seems to have played an essential part in social interaction. Music habitually accompanies religious and other ceremonies. Some anthropologists have speculated that vocal music may have begun as a special way of communicating with the supernatural; a way which shared many of the features of ordinary speech, but which was also distinctive.[4]

---

[3] *Webster's New Twentieth-Century Dictionary, Unabridged,* 2d ed., s. v. "music."

[4] *Music and the Mind* (New York: Free Press, 1992) 2, 17.

Friedrich Nietzsche was both a philosopher and a musician. In *The Birth of Tragedy* he writes that "language can never adequately render the cosmic symbolism of music."[5] Although we may reject much of Nietzsche's philosophy, he can still instruct us about the primacy of music in communicating the ultimate mysteries of life. Great hymnody joins music and doctrine to communicate the richness of the faith. Good youth ministers stand in awe of music, wanting to understand more of its nature and its affect on young people. Storr points to its influence and how it must be evaluated:

> Although science can define the differences between tones in terms of pitch, loudness, timbre, and waveform, it cannot portray the relation between tones which constitutes music. . . . Music has often been compared with mathematics; but, as G. H. Hardy pointed out, "Music can be used to stimulate mass emotion, while mathematics cannot." . . .

> The power of music, especially when combined with other emotive events, can be terrifyingly impressive. At the Nuremberg rally of 1936, the thunderous cheers of the vast crowd eventually drowned the music of the massed bands that played Hitler in. But the bands were there long before Hitler appeared, preceding his rhetoric with their rhetoric, preparing the huge gathering for Hitler's appearance, binding them together, arousing their expectations, aiding and abetting Hitler's self-dramatization, making it credible that a *petit bourgeois* failure had turned himself into a Messiah. The Greeks were right in supposing that music can be used for evil ends as well as for good. There can be no doubt that, by heightening crowd emotions and by ensuring that those emotions peak together rather than separately, music can powerfully contribute to the loss of critical judgment, the blind surrender to the feelings of the moment, which is so dangerously characteristic of crowd behaviour.[6]

---

[5] New York: Vintage, 1967, 55.
[6] *Music and the Mind*, 3, 46.

Because they spend time in the youth culture, youth workers and teachers are sometimes better able than parents (who should still try) to help young people discriminate points at which music may encourage adverse behavior or lead to a loss of critical judgment. We should understand the nature of music and its basic elements—beat, tone, melody, harmony, instrumentation, and lyrics. We want to make young listeners more aware of the lyrics, beat, and volume of contemporary music, along with the lifestyle of its performers, as we ask informed questions about their music.

REFLECTING THEOLOGICALLY ON MUSIC

Martin Luther believed that music was the second most powerful form of communication, after the preaching of the Word. His borrowing from popular music for hymns of the church is widely known. Percy and Ruth Crawford used the sound of big dance bands to give birth to the Christian choruses of the 1930s and 1940s. Larry Norman refused the devil a monopoly on rock music in the 1960s and 1970s. The line between secular and religious music is neither distinct nor absolute. Instead there is a continuous historical relationship between the music of this world and the music of faith, between pop music and church hymnody.

Music should, and according to the Bible did, praise the Lord. In the beginning of creation the morning stars sang together (Job 38:7). The heavenly host glorified God in song before the creation of the world and will, together with us, through all ages.

> You are worthy, our Lord and God, to receive glory and honor and power, for you created all things, and by your will they existed and were created. (Revelation 4:11, NRSV, see also Revelation 19:1ff.)

We celebrate the Christmas story, in which heavenly hosts sang joyously to shepherds (Luke 2:13-20).

The rebellion and fall of humanity from God's intended paradise created a rift between work and worship, work and play, secular and sacred. Perfect worship was interrupted by cultural needs. The first song in the Genesis stories is not a song of praise; it seems to be a romantic lyric of a man for his woman (Genesis 2:23). It is followed by Lamech's song of personal retribution after committing homicide—a social reflection on personal violence (Genesis 4:23-24). The Bible is full of hymns praising God and songs of the human condition. Scripture has its war songs (Exodus 15:1-18 and 20-21) and odes to love (Song of Solomon), along with ancient liturgies of tabernacle/ark (Numbers 10:35-36; 1 Chronicles 16:8-36), temple (2 Chronicles 5:13; Psalms 84; 121-134). It is filled with songs of personal devotion like Psalm 141 and the Magnificat. The trumpets at Jericho felled the city's protective walls (Joshua 6:4-5), and David's harp calmed the troubled spirit of King Saul (1 Samuel 16:23). The consecration of Solomon's temple was celebrated with loud and exciting music:

> The priests came out of the holy place . . . [and] the Levites who were singers . . . with cymbals, harps and lyres, . . . and with them a hundred and twenty priests blowing trumpets . . . the trumpeters and singers were heard as a single voice praising and giving thanks to the LORD. (2 Chronicles 5:11-13, NAB)

Few Bible readers today realize how much of the Bible was written in song and poetry. Ancient people—and some tribal people today along with modern young folk—live much of their lives to music. Through history, tribes have worked to music, gone to war with song, celebrated God (or the gods) in hymns, told their history in lyrics, and reflected about life in poetic stanzas. Ideally all songs should be directed to God, the center of our lives and existence. All music, then, would be an act of worship. But in our present life we must distinguish between music of entertainment and music of worship.

From a theological perspective, it is human rebellion and sin that cause a cleavage between Christ and culture. Since humanity's fall, and until our final redemption, our individual and corporate lives can never be completely whole—Christ and culture will always be in some sort of tension. We must deal with temporary distinctions like secular and sacred. Still, we aspire to wholeness and strive toward the integration of our lives and the world, our play and worship, God's kingdom and our culture.

"Worldly" songs have inspired some of the great hymns of the faith; Wesley, Luther, and others took some of their tunes from the tavern and love nests. On the other hand, some secular music has roots in religious or gospel songs; rhythm and blues, soul, and rock have deep religious roots.

Like drama, music seems to have been given to humanity to relieve and to inspire. We may understand humor, wine, and music as divine palliatives for human tedium and suffering.

> Being cheerful keeps you healthy. It is slow death to be gloomy all the time. (Proverbs 17:22, TEV)

> [God causes] grass to grow for the cattle, and plants for man to cultivate, . . . and wine to gladden the heart of man. (Psalm 104:14–15, RSV)

> I would have [liked to send] you away with mirth and songs, with tambourine and lyre. (Genesis 31:27, NRSV adapted)

> The father said to his servants, "Quick, . . . bring the fatted calf and kill it, and let us have a feast to celebrate the day . . . (with) music and dancing. . . . (Luke 15:22, 23, 25b, NEB)

Obviously, alcohol, humor, and music can be abused, and sincere Christians will disagree (often because of cultural differences) on their proper use.[7] We must tolerate

---

[7] We will not enter into the debate about Christians imbibing wine and beer except in the following ways: to note the controversy on this matter; to recognize the danger of teenage drinking; to discriminate between total abstinence, a moderate glass of wine or beer at a meal, and drinking with friends to get drunk; to distinguish wine and beer from hard liquors; to acknowledge the need to avoid offending young believers; and to acknowledge important cultural differences that make wine and beer acceptable in some Christian cultures (such as European) and taboo in others. In most cultures youth ministers do not drink any alcoholic drink with young people.

differences regarding the place of comedy, alcohol, and music in the Christian life. The Bible does not tell us how we are to use and to judge popular music. A theological and cultural framework based on Scripture and social understanding is necessary. We move toward a more mature understanding of music as we consider its many functions.

THE FUNCTIONS OF MUSIC

First, we need to appreciate what music does in our lives. Music is one of the deepest and most holistic forms of human communication, speaking to us physically, emotionally, intellectually, and spiritually in ways that touch us deeply. Music can say things that no other form of communication can. We may think of music as a kind of cosmic communication—expressing our ultimate longings for union and significance at levels that finally demand communion and affirmation from God. Youth ministers and parents should begin to consider the music of young people from the standpoint of communication.

James Lull is a writer, social analyst, and performer who has edited an important book entitled *Popular Music and Communication.* He describes it as being about "the role of music in human communication, especially as it pertains to the sociocultural behavior characteristic of youth."

> Music is a passionate sequencing of thoughts and feelings that expresses meaning in a manner that has no parallel in human life. It is a universally recognized synthesis of the substance and style of our existence—a blending of personal, social, and cultural signification that is confused with no other variety of communication. . . . Popular music is a unique and extremely influential communications form that deserves serious analysis— not just on the street and in the popular press, but in the scholarly literature and classroom as well.[8]

---

[8] Second ed.; Newbury Park, Calif.: Sage, 1992, 1.

Young people listen to music with their bodies and emotions. Rhythm and beat touch them in unique ways. In a moment they may pass from stress to mellowness, from depression to ecstasy, or from lethargy to high energy. A particular song may coax them from deep feelings of rejection to a secure sense of belonging.

Although we as leaders are theologically interested in the lyrics of popular music, we must remember that for most young people *beat* comes first, then *images*—much of today's music is being watched, as well as heard, in music videos—and finally the *words*. Suggestive meaning is conveyed to young viewers. As with all popular media (including the evening news), much of this music is sexual and violent in content.

Adolescents are struggling to find clear personal identities apart from their parents. Their life task involves a quest for relationships and intimacy. They must find some direction for the future, and some hope for the world. As they watch and listen to music, young people are taking in messages that promise them romance and significance. What they hear may be a superficial or empty promise of personal enlightenment, a sharing of common struggle, and a sense of community and belonging. A teenager listening to the radio full blast may be "spacing out"—or getting in touch with some profound issues of his or her soul. We may not recognize moments of deep religious significance in the life of a particular listener. Running through music and all the popular arts is a quest for some ultimate statement. It is part of a universal groping for meaning, union, and significance.[9] In classic rock, like The Doors' "Break on Through to the Other Side" and Led Zeppelin's "Stairway to Heaven," as well as in more recent rock, one sometimes sees that quest leading, in the absence of God, to an

---

[9] See Steve Turner, *Hungry for Heaven: Rock 'n' Roll and the Search for Redemption* (Downers Grove: InterVarsity, 1995); Bill Flanagan, *Written In My Soul: Conversations with Rock's Great Songwriters* (Chicago/New York: Contemporary, 1987); Timothy White, *Rock Lives: Profiles and Interviews* (New York: Holt, 1990).

ultimate high in death—whether through drugs or through violence.

We hear music in the life of a teenager as communication, as elixir and aphrodisiac, friend and support group, mentor and spiritual guide. Listening to current songs helps youth leaders understand and "get into" the hearts of young people. Asking about their favorite music and discussing how it makes them feel allows us to hear what young people are exposed to and, sometimes, to hear the deep cries of their hearts. I know that many young people find in their favorite songs statements of hurts, fears, and hopes they cannot express—even to their closest friends or (perhaps especially) to their parents. One of the reasons they turn it up so loud may be that no one is listening to what they need to reveal.

Jackson Browne once asked if he was the only one who heard the screams and the strangled cries. The shrunken, high-pitched voice in Missing Persons' "Words" asks plaintively—to no one in particular—what words are for if no one cares or even listens anymore. The group goes on to voice the frustration of not being heard or even noticed; the singer threatens to dye his hair blue. It seems to many young people that no one hears, no one cares, except the stereo and his or her favorite group. For those who care, it is a privilege to listen to another's heart, and music can open a door to the inner world of many teenagers.

Through their music we not only enter the hearts of young people but can also be introduced into their culture. Popular music is the tribal music of the youth culture. It is a distinguishing mark of youth culture, a link to their particular group of friends, and a very personal badge of social identity. Attack it, as many Christian music critics have done, or even focus on the evident negative features of the music, and you will be identified as a "tribal enemy." Among the many substitute markers adolescents have created (getting a license, getting drunk, losing their virginity . . .), music separates them from adults, takes them into another world, allows them solitude, teaches them lessons, and brings them back, joined to their cohorts, as new persons. We should not be surprised when this music of the youth culture (though often written and performed by middle-aged women and men who, to some degree, stay in the youth culture to exploit it) tries to shock adults, who are seen as intruders. Unfortunately it is becoming more and more difficult to shock people who have been desensitized to so many sensationalized images of sex and violence.

Popular music not only is a key to understanding the youth culture but also identifies specific groups within that culture. Different types of music are the adhesive of various subcultures. From junior high or middle school on up, we can begin to identify various groupings and types of young people by their favorite music.

Rap music originated in the hip-hop culture of the Bronx, reggae from a particular culture of Jamaica. The various forms of heavy metal—industrial, gothic, or death—originate from a working class background. Straight-edge heavy metal is an interesting "clean-cut" variety and part of a punk subculture. Alternative music tends to react against dominant trends and is claimed by thoughtful youth who would like to be seen as justifiably angry and possessing a unique commitment to integrity. Rave/house/dance music has dominated the 1990s. It attracts a slightly older crowd for the most part.

Many different forms of music find their way onto the pop music scene. The reggae music of the Rastas, the early dance and rap music of inner city clubs in the 1970s, grunge music in 1980s Seattle coffeehouses, punk and neo-punk, rave, ska, and many forms of dance music may all be seen as folk music in their beginnings. As soon as any group expression becomes commercially successful, it becomes *popular* music. Similarly, when alternative groups become entrenched at the top of the ratings charts, they become mainstream. Our studies of pop music and subcultural lifestyles are necessarily intertwined and provide us with cultural insights that feed our missiology and practical theology.

CRITIQUING THE MUSIC OF YOUNG PEOPLE

We may never enter more sacred territory or touch more personal sensitivities than when we challenge young people about their music. To them their world of music may be culturally off limits to adults or even a spiritually sacred and private compartment of their lives. They know their music has been used to shock adults, and they sense judgmental attitudes before we speak. Once, speaking at a college convocation, I treated the music popular among many students very positively and the lyrics of the Smashing Pumpkins with all due respect. Still, one student interrupted with protest and misinterpreted my remarks, to the chagrin of many of her classmates, who apologized to me. We must find the proper balance of interest, affirmation, questions, and information, in order to sensitively and compassionately broaden their tastes and aid their discrimination regarding music's function in their lives.

Many teenagers soak up ideas and values without being fully aware that they are doing so. Few realize, for instance, how sexist and degrading to women the words of much classic rock, heavy metal, or rap may be. We forget how often men write music for women to sing that reinforces a false and degrading mythology that men like to believe about women. It is the old myth of the desperate female waiting to be relieved and fulfilled by a sexual hero. It is difficult to determine the extent of the relationship, if there is one, between such fantasies and rape or sexual harassment. What we can say from many different sources is that the prevalence of sex on demand and sexual violence in movies and music have desensitized general viewers and have instigated action in those most vulnerable to such suggestions.

Much has been made of music with occult and destructive messages.[10] We would urge youth ministers to

---

[10] Robert G. DeMoss Jr., *Learn To Discern* (Grand Rapids, Mich.: Zondervan, 1992); Tipper Gore, *Raising PG Kids in an X-Rated Society* (Nashville: Abingdon, 1987); Walt Mueller, *Understanding Today's Youth Culture* (Wheaton, Ill.: Tyndale, 1994).

know their young people and discuss with them the most productive approach to the negative aspects of various kinds of music. Some music does have occult and destructive messages. These may amount to nothing more than an attempt to shock and to sell. Marilyn Manson, for instance, implies to some reporters that he is truly antichrist and a follower of Lucifer. In what may be a more authentic interview with *RIP,* Marilyn Manson says,

> I find it most entertaining that people miss my irony, and they've played into the joke that I have laid out and made fools of themselves. The instances when people misconceived me as a devil worshipper or misconceived me as a sexual deviant—they don't realize that they're actually reading their own game and they're only hurting themselves. [11]

In working through their own personal problems, such musicians may be exploiting the market for their own gain as they push musical boundaries and advocate a philosophy opposed to their own Christian and middle-class backgrounds.

Superficial critics are sometimes offended by music intended as a parody. Critics of popular music who are mainly negative, or treat all rock music as heavy metal, or look primarily for the satanic, should be heard with caution. A much deeper and broader analysis is needed. What may be found in 10 percent of popular music should never receive 90 percent of our consideration. To focus on occult messages and symbols hinders the crucial consideration of more prevalent images that demean or seduce.

Any strictly negative approach is a counterproductive way to deal with the music of young people. Nonetheless, along with reading positive reviews and books about popular music, we should also hear negative opinions. Martha Bayles condemns contemporary American rock because it has been polluted by European "perverse

---

[11] Chuck Dean, "Smells Like Mean Spirit," *RIP* 10, no. 11 (November 1996) 44.

modernism."[12] In an article entitled "Rock Music's Din and Decline," John Leno applauds Bayles's description of current music and seems to treat the music of young people as a pathology:

> What Bayles calls "today's cult of obscenity, brutality and sonic abuse" is shaping the dominant youth culture—selling nihilism, dehumanized sex, ugly excess and casual cruelty. It functions to whip up anger among young males and provoke extreme reactions. If the spread of this stuff into the mainstream isn't a social problem, what is?[13]

I am not dismissing the content of such critiques, but only noting Bayles's biases (for early rock and against British groups). More important, can such negative approaches encourage productive dialogue with young consumers of popular music?

With young listeners we need to appreciate positively the prophetic cries against pollution, mindless conformity, greed, materialism, war, and prejudice in current songs and classics from the past. Popular music that speaks out more clearly against idolatry and injustice than does the church, for instance, should be heard. Significant social critiques abound in heavy metal and tough rap music.

Youth leaders do well to know lyrics expressing important themes in the lives and dreams of young folk. This knowledge does not necessitate hours of watching music videos or listening to the newest releases. The high school crowd has already done that research. Our discussions with young people should include, among other things, questions about current television shows and their favorite music. We add information from these conversations to what we are reading in newspaper and magazine reviews.

Songs that we should consider do not have to come off the top hits of the past week. Some young people are "into oldies," and most are familiar with, or are willing to listen

---

[12] *Hole in Our Soul: The Loss of Beauty and Meaning in American Popular Music* (New York: Free Press, 1994).
[13] *U.S. News & World Report* (May 30, 1994) 19.

to, songs of the past. If we are willing to listen to and talk about their music, young people will usually give time to hear about our old favorites. Besides, conversations and sessions about music should raise the level of their discrimination about mass music as well as stretch their appreciation of all different kinds of music. It is sad to see young people divided from one another by their music.

Few things are more important to young people, or serve as a better bridge into their inner world, than music. It is therefore important to further our theology of music by reviewing its many forms and functions. The following points may guide our analysis of music as it affects young people. We should understand, collect, and discuss music in terms of:

- art,
- rites of passage,
- the "tribal music" of a special culture,
- images in videos,
- play and dance,
- entertainment,
- prophecy,
- lament,
- and especially commercial enterprise.

Does this music hurt anyone or hinder their growth? Does it contribute to someone's relief, healing, and empowerment? The ethical standards implied in these questions are our basis for analysis and critique in the world of youth, as everywhere else. Such questions will help us to understand how God is speaking, or being spoken about, in popular music.

It is our high privilege to live among young people and to share in their culture. From our own experience and studies and from what we learn from them, we can help young people evaluate their use of time and their internalization of media. Hopefully our gathering of information and exegesis of culture will merge with their processing and empowerment.

USING POPULAR MUSIC IN YOUTH MINISTRY

Young people, along with all of us, are searching for justice and peace, love and significance. Take a moment to ponder how important these themes are among young people. To the extent that they are not finding these human needs, they may turn to revenge, drugs, sex, and violence.

Consider how frustrated a young man or woman can become. Discrimination, dysfunction, rejection in society, in family, or among friends may be building up an incredible reservoir of anger. Young people may find more that speaks to their feelings and issues in music than they do at home, at school, or in church. You may be of some help in reminding them of God's promise of justice, peace, love, and significance.

Adolescents are idealistic and altruistic; they are concerned about the state of the world and of their society. The human heart demands an outcry regarding injustice and duplicity. Issues overlooked by preachers have often been picked up by popular musicians, whose medium is more attractive to young senses for all the reasons we have explained.

Although the Bible (especially Psalms) is filled with laments, young people today are given little opportunity for public cries of personal and corporate pain. We can be glad that many find in rock music what has been denied them at school and church. Scripture repeatedly records the cries of people; at times there was none to hear except the Lord. Where contemporary music gives voice to cries that young hearts may find it hard to express directly to us, we ought to be listening. Where it expresses the hopes and needs of their lives about which they may find it awkward to talk, we can hear and present the gospel.

Along with its hedonism and escapism, modern music is an expression of hopes and fears that reveals inner thoughts of many young people. The themes and lyrics of this music can be used in sharing the good news. In a deep sense, everything in this world, including its music, points to the reality of Jesus Christ. In the spirit of Psalms 34:15; 106:44; and Isaiah 52:7, we should listen sensitively and thoughtfully to the sounds of contemporary music.

QUESTIONS FOR REFLECTION AND DISCUSSION

1. How precious is music to you, and how deeply have you considered its effect on you recently and in the past? Have you spent time reflecting on music theologically?
2. With what in this chapter do you most agree or disagree?
3. How can the story of Hitler's music be discussed in regard to the positive and negative mass influence of music today?
4. What questions about popular music do you want to pursue further?
5. How do you listen to music with young people? How would you like to deepen this experience?
6. How might you use Colossians 3:14-17 in a discussion or unit on popular music?
7. How many different ways do you use music in ministry? How could this aspect of your ministry be broadened or enriched? What resources and books about music in youth ministry do you have available?

10 A THEOLOGY OF SEXUALITY

Sex and Spirituality

I've always been told that sex is like candy: once you're introduced to it, you never get enough. And boy, is that the truth.
—Sophomore female, 1989

Come on, sex has nothing to do with love or friendship. It's as meaningless as eating. Sometimes it's wonderful, other times it's gross and no fun. Lighten up on this relationship stuff. The phrase "to death do us part" means nothing anymore. All we can do in this world is get as much pleasure as possible. If that means risking AIDS or pregnancy, so be it. Where is all this love you're talking about?
—Teenage correspondent in "Ask Beth,"
The Boston Globe, 14 January 1993

Jesus said, "From the beginning of creation, God made them male and female . . . and the two shall become one flesh; consequently they are no longer two, but one flesh."
—Mark 10:6, 8, ASV

THE NEED FOR A THEOLOGY OF SEXUALITY

Many youth ministers do little deep theological reflection about sexuality. When the subject is addressed, it is often discussed more in terms of standards than underlying principles. We must face our own sexuality honestly and then probe the mystery of this mighty force.

Young people in modern societies are sexually aroused through media and peers at a remarkably young age—with marriage a distant and remote possibility. Furthermore, contemporary youth culture is like a social science laboratory in which society has decided to study adolescent frustration by maximizing sexual stimulus and postponing the economic and emotional viability of marriage.

Driving home from a family vacation once, Whitney Houston's "Saving All My Love for You" came on the radio. It is a pretty song—attractive, technically well done, and capable of sticking in your mind for days. You may even have hummed it in the elevator, restaurant, or dentist's office. I heard my sixth-grade daughter singing along in the back seat—before her older brother convinced her to be quiet. The tune was familiar, but snatches of the lyrics my daughter was singing piqued my interest. When we arrived home, I asked her if she could write out the words for me so I could use them in a class. I still have her sheet written out word for word from memory.

The song starts out sweetly, describing the few moments the two lovers can share. In the next line the lover reminds her guy that he has a family and is needed there. Although she realizes she must always be last on his list, no other can ever fulfill her longings, so she is saving all her love for him. The song goes on to speak of tonight as the night when all her feelings, longings, and frustrations are going to be fulfilled—all night long.

What happened next with my daughter is a lesson in itself. We talked about the song; my daughter had not noticed the implications of the words. When she took a good look at them, she agreed with me that the song involves a case of adultery. She saw it, did not approve of it, but was not particularly bothered by it. Most of us have gotten many such responses, "Of course it's wrong, but what's the big deal?" Still, the conversation seemed profitable for both of us.

The sexual picture of our times is grim. A study by Guy Dorius, Tim Heaton, and Patrick Steffen reviewed the research and cited the following results:

According to a study by Sonenstein, Pleck, and Ku:

- 33 percent of males had sex by age fifteen,
- 86 percent were no longer virgins by age nineteen.

Using data from the National Survey of Family Growth (1988), Pratt concluded:

- 25 percent of females had sex by age fifteen,
- 80 percent were no longer virgins by age nineteen.[1]

Many other studies suggest that only about half of sexually active teenagers use birth control or protective devices. Furthermore,

- around one million teenage girls became pregnant every year,
- about half of these pregnancies resulted in live births,
- four out of ten resulted in abortions,
- one out of ten resulted in miscarriage.

The rate of births to unmarried teenagers between 1960 and 1991 rose almost 200 percent, despite the increase of sex education (according to the National Center for Health Statistics, Centers for Disease Control).

Some conservative groups criticize these studies for exaggerating sexual activity or for giving implied social sanctions to such behavior. Our society's divisions on this important issue run so deep that serious dialogue about the subject is hindered. We have a problem here: teenagers (including Christians) are having sex, often hurting themselves. Many churches and Christian youth organizations either are doing little about it or are approaching it in a way that excludes those who need guidance most. The teaching may be fine for those who have clearly decided to wait, but those already sexually involved or on

---

[1] Guy L. Dorius, Tim B. Heaton, and Patrick Steffen, "Adolescent Life Events and Their Association with the Onset of Sexual Intercourse," *Youth and Society* 25, no. 1 (1993) 3-23, citing F. L. Sonenstein, J. H. Pleck, and L. C. Ku, "Sexual Activity, Condom Use, and AIDS Awareness among Adolescent Males," *Family Planning Perspectives* 21 (1989) 152-58; and W. F. Pratt, "Premarital Sexual Behavior, Multiple Sexual Partners, and Marital Experience" (paper read at the annual meeting of the Population Association of America, Toronto, 1990).

the brink may not hear anything that makes sense for them. Most parents are not sure what to do; many simply tend to hope for the best.

APPROACHING SEXUALITY IN OUR TIMES

Parents and youth leaders must be able to relate with compassion and a positive approach to sons, daughters, or young friends who are having sex before marriage. It is very difficult when your young daughter is already sleeping with her boyfriend, or when a young man you have led to faith becomes sexually involved.

Parents and youth ministers have different relationships with young people, but they should be able to minister together. In love with firmness, parents must set and explain the rules and boundaries of their home. Youth workers must approach the situation with interest, respect, and concern. Both parents and youth ministers should convey to sexually active young persons a strong rationale and practical guidelines for sexual abstinence before marriage. Many of our young people are waiting until they are married to have sex, and we must prepare and encourage them in godly standards. Still, the studies and our experience with youth show that many others are not waiting. In a postmodern, media-influenced age, abstinence works only by the grace of God and on the grounds of a solid and relevant theology of sexuality.[2]

We are on the side of abstinence, *and* we want to be realistic and unconditionally compassionate with all young people. We must realize that we deal with sex most successfully as we help young people work out their own personal

---

[2] Music and other media should be brought into these discussions. The Shades were presented in the late 1990s with a vibrant and sexy image by Motown Records. Still, they believe that loving is much more than sex. Their song "I Believe" rejects one night stands, talks about slowing it down, and looks forward to a love that lasts. Christian pop music goes further still: see the 1994 *True Love Waits* album with strong messages from DC Talk, Michael W. Smith, Newsboys, Petra, DeGarmo & Key, and others.

identities, their worldviews and values, and their relationships with others.

Many experts on adolescent sex in the 1960s and 1970s followed the sexual revolution toward permissive freedom. "Have fun, but be responsible"—whatever that meant in specific situations. During the 1980s, however, most secular specialists took a more conservative stance. They came to question whether teenagers were emotionally mature enough for sexual intimacy, for keeping themselves from unwanted pregnancies, and for avoiding sexually transmitted diseases. In the 1990s we are seeing new ideas and permissive trends producing ambivalence among experts and confusion among youth.

A contemporary liberal opinion comes from University of Minnesota sociologist Ira Reiss and from Harriet Reiss, who see a society that has given teenagers permission to have sex. They do not see the answer in withdrawing that permission but in helping them to know when and why to say yes to sex and when and why to say no: from kissing to intercourse teenage sex should be honest, equal, and responsible.

> All sexual encounters should be negotiated with an honest statement of your feelings, an equal treatment of the other person's feelings, and a responsibility for taking measures to avoid unwanted outcomes like pregnancy or disease.[3]

This same sociologist does not believe that soap operas, Madonna, movies, and videos are strong influences for early sex.

Deborah Haffner, president of the Sexuality Information and Education Council of the US, sees everything in the culture telling children, even eleven- and twelve-year-olds, that they should go for it. She and her agency are calling for sexual gradualism, education that would encourage teenagers toward unpressured discovery of sexual feelings and activities short of intercourse. She suggests a

---

[3] Ira Reiss and Harriet Reiss, *An End to Shame: Shaping Our Next Sexual Revolution* (Amherst, N.Y.: Prometheus, 1990) 219.

cautious use of what used to be known as the "sexual bases" rather than immediate and full sexual intimacy.

Society should encourage adolescents to delay sexual behaviors until they are ready, physically, cognitively, and emotionally for mature sexual relationships and their consequences.[4]

Reiss and Reiss do see the dangers of teenage sexual activity. Although they don't think it possible to tell kids they can't have sex, they nevertheless encourage adults to offer teens help and advice:

Growing up sexually in America is like walking through a minefield, and few escape unscathed.[5]

[Adult society's] waffling, our internal conflicts, our ambivalence, and our dogmas about sexuality are major blocks to thinking clearly and to understanding today's grave sexual problems. We currently seem to act to encourage both the pleasures and dangers of sex, with little awareness of how to maximize the chances of obtaining one without the other.[6]

When one makes an unbiased comparison of promoting abstinence vs. promoting condom use, the results are obvious. Vows of abstinence break far more easily than do condoms.[7]

Having listened to these two experts, it is time to ask ourselves, as youth leaders or parents, What specific guidelines *are* we to give our young people these days?

- "Nothing below the waist."
- "Just keep all your clothes buttoned up and zippers closed."
- "Do it all standing up; no lying down."
- "Kissing is all right, but no French kissing."

---

[4] Deborah Haffner, ed. *Facing Facts: Sexual Health for America's Adolescents* (New York: Sexuality Information and Education Council of the United States, 1995) 4.

[5] *An End To Shame,* 19.

[6] Ibid., 30.

[7] Ibid., 125.

These rules made more sense in the 1940s and 1950s. At one time movies showed a car driving up to a house, someone getting out of the car, walking up the sidewalk, ringing the bell, and being let in. Now audiences are supposed to know characters are going from point A to B, and it happens in a flash with no plodding details. Similarly, love making used to begin with holding hands, move to arms around the waist, a gentle kiss, a longer kiss. People talked in terms of kissing, necking, and then petting. Today's films, however, show a look of attraction, mouths opening wide for deep kissing, clothes falling off and the couple going prone. Young people have been raised on this. No matter how much or little television they've seen, this instant way of life and satisfaction has been absorbed from the culture.

We have passed the age of restraint (as Haffner has observed above). There are no longer progressive stages from hand-holding, to kissing, to necking, to petting, and so on. We are in an age of instant intercourse. Most studies show that the standards of young people of faith and those with a church relationship are not far different from those of secular orientation. In regard to sexual norms, cultural norms seem to be very influential.

The rules above are inadequate because they do not rest on a strong theological foundation. If negative restraints are inadequate for our young folk, we must seek an approach that is positive and powerful. "Just say no" is not a strong enough way to handle overwhelming temptations. First, sex is too powerful for "just." Second, if you wait until you have to say something, it may already be too late. Finally, as Paul reminds us, positive and offensive measures against the easy path of temptation are stronger than any defensive means, "Don't allow yourself to be overpowered with evil. Take the offensive—overpower evil by good!" (Romans 12:21, Phillips). Young people seek a way to live an exciting and affirmative life—a way of life that says yes rather than no.

We need to understand more of what it is like for a young person in a position where he or she needs to say no.

It will help us to understand why it is not usually enough to just say no. As we contemplate the power of hormones, media, and peers in the experience of a young person, we will better appreciate how difficult it is for a mere no to overcome passion. As adults, we must have a clearer vision for positive thinking and living in today's youth culture. We must help young men and women live a dynamic yes to their own sexuality, to the fullness of life, to challenging activities, to supportive community, to the law of God, and to God's loving presence in and for them.

But before we can help young people deal with their sexuality in a society that bombards them with highly titillating messages and icons, we must deal with our own sexuality and come to a sound theology of sexuality ourselves by addressing the following questions.

- How do we define sex and sexuality?
- What is the nature of sex and the sexual drive?
- How does God intend the sexual drive to operate in a single person and how should married people appreciate and love those of the opposite gender?
- How do we handle our sexual temptations and fantasies?

Then we must go on to deal honestly with our responsibility to teenagers who are awash in sexual come-ons and powerful peer pressures.

- How can today's teenagers develop a healthy sexual identity? What is God's intent for male and female?
- How should young folk deal with their sexual energies? Why has God endowed them with such powerful passions?
- Can we tell teenagers and those in their twenties that sexual activity should wait for marriage?
- What guidelines can we give them as to the level of sexual intimacy they should have before marriage?

DEVELOPING A THEOLOGY OF SEXUALITY

Any theology of sexuality must begin with God, who is the divine model and is therefore the exemplar of all that we are and should be. God created human beings, as we have been saying, with basic drives for *union* and *significance*. We are meant to love and to serve. We do so with a divine energy that strives within us for life in tune with one another and creative work. We long to be at one with God and one another (communion) and to serve and be affirmed by one another (service). In this we find love and worth. This is the first step in working out our understanding of sexuality.

The next step is to understand how the divine model is expressed in the blessed Trinity and how the Trinity is a divine model for human life. The eternal flow of love and light (or wisdom) is the bond of perfect unity. God's unity (as emphasized in Judaism) is reflected in the diversity of roles (the Father, the Son, and the Holy Sprit) from our Christian perspective. The Father is revealed through the Son while the Son defers to the Father and promises the Holy Spirit. In the eternal triune God there is no hint of superiority or discontent. Father, Son, and Holy Spirit enjoy perfect union and significance. The holy Trinity is supreme love and worthiness (unity and significance). God has placed these holy drives toward union and significance in human nature. They are what loving and living are all about.

In reading the Genesis accounts of creation, I am struck by the fact that it was good for Adam and Eve to be created; it was not good for Adam to be alone and incomplete; it was good for Adam and Eve to be joined together. Aside from the idea of holy celibacy, and from a divine perspective, there is an incompleteness about manhood apart from womanhood and womanhood apart from manhood. It is an incomplete reflection of the divine. The bond of marriage provides what might be called a "reflective completion," a completion and wholeness reflecting divinity. Still, marital bliss is a pale reflection of heavenly glory and the union we will experience in God.

Human marriages are, moreover, secure only as a partnership of three: man, woman, and God. The Lord is the crucial third factor or partner in all healthy relationships. Those who are single are promised a special "marriage" to, and unusual support from, the Lord. Separated from our source we flounder and fade as mere shadows of ultimate reality. Following the Creator's plan for sex and marriage, human beings find fulfillment of their drives for union and significance. It is in this sense that the church speaks of matrimony as a sacrament. Marriage is a visible expression of an unseen reality: the love of the holy Trinity. In this light we begin to understand sex theologically. At first it sounds strange to speak of the sacrament of sex. (Our understanding of sex as sacrament will grow as we work on this theology of sexuality.) We slowly come to understand sex as a visible expression of the union and significance enjoyed in the blessed Trinity. It is a part of a larger creative drive— our loving force and creative force.

Take a moment to define sex. It seems like everybody talks about sex. Do we know what we're talking about? As we work on this question, we realize we're talking about gender, sex, and sexuality. *Webster's New Twentieth-Century Dictionary Unabridged,* 2d ed., combines all three ideas under its definition of sex: our gender as male and female; all that distinguishes women and men from each other; and the expression of our sexuality or the fulfillment of our sexual desires. The term gender has been properly restricted to its use in grammar, but colloquially it distinguishes our sexual identity, male and female, and in this sense it will be used here. To define sex, which we still haven't done, is not an easy thing, is it? What, precisely, do you mean when you talk about sexuality? To see our sexuality only as a genital expression is extremely limiting, if not damaging to our health, wholeness, and theological understanding. But that is how sex is considered from most nontheological and nontheistic points of view: mere mutual relief from sexual tension, desire for attention, and orgiastic euphoria. It is that powerful experience you dream about at school or work and try *to have* on off-hours. And if you cannot have it, you watch it.

Many powerful people in this world seem to think that sex is a deserved and expected reward. Only on such terms can we begin to understand the capers of many of our political and religious heroes. Newspapers and inside biographies report leaders who considered their sexual dalliances a dessert after the meal of public activity. An astonishing number of pastoral counselors and preachers have fallen prey to a form of sexual addiction. Students and workers, too, can look for this kind of "reward"—especially when they do not know how to nurture themselves appropriately.

The Russian theologian Nikolai Berdyaev describes the possible slavery of sex (unfortunately using generic masculine language):

> The erotic lure is a lure that is particularly widespread, and slavery to sex is one of the very deepest sources of human slavery. The physiological sexual need rarely appears in man in an unmixed form, it is always accompanied by psychological complications, by erotic illusions. . . .
>
> Erotic love always presupposes deficiency, unfulfilledness, yearning for fulfilment, attraction towards that which can enrich. There is *eros* as a demon, and man can be possessed by him. . . .
>
> With sex, which is a sign of deficiency in man, is connected a particular longing. And this longing is always stronger in youth. . . . The greatest triviality may be connected with sex. Not only the physical aspect of sex, but also the psychical is profaned.[8]

Augustine, one of history's great philanderers before his conversion, finally came to say: "Our souls are restless until they find their rest in Thee." Among his problems in accepting Christianity was trying to imagine going to bed without a woman. In his dictum we find the secret of our sexuality. God has placed in human creatures a restless and surging passion for himself. Thank God it is there! It is the drive for *knowing* and *communicating*—both of which are related to sexual intercourse. To have sex with someone is the ultimate human communication; it is to enter

---

[8] *Slavery and Freedom* (New York: Scribner's, 1944) 222–23, 225, 231.

literally into each other's being; it is "knowing" in the
biblical sense. That is why the Creator has guarded sex so
carefully within marriage. "The one who made them at
the beginning 'made them male and female' . . . 'a man
shall . . . be joined to his wife, and the two shall become
one flesh' . . . they are no longer two, but one flesh"
(Matthew 19:4-6, NRSV).

Berdyaev further describes sex:

> Man is a sexual being, that is to say, he is a divided half, he is
> incomplete and he feels an urge towards fulfilment, not only
> in his physical nature, but psychologically also. Sex is not
> merely a special function in man, connected with his sexual
> organs, it flows through the whole organism of a man. . . .
>
> Sexual energy is life energy and may be the source of the
> urge of creative life. A sexless creature is a creature of
> lowered life energy. Sexual energy may be sublimated, it may
> be detached from specifically sexual functions and be di-
> rected towards creativeness.[9]

We begin to see the weakness of thinking of sex
merely in a genital way. The impulse to seek a vision of God,
union with the Most High, flows out of the same passion
we have for communion with significant others around us.
It *may* involve sexual intimacy with a lifetime partner. Or it
may be beautifully expressed by those who are single—in
freedom for a special relationship to God, to express their
creativity, to care for themselves and for others.

We need to understand how single people are to express their sexuality. Families in contemporary society can
barely find enough support from the church. Single persons
find even less. The frustration, even the anger, of single
Christians who hear support given to married people but
not to single people is understandable.

How are the unmarried to understand and use their
sexual energies? Must they simply repress their sexuality?
Can they separate it from the energy needed to pursue

---

[9] Ibid., 223, 231.

ultimate union and significance? Were Jesus and the saints devoid of sexual energy?

Such questions demand a broad view of sexual energy—one related to love. Christ loves the church *as* husbands and wives love each other (Ephesians 5:1-2, 25). The sexual language of the Song of Songs (or Song of Solomon) has been used since at least the first century AD as a metaphor for our striving after and attaining union with God. It is important to see the connection between sexuality and spirituality—both are striving for union with another, both involve relationship and communication. A divine energy seems to drive human sexuality and spirituality.

Our Lord Jesus Christ in his humanity was a sexual person. In his incarnation Christ did not empty himself of sexuality. Sexuality can hardly be conceived as a totally dormant energy in Jesus as he walked our way of life and was "in every respect . . . tested as we are, yet without sin" (Hebrews 4:15b, NRSV). Rather, his sexuality, without genital expression, animated his life in pure and positive expressions of love and compassion. Jesus Christ is the great example, for single and married alike, of the healthy use of those energies that produce a longing for union with God and friends.

Christians, then, find it impossible to define sex apart from love and union. Love, the passion to belong, to communicate, and to serve, has an erotic side, which one must keep in its proper place. A nursing mother feels love for her infant and may enjoy pleasure in its sucking at her breast; a father may feel sensual pleasure from contact with his small child. But these are and should be different feelings from what we experience in lovemaking. Emotions leading us toward union go beyond genital attraction. They are part of a larger energy. To deal with sexuality we must have a sense of this drive toward union.

Passionate singing and speaking also draw on sexual energies. I have talked with many gifted Christian communicators and musicians. Those in such a spotlight experience a special rush of creative flow. After great performances many feel especially vulnerable sexually. Rock stars have commented on the same phenomenon. There is more than one reason that Christian leaders have been tempted after dramatically successful performances, but it seems clear to me and to many others that powerful spiritual or artistic communication flows from the same energy from which sexual desires find their source. That energy should drive us in the direction of ultimate union—and from there to deeper, godly relationships with others. Any substitution of physical union for that ultimate spiritual union is disastrous at worst, and at best trivializes our human existence. Agnes Sanford, a popular Christian speaker and author, in her lectures on sexuality, would recommend what may sound odd or simplistic. In regard to frustrated sexual energy, she advised people to "lift and shift" the creative force. God has provided alternatives for the use of sexual energy.

The Creator has wasted nothing. God has not wasted sexuality on the single or celibate person. I used to ask my students who is sexier: Madonna or Mother Teresa? Mother Teresa is not sexless. She is more full of vibrant sex than a sex object or boy toy. At first glance a current sex goddess may appear sexier, but finally she (like Madonna in *Truth or Dare*) admits to being sexually bored, and her sensational popularity, her sexual attractiveness, may decline as tedium, if not nausea, sets in. All who seek satisfaction in her sexual delights will eventually become bored. Young people need to realize that their greatest sexual fantasy, separated from love and apart from the fullness of life, is nauseating and fatal. No mature human being can watch extremely sexy rock videos for an hour or so without feeling a deep sadness and regret for their use and abuse of those who appear in them and the degradation of those who watch them.

Contemporary male celebrities claim, and have written books about, having sex with hundreds, even thousands, of women. I have heard children quote the sexual statistics of their athletic role models. How are we to understand this recreational—even competitive—use of sexuality in our world? Such perverted conquests must reveal a loss of real power and fulfillment—a lack of wholeness.

In Madeleine L'Engle's book *A Severed Wasp,*[10] a rather disturbing image gives its name to the title and theme of her work. A wasp settles on a honeyed dessert and proceeds to gorge itself. One of the characters severs the wasp at the thorax with a table knife. But the wasp continues to ingest the honey, seemingly unaware that it is now only half a wasp. Those who enjoy sex as an end in itself are like the wasp. Their enjoyment of the pleasures of sex may be similar in its euphoric feelings to sex within the bounds of a loving, committed relationship. Indeed, new liaisons can be more exciting. But the momentary enjoyment is a fragmented joy, and the end of sexual infidelities is death rather than life. "The adulteress . . . forsakes the partner of her youth . . . her way leads down to death" (Proverbs 2:16b-18a, NRSV, see also Proverbs 5:5 and 7:17-27). Any breaking of the Ten Commandments is wrong, not primarily because it violates a law, but because it violates relationships.

Sexual promiscuity is bound finally to end up in using others—as the means for one's own personal relief—in a way that moves toward the destruction of oneself and the objects of one's lust. Idolatrous sex, exploited sex, and sexual abuse will lead to the degeneration not only of the unlawful or careless but also of the innocent. The weak and innocent (such as children of AIDS or of divorce) suffer along with—and often before—those who transgress. No matter how we analyze, explain, or interpret them, rape, abortion, and AIDS are paradigms of something gone wrong in nature; they are not what the Creator intended.

In the secular arena as well as in the Christian arena, we must teach the high dignity and responsibilities of human relationships. Anything that hinders the growth of individuals and the peace of community is not acceptable. We cannot accept a moral philosophy based on the way things are; we must strive toward a higher view of the common good. Recreational sex violates human relationships and demeans personal identity. Indeed, it is a weakness

---

[10] New York: Farrar, Straus, Giroux, 1982.

in personal identity (and a strong sense of gender is part of that identity) that leads many young people into reckless sexual experiences. If I do not know who I am, I am not sure of my personal boundaries. Good parenting, education, and youth ministry focus not on negative cautions but on the building up of positive identities and relationships. In contrast to those who exploit sex for pleasure and profit, saints continue to be turned on by human contact until they die.

Sex is challenging, exciting, beautiful, fun—characteristics that are high priorities for young people. Hang-gliding, parachuting, motorcycle racing, rock climbing, snowboarding, skateboarding, surfing, and mountain biking are also exciting, beautiful, and fun. They operate on laws of nature that, when violated, spell disaster and death. Still, people approach extreme sports with a very positive attitude. In this positive mode, they are instructed and learn the discipline involved. Such discipline does not take away from the sport; it enhances its challenge and satisfaction. When we become careless in regard to sexual restraint, we can greatly damage ourselves and others. The greatest challenge regarding sexuality for teenagers is that physical fulfillment can stand so far off. Many young people, however, are facing this negative constraint in a very positive manner. Youth leaders with new insights can bring great encouragement by explaining sexuality as a part of a larger energy used for deeper relationships and communication.

In short, sex is part of our vibrant, creative energy. It is relational—a vital aspect of our communicating and communion with others. This is why it is useless to try to subdue sexuality by restraints or by denial. Those who are crippled in their communicating, their knowing, or in the way they relate to others—be they great leader, counselor, teacher, or whoever—will usually feel sexually frustrated. Those who neglect their God, their neighbors, or themselves may experience sexual unrest. More and more young people are pursuing purity rather than appeasement in their sexual lives. They are becoming integrated rather than patchwork selves.

In discussions about sexual problems counselors may encounter young people with sexual dysfunctions. But complaints of inordinate lust and masturbation often turn quickly to deeper problems of self-esteem and self-nurturance. If our creative flow of love, which is meant to foster personal wholeness and to spill over to our neighbors, is thwarted or neglected, it frequently emerges as an unhealthy craving for genital satisfaction.

If we see love in this way, we understand how Christians, single or married, can turn their sexual energies in many healthy directions besides genital expressions. Wilderness challenges, music and drama programs, service projects, and just having fun hanging out together will take the place of transitory or frustrating relationships. When struck with seemingly overwhelming temptations, we need to ask ourselves:

* Have I attended to the child within me adequately?
* Am I allowing myself creative activity?
* Am I experiencing the love of God in a deeply personal way?
* Am I in significant relationships with others?

If we cannot answer these questions satisfactorily, or are not able to experience the fulfillment in our lives of the principles behind these questions, we may need a counselor's help. It may also be important to find a spiritual director (since we are speaking theologically here). Underlying questions of spiritual direction are: What kind of a *lover* are you these days? How are you loving yourself? How are you loving others? How are you loving, and receiving the love of, the Father, the Son, and the Holy Spirit?

Finally we come to definition: Sex is the passion that drives us toward union. That drive may be directed in a genital, artistic, altruistic, or spiritual direction. We are trying to see sex as a sacrament of ultimate union with God. Sex is a visible manifestation of our need to be sought after and to be joined in meaningful relationships.

Those for whom the spiritual aspect of sex is still enigmatic should consider the Song of Songs. Here is a book in which lovers make explicitly sexual statements.

How beautiful you are! Your eyes are like doves. . . . Your lips are like a scarlet thread. . . . Your two breasts are like two fawns. . . . You are altogether beautiful, my darling.

My beloved is dazzling and ruddy. . . . His locks are like clusters of dates. . . . His eyes are like doves. . . . His abdomen is carved ivory. . . . His legs are pillars of alabaster. . . . His mouth is full of sweetness. And he is wholly desirable. (Song of Songs 4:1, 3, 5, 7; 5:10–12, 14–16, NASB)

Most of us see the Song of Songs as primarily a paean of praise for earthly love. Those who seek *a vision of God above all* also find this book pointing to the passion that draws our Lord to us and us to the Beloved. The great mystics, Jewish and Christian, have held this section of the poetic writings to be the holy of holies in Scripture.

Our sexuality defines us as one of God's two created genders. Furthermore, sex is:

- an extremely pleasurable aspect of love;
- a bonding between husband and wife;
- an energy that nurtures our own souls;
- a creative flow that fosters healthy relationships and human communities;
- and above all, part of a holy passion for divine union.

Difficult and controversial issues such as masturbation and homosexuality still remain. The lack of emphasis in Scripture on these issues should keep them from being prime targets of ecclesiastical, pastoral judgment.

DEALING PRACTICALLY WITH WHOLESOME LIVING AND SEXUALITY

As you approach the subject of sexuality with teenagers, consider the following:

1. Understand sexuality. Be able to define and describe sex in your own words. Consider how you and your adolescent friends are dealing with sex physically, emotionally, relationally, socially, and spiritually.

2. Deal with your own sexuality: your own gender issues; your sexual fantasies, temptations, repression, etc.; your embarrassment about the topic in public; and the way you process this issue with your leadership team and friends. 3. Know where your faith community stands on important issues. Be aware also of the attitude of your town or city, class, or ethnic group. Know the concerns of the parents of your young people; discuss any units on this topic with your adult committee. Be sure that you and the senior pastor, or your immediate director in an organization, have discussed these issues and that they approve of what you intend to teach. 4. Respond openly and appropriately to all inquiries from young people. Do so on the spot, in your next session together, or privately. 5. Let male leaders deal with boys; female leaders with girls. Depending on your maturity and the situation, allow for some careful exceptions to this rule. Some group sessions should be for girls and boys alone; others as coed discussions with shared male/female leadership. 6. Develop a unit on sexuality even where young people are not asking for it. Begin with an understanding of sexuality and emphasize its relational aspects.

- Be sure to use materials from their media.
- Use brief video clips or songs to initiate discussion.
- Clear these discussion starters with the senior pastor and your committee.
- Be sure you and your leaders are not projecting your own issues on young people.
- Always use help from leaders among youth.

7. When you do not feel fully prepared to deal with some aspect of sexuality, bring in some experts cleared by the senior pastor and your committee. 8. Don't overemphasize the topic. You should be teaching them that there is lots more to life than sex. Emphasize creative group activities and dynamics.

Imagine asking some ninth or tenth graders what issues they would like to discuss in their group. Instantly, a bright mischief-maker yells out, "Sex!" And everyone laughs or smiles with a look of "We've got you!" on their faces. You might pause for a long moment. Then look them squarely in the eyes and ask them with love and respect: "And do you want to talk about the *biological* or *the relational* aspects of sex?" Most often they will tell you they are tired of hearing about penises and vaginas in gym or health classes. They want to know more about the relational side of sex (meaning when and how to do it).

Leaders (a male and female team) should then be able to ask:

- What do you want or need in a relationship?
- What are some of the best relationships you have seen?
- How can people hurt each other in a relationship?
- What is wrong with some of the adult relationships you have seen?
- What hurts you or your friends most in some relationships?
- Can you think of any way in which you have failed in a relationship? What can you do about such failures?
- How do you think God might help men and women get ready for healthy relationships?

These questions are an outline for a theological discussion about sex for junior or senior high students. Of course, there is more. Next, the group can try to find practical and profitable agreement in the following statements.

- Sex is God's gift to us (we might say it was invented for our pleasure).
- Sex is a natural and beautiful human function.
- Like anything else, sex can be distorted out of its appropriate context.
- Sex isn't everything; just think—really think—of trying to make sex the main thing or the whole thing in your life.
- Sex can be used in a way that can deeply hurt people.
- Sex should be enjoyable and significant for a whole lifetime.
- Sex is about love and relationships.

- It helps to discuss our sexuality in a group that cares about friendship, fun, community, and service. All adolescent issues of identity are clarified by friends.

These are the understandings (backed by biblical and church teachings) we share with young people. Out of such discussions we may find ourselves asking questions such as:

- Can a group of friends sometimes be more fun and more supportive than a date?
- Where do we see ourselves these days, and how do we want to grow?

We will sense that we are providing help at the edge of growth in many of these discussions. Having been honest about our own sexuality and vulnerable as to our own struggles—and admitting that we do not have all the answers—we can be of great help to those young people searching for real answers and solutions in their own lives.

After sessions on this topic, students have sometimes asked me further questions:

- If I know many of my young people are having sex, should I encourage them toward safer sex? Should I ever inquire about these matters?
- To what extent should a leader question gay teenagers about their sexuality if such questioning may cause them to withdraw from their faith? Should gay teenagers who are vocal about their identity and rights still be welcomed at church and in youth groups? If I know someone who is gay but has not disclosed it, should I ever question them on this?
- How and to what extent should I use Scripture to prove my points?

The answers to these questions rest mainly in the situation, in our relationship to young people, and in the standards and style of our faith community. Our understanding of Scripture, our experience of human life, our self-understanding, and our relationship to our church or organization are critical factors. Equally important is our relationship with the young people involved. Do we feel deep compassion toward and have high hopes for these young friends? Do we understand their view of life, the world, and themselves? Are we willing to let them help us answer the questions above? Remember that their faith is always more important than sexual standards at a particular point in their lives. Such a style and approach will produce more benefit than dogmatic answers and judgments.

Our approach to sex and sexuality with young people should be primarily in the spirit of true celebration—an assured sense of the delights and holy possibilities of this vital life force. Sex is part of what God described as good—and, we might add, it is fun. Young people should see in us an unembarrassed and frank approach to sexuality. We need to explain biblical principles from a positive and confident posture. Seeing these qualities in us will help them sense the relevance of Christ's teaching about sex.

PASTORAL COUNSELING ABOUT SEX IN AN ADVERSE SOCIETY

Premarital Sex

We cannot avoid the nitty-gritty questions about how far to go sexually. We should always try to put them in the context of the above relational issues. More specifically, however, if the rules of the past do not work so well today, what are we to do?

Our assumption is this: If two American teenagers—who have been programmed for several years by the media to expect sexual climax as a sign of a positive relationship—come together over a period of time in romantic and intimate settings, then sooner or later they will probably have sex. Our general advice to young couples is to place themselves in settings other than intimate.

A corollary of the above assumption might be: It is very difficult for a couple who are engaging in any level of erotic arousal to regress to a lower level of physical intimacy together. In such a case the only way to avoid continued petting or intercourse is usually physical separation. This separation may even involve a move on one of their parts or at least a significant shift in schedules.

A third postulate: It is possible for teenagers to have fun and find real support in a friendly group. In such groups many teenagers have learned to stick together, to meet their need for companionship, to create all kinds of activities, to be open to others, and to find challenge and fulfillment in serving. Youth ministers today are increasingly interested in wilderness camps and service projects. Groups of friends who get together for healthy fun should be affirmed and praised.

There is an ongoing debate among youth leaders as to the necessity and benefits of teenage dating. I do not think it should be condemned out of hand. Many of us think, however, that creative group activities in the teenage years build healthy relationships and can prepare young people for serious dating later on. It is much more difficult to become good friends than it is to become good lovers in our world today. Healthy friendship involves security in a clear personal identity that allows one to be vulnerable. We hope that young people will work at becoming friends before becoming lovers. Careful thought, prayer, and counsel are a proper prelude to marriage commitment—probably with a shorter and more purposeful engagement period than in the past when there was less pressure toward sleeping together.

David Elkind[11] and many others have pointed to a critical need of today's teenagers. It is for time and place, safe from violence, undue pressures, and confusing messages, to be with a concerned adult and supportive friends. They need to catch up with what has been missed in a hurried childhood. Their socially-conditioned patchwork selves are in critical need of integration. Wholesome fun and challenging experiences with a group of friends provide opportunities for exciting growth.

Even today some couples begin dating in high school, develop a strong friendship along with romantic ties, stop

---

[11] *All Grown Up.*

short of petting and intercourse, and go on to marry in college or just after. Their restraint should be admired and encouraged. Here, however, we are exploring how we can minister to the majority of young people who will follow current trends and norms for premarital sex. Let us strongly encourage group friendship.

How can we be firm, accepting, and realistic as we minister to teenagers and college-age young people who are in love and cannot soon get married? In general, many of us believe we should point to the high standards of Scripture and our Lord Jesus Christ. "This is the right way, we realize how hard it is, we are willing to help you in any way you'd like, and we understand if you fail." Provocative studies from the book of Proverbs, Song of Solomon, 1 Corinthians, and Ephesians will help young people determine their personal philosophies of sexuality. They will find much to ponder in the words of Christ regarding sex and marriage in Matthew 5 and 19.

In most cases today, it seems best for romantic courtship to be short. A couple in their twenties may take a year and a half or more to grow as friends, to talk with family and friends, to develop their friendship and reflect on their values and goals, dreams, and fears. Their courtship should include very clear counseling. Part of courtship's function is the development of mutual discipline. Few today can endure a prolonged courtship with sexual fidelity to biblical standards.

The implications of a biblical standard of sexual conduct for the contemporary youth culture are radical. If young people cannot "go together" safely in our society today (and the studies seem to show that they—including Christians—cannot), let's not try to develop rules for boy-girl special relationships. The old advice "stay on first or second base until you're engaged," or "nothing below the neck," or "just keep all your clothes on and fastened," does not seem to work in many cases. Let's develop alternatives such as the "special friendship groups" suggested here.

Some will object to this depreciation of dating and say that young people need special relationships by which to develop socially and to be ready for marriage. There is some truth in such an argument, and it poses a difficult dilemma. Some young folk will need a temporary boyfriend or girlfriend. Others will be sure they are in love and are going to be married—and may indeed marry their high school sweethearts. But let youth ministers concentrate on uncoupled good times among close friends. Let's have fun (games, etc.), be stretched (ropes courses, adventure camping), be taught (clear instruction and deep discussions), and serve (empowerment and opportunity).

Here is the reality: Some teenagers will have sex, and some young adults will live together. Some will admit their sexual activity, others will not. Should they be thrown out of home or rejected from youth group? I think not. Consider how many we would be throwing out; and think how difficult it would be to determine who is being honest. These types of situations present us with fine opportunities to discuss and practice grace and forgiveness.

Christian homes and youth groups are not being asked to compromise and accept the prevalent standards of the secular world. Parents are expected to set limits for sons and daughters in high school and to establish the rules for their home. In most cases it will be the relationships, instructions, and modeling of early years (from birth to puberty) that provide for acceptance of these limits. Parents of teenagers can do little to rectify deficiencies of earlier ages; it is now time to negotiate without capitulation and within reasonable limits.

These negotiations between parents and teenagers as students progress through junior and senior high school years will vary according to parental styles. Each home will deal differently with a situation in which the son or daughter is sexually active. Standards of the parents should not be violated in the home itself. A parent cannot, in most cases, stop a teenager from having sex if they are determined to do so. But the parents can and should control what goes on in their home. Continued violations may lead to the necessity of older teenagers living elsewhere.

Teaching that is biblical and relevant should make clear to youth groups the high quality of Christian lifestyles. Sexual conduct is important, but sexual sins are not the most heinous crimes. If leaders sense that a couple is sleeping together, they should give that couple pastoral counseling. Pastoral theology (that is, the kind of theology we are doing in most of this book) always maintains God's high standards while it realizes human weakness. It is strong on grace. Church traditions will vary in terms of the approach to sexual issues among the young, but generally speaking those suspected of sexual intimacy outside marriage should be counseled with respect but not placed in positions of leadership. Sexual sins are forgivable—though the church has sometimes found it difficult to practice the model of a compassionate Christ. Institutional judgments are safer and easier than the working out of corporate compassion. "Jesus said, 'Neither do I condemn you. Go your way, and from now on do not sin again' " (John 8:11, NRSV).

Compassion, as we have learned it from our Lord Jesus Christ, is a key to dealing with these difficult issues. We cannot simply say to young people today, "We love you, but we hate your sins!" Adolescents can often sense when we even think in those terms. If you do not know how judgmental such a statement sounds to them, you do not know young people. What they hear when you say something like that is: "We hate you and your sins."

A word should be said about various counseling situations. First, consider the differences among *preaching* (which is the proclamation of truth: Do you hear it?), *teaching* (which includes explanation and discussion of the truth: Do you understand it?), and *counseling* (which allows people to clarify their own life view and work out their own issues according to their personal values: What are you going to do with it?).

Homosexuality

Let's consider pastoral counseling of gay teenagers—or those who think they are gay. On the one hand, many teenagers pass through a stage in which they have homosexual feelings or experiences. A homosexual experience, or several relationships, does not mean that the adolescent is gay. On the other hand, a person may be have a gay orientation from the time he or she can remember.

The general hostility of the youth culture, the judgment of the church, the fear of parents and siblings, the lack of support from lifelong friends—all can make life for the homosexual teenager exceedingly difficult. The goal of this stage of life is working out one's identity (gender, personality, and related characteristics) a sensitive task at best. A secondary concern of adolescence is how others see you and think of you. Like anyone else, a gay teenager needs to feel accepted in a community that gives him or her feedback. Lack of positive feedback has contributed to an alarming rate of suicide among gay teenagers. Very few Christian organizations or churches provide an environment where the gay person can determine personal identity, develop relationships, and consider a worldview and future life direction. Both churches who are moving toward legitimating homosexual unions and those who see homosexual activity as contrary to Christian standards have failed generally to provide questioning teenagers with a receptive and redeeming community.

Youth leaders should enter such pastoral relationships with a humble sense that we have a lot to learn—not only about homosexual orientations but about this particular individual (we must avoid stereotyping) and about our reaction to gays (we can learn much about ourselves from counseling others). Few heterosexuals have any sense of the pressures gay teenagers feel from parents, family members, peers, society, and the church. Their greatest need in coming to us is for an older, trusted friend. In most counseling situations, youth ministers are bridges to professional counselors or agencies.

Abortion

Youth ministers may also have to counsel girls who are considering an abortion or who have just had one. This situation puts us in the middle of one of our country's and the church's most emotional debates. Our society is pondering how a secular and pluralistic nation distinguishes the natural rights of a fetus from those of a mother. That is the national debate, but here we are face-to-face with someone who is scared and pleading for counsel and support.

We would like to believe that everyone feels that the termination of a potential life is sad and regrettable. We would hope for a discussion that goes beyond a woman's rights vs. fetal rights to a consideration of the mystery and dignity of life and the unfortunate choices among greater and lesser evils faced by many young women—and sometimes by their male partners. On one side of the debate are those who see the issue as one of a woman's right to choose, a right long neglected by society. They believe abortion may sometimes be necessary in rational planning for a mother's and family's long-term welfare. The other side argues for the sanctity of all life, for acknowledging the fetus as a developing person. They see themselves as advocates for the rights of the unborn and most vulnerable, and they fight against what they see as a society's general trend toward moral decline.

Significant questions underlie this debate:

• When does human life actually begin?
• Who has the right to determine when life begins or the competing rights of fetus and mother?
• How do government, religion, science, and power groups interact on such issues?
• How can laws be made that deal justly with rich and poor alike?
• How can this debate lead people to consider more carefully the moral and religious bases of their personal and social lives?[12]

Without attempting a resolution of these difficult questions, we urge youth ministers to know the position of their own faith community, to give it careful thought and biblical study personally, and to understand its pastoral implications

---

[12] See Dean Borgman, "Abortion: Topic Discussion," in *Youth Workers' Encyclopedia* (Austin, Tex.: NavPress Software, 1996).

in their ministries. Two stories (with names changed) will help us see the practical complexity of this issue.

Mary has just completed an M.S.W. and is now a social worker; she is also a volunteer youth minister. Michelle comes to her crying. "Mary, you just can't be pregnant in this high school. Nobody has ever walked these halls pregnant. And my parents would kill or disown me." Mary is understanding and helps her through the abortion process. A couple of years later Michelle comes into serious doubt and guilt. She comes back to Mary and wants to know how a Christian leader could have aided her in the termination of an unborn life. At this point, both women may need pastoral counseling. Michelle may be grieving the loss of a child and a trusted leader; Mary may be overwhelmed by the loss of a young friend and by a sense of guilt.

Jane is a young staff member of a national Christian youth organization. All her instruction has been pro-life. Susan tells Jane that her close friend, Tracy, is pregnant and planning on having an abortion. After a great deal of prayer, Jane asks Tracy to come to her apartment. Tracy senses what is coming but has a good relationship with her leader. They have a good discussion. Tracy promises to think the issue over. She does and decides to have an abortion. Jane sees Tracy several times over the next few days and becomes stronger and stronger in her arguments against abortion. To Tracy, as well to Susan, Jane is becoming dogmatic, angry, and highly judgmental. They feel betrayed and condemned. Tracy has the abortion without the support she needs. Her and Susan's relationships with Jane are never restored. Jane confesses to her supervisor that something went wrong and is sure she would handle the situation differently in the future. Like Mary, the other volunteer leader, Jane needs wise and sensitive supervisory help or counsel.

These true stories are intended to give us compassion for those who wrestle personally, usually unpreparedly, with this issue. They also demonstrate our need for professional and pastoral advisors in youth ministry. We must approach the abortion issue with a great respect for life—the life of the mother, the life of the unborn, and all others affected. We need to listen to all sides of the debate. It is a most important discussion to have with young people before dating and sexual contact. It is a matter about which you may have a strong opinion. In your pastoral role, however, you may be asked to support someone who has taken a course of action opposed to your view.

CONCLUDING REFLECTIONS

Pastoral theology must deal with complex issues, and sexuality is the most difficult in many ways. How can a Christian live with a spouse who does not believe or does not love anymore? When does a woman leave an abusive husband? How and when does a girl respond to what she considers an inappropriate remark or touch from a prominent and respected church leader? If two Christians are living together, must they separate before being married in a Christian ceremony? Life is not all black and white; much of it can be gray and complex. Solutions to moral problems are not always clear. Youth ministers must serve young people with loyalty to the positions held by their church or organization.

Pastoral counselors and youth ministers are called on to exhibit the holiness of God and the compassion of Christ. Our times call for both high beliefs and a deep sense of grace. With our Lord we stand firm against sin, yet we are gentle in tending the flickering wick or the broken reed.

As we approach the subject of sexuality with young people, let us have a very high view of sex. It is great, it is beautiful, it is a sacrament! We look young folk in the eye and plead, "Don't get cheated by illusions that lead over a cliff or by short-cuts that lead to dead-ends. Don't let the media or peer pressure rip you off. Don't miss any of the joys God has for you in this life and through all eternity. 'Delight yourself in the LORD; And He will give you the desires of your heart' " (Psalm 37:4, NASB).

If you are still trying to find ways to *control* the sexual behavior of the young people in your ministry or of your own sons and daughters, you have not gotten much help

here. But if your desire is to help young people grow
toward their full potential, if you are willing to give them
the freedom to fail, if you are able to forgive, and if, above
all, you are willing to learn from young people as any
effective parent and youth leader must do—then perhaps
there is hope for us all in a world filled with pitfalls. From
the darkest night there comes the brightest dawn. "Where
sin abounds, grace does much more abound." Or as we
might put Paul's declaration in paraphrase: "When the sin
of this world seems completely overwhelming, God's grace
is still triumphant" (Romans 5:20).

QUESTIONS FOR REFLECTION AND DISCUSSION

1. In what ways are you happy about your sexuality? How comfortable are you in your manhood or womanhood? Are you
   able to express attraction and love to other creatures in a
   powerful and free way? What kind of lover are you? How
   does this work out for you on genital and nongenital levels?
2. In what ways are you not happy with your sexuality? To
   what extent do you feel unsure of what it means for you to
   be a woman or a man? To what extent are your genital
   drives a distraction and difficulty for you? To what extent is
   the flow of love and creativity restricted in expressing itself
   to others? Who might assist you in any of these issues?
3. How would you like to grow sexually and spiritually? How
   are the sexual and spiritual aspects of your life related as
   you pursue holistic growth? Might counseling or spiritual direction be of help to your growing?
4. How have you been most effective in teaching or counseling teenagers about their sexuality and sexual behavior?
   What frustrations have you or they had? What might help
   you become more natural and effective?
5. What kind of help do young people in your group need
   from you, your team, and possible resource persons? How
   can you improve your curriculum of sexual education?
6. What can you do to move from negative to positive in sex
   education and social life in your group?
7. Are the young people to whom you minister given enough
   opportunity for celebration and intimacy in their worship
   and play? What more could be done?

11 THEOLOGY WITH HEART AND HANDS

Living Out Your Whole Theology

Here is my servant whom I uphold, my chosen one with whom I am well pleased. . . . A bruised reed he shall not break, and a smoldering wick he shall not quench, until he establishes justice.

—*Isaiah 42:1, 3-4,* NAB

The Son of Man has come to search out and save what was lost.

—*Luke 19:10,* NAB

The Son of man came not to be ministered unto, but to minister, and to give his life a ransom for many.

—*Mark 10:45,* KJV

THEOLOGICAL PERSPECTIVE

Theologians who study and work with young people may come up with unique definitions of theology. Theology is understanding God's love in action. It involves translating the story of Christ from the Gospels into our time and place. Theology is thinking about God's perspective on our various cultural situations.

Living out this theology and explaining it to young people call for theology with a heart, theology that reaches out to real situations, touches deepest hurts, brings freedom to those oppressed, and empowers those deprived of opportunity.

ANOTHER LOOK AT ADOLESCENCE

We consider youth or adolescence as a transition from childhood to adulthood. Such a transition has always existed, and the nature of the transition is affected by the stages of human development and puberty. But the pattern of adolescence is determined by each society.

Young people have played important roles in historic events as disparate as the Children's Crusade in the thirteenth century and the American revivals at the turn of the eighteenth century.[1] The worldwide Christian Endeavor movement of the late nineteenth and early twentieth centuries may be considered an outcome of those early revivals. Mandatory high school in the Great Depression created a youth culture with its own school life, dances, and norms. A new youth culture, with high school athletics and dances, music and movies, emerged in the 1940s. When it came it demanded new approaches. Youth ministers had to leave churches and safe adult sanctuaries for places where young people gathered. This idea of entering the youth culture in an incarnational manner was developed during the 1940s particularly by Jim Rayburn and Young Life. This emphasis on relationships and a ministry of presence has become a hallmark of relevant youth ministries today.

Revolutionary changes in family and media from the late 1960s through the 1980s produced new and profound effects on the youth culture and on the lives of individual young people. The dramatic weakening of family and communal life since the 1960s—along with the growing power of the media—has forced children to grow up quickly without adequate time to integrate a clear sense of their

---

[1] See Dean Borgman, "A History of American Youth Ministry," in *The Complete Book of Youth Ministry* (ed. Warren Benson and Mark Senter; Chicago: Moody, 1987) 61-74.

own personal identity, values, and idea of truth. This social revolution had such drastic implications for children that four social critics sounded an alarm within the space of three years.[2] In two of his books, acclaimed child expert David Elkind explains how, in a new social climate, children are pushed to pseudomaturity, forced to learn by imitation rather than by integration, shaped into "patchwork selves," and left with a new kind of stress. We have not only forced children to grow up quickly, society has also extended the length of adolescence—it takes longer to enter adulthood than ever before. This prolongation of adolescence strengthens the subculture of youth and adds the ambivalence of being, at the same time, grown up but not an adult. Most experts agree that young people today have a special need for a safe place and caring mentors. This is the basic social challenge of youth ministry.

REMINDERS OF YOUTH'S HURT

When this stress among young people is aggravated by personal hurts or lack of family and community support, it can produce enormous amounts of rage and reckless abandon. It is a law of nature: young people who have been hurt tend to hurt themselves or others. The stories found in *Go Ask Alice* and *Vivienne* offer descriptions of young, white, well-to-do women who, despite their privilege and nice parents, turn stress and low self-image into self-destruction.[3] Sex and drugs that were used to relieve stress only heightened their anxiety and pain, causing greater stress. Casual affirmations from caring adults could not find their mark. Just as these girls seemed to be discov-

---

[2] Elkind, *The Hurried Child* and *All Grown Up;* Postman, *The Disappearance of Childhood;* Vance Packard, *Our Endangered Children: Growing Up in a Changing World* (Boston: Little, Brown, 1983); Winn, *Children Without Childhood.*

[3] Anonymous, *Go Ask Alice;* John E. Mack and Holly Hickler, *Vivienne: The Life and Suicide of an Adolescent Girl* (Boston: Little, Brown, 1981). See also Pipher, *Reviving Ophelia.*

ering a way to cope, sudden depressions led to their suicides.

Say You Love Satan, mentioned earlier, describes a young man growing up in the midst of affluence and advantage.[4] Such a seemingly positive environment is no sanctuary from rebellion, heavy metal music, drinking, and drugs. In this case there was also dabbling in the occult and, most tragically, the vicious murder of a young friend.

The late 1980s and 1990s brought a rise in violent behavior and cries of anguish among young people as evidenced in news reports, studies, and music. We need a theology adequate to answer these cries for help and screams of rage. From all sectors of our society come stories, not easily explained, of troubled youth who will not be easily served.

Jamie, a tough high school junior, got angry with Amy, his pretty freshman girlfriend. So he took her out into the woods and slit her throat as she screamed, "Jamie, I love you; I love you." He came back and laughed to his friends about her last words. Then he got one of them to help him put her body in a plastic bag and dump it in a pond. As he did, he commented, "It sucks to be Amy." Jamie was not a product of big-city violence, but behind his story are family troubles and drugs, including steroids. With his mother's help he tried to break out of prison, where he will now spend much of his life.

The case of Brenda Adams received national attention. Brenda, a studious, well-liked girl, was returning from a party when she was suddenly set upon by girls on a stealing binge. Brenda would not surrender her coat, and in a few minutes she was dead. Felicia Morgan, who did the shooting, was defended as innocent by reason of temporary insanity induced by posttraumatic stress. What had her life been like? Her favorite uncle and cousin were both shot to death. Her father shot at her mother for not putting enough salt in the gravy. Loaded guns were kept in the apartment, her mother reported, because "it was a bad marriage."

---

[4] By David St. Clair.

Felicia had been raped when she was twelve years old. She experienced not only violence in her community but also racism and class inequality in society at large. Leaving aside for a moment the whole matter of just sentencing, what do the Felicias of this world need? Besides the justice of punishment, such offenders also need deep therapeutic help, a new sense of the meaning and dignity of life, true remorse, and a new sense of self-worth and responsibility.

The age of the violent has dropped strikingly in the 1990s. The near South Side of Chicago saw a murder by eleven-year-old Robert "Yummy" Sandifer, and then his murder by teen gang members who thought he might be forced to inform on them. Within days another eleven-year-old in the same neighborhood was arrested and charged with bludgeoning an elderly neighbor to death.

Trouble often comes to a town or neighborhood in large doses. Within weeks, residents were dealing with the chilling story of five-year-old Eric Morris, who wanted to do the right thing and was too weak to defend himself. With his brother Derrick (age eight), he visited a fourteenth-floor abandoned apartment used as a clubhouse by some boys. The Morris brothers were told to go steal some candy for the others. When they refused, two boys (older but not yet in their teens) grabbed little Eric and dangled him out the window. Derrick was able to fight off the others and bring his brother back in. But the boys managed to do it again, and this time Derrick was hit and bitten by others. In the melee, Derrick lost his grip on his brother, and the others dropped him.

"It was horrible," said Monique Jackson, fourteen, who watched from outside the building as she was returning from the market. "He came down waving and screaming."[5] Joanne Mitchell, twenty-eight, an eleventh-floor resident of the Ida B. Wells housing project, put it well for the community and all of us when she asked, "What goes on in a child's mind to do that to a baby? What kind of kids are we raising?"

---

[5] Stephen Braun, "Childhood Savagery Revisits Chicago's Tough South Side," *Los Angeles Times*, October 15, 1994.

We must find some answers. Relevant theological endeavor demands bringing earthly realities and behavioral studies together with principles of faith. I hope that this study of human growth and understanding of changes of critical systems around children and youth has provided new understanding. Human beings are created to belong to significant groups, to find significance in a just society. Children must have attention from their parents and loved ones, and adolescents must have healthy challenges to prove themselves.

Studies from the 1950s to the present find a striking correlation among impoverished neighborhoods, juvenile delinquency, and drug abuse. The highest concentrations of drug users are found in the communities displaying the highest rates of juvenile court delinquents, of boys' court cases, of tuberculosis, and of infant mortality—which are also the communities of lowest income in the city.[6]

Behavioral sciences demonstrate the dilemma of youth growing up without support and opportunity. Young people may be drawn into a culture of violence or drugs because they see no opportunity for themselves elsewhere, because they have not been prepared to distinguish themselves in a positive, healthy way. The violent gang member takes everything he has seen on television—all the lessons of consumption and acquisition, competition and success, considers how he can most likely acquire the money it takes to buy what he sees advertised and owned by his role models, adopts the value system of the only social group who will accept him, and "goes for it." Young males and females, in

---

[6] Isador Chein, "Human Misery," in *The Road to H: Narcotics, Delinquency, and Social Policy* (New York: Basic, 1964), cited in Elliot Currie, *Reckoning: Drugs, the Cities, and the American Future* (New York: Hill & Wang, 1993). See also Harold Finestone, "Cats, Kicks, and Color," *Social Problems* 5, no. 1 (1957); Richard A. Cloward and Lloyd Ohlin, *Delinquency and Opportunity* (New York: Free Press, 1959); Kenneth B. Clark, *Dark Ghetto: Dilemmas of Social Power* (New York: Harper & Row, 1965); Harlem Youth Opportunities, Inc., *Youth in the Ghetto: A Study of the Consequences of Powerlessness and a Blueprint for Change* (New York: Harlem Youth Opportunities, Inc., 1964); Ianni, *The Search for Structure.*

different ways, are pushed down from the larger society and drawn into "oppositional cultures," involving pregnancy, drugs, crime, and violence. To those outside, such delinquent behavior may make no sense; it consists of pseudowork (hustling or gang activities) and antisocial behavior. It leads to poverty, dependence, and death. But from within, life on the streets is a natural alternative to socially acceptable dead-end alleys.

Ghettos, suburban towns, and rural areas share many of the same problems; drugs, crime, and violence are everywhere. Of course, different communities treat these problems differently. The same crimes that take African-American youth in the city to court are frequently settled at the suburban police station after parents are called. But guns and death (often the result of drunken driving) are now ubiquitous.

Hurt and neglect come to children in all of society. The private pain and low self-image of wealthy white girls may lead to anorexia or bulimia (one million teenage girls are afflicted with eating disorders, according to a Gallup Poll).[7] Peggy Orenstein spent four days a week for one year with eighth-grade girls from two California schools. One school might be described as wealthy, white, middle class; the other a school of minority students in a poorer section of the city. She also studied such research as the American Association of University Women's report, *Shortchanging Girls, Shortchanging America.*[8] The conclusions of her experience and study are important for all parents and workers with youth:

> For a girl, the passage into adolescence is not just marked by menarche, or a few new curves. It is marked by a loss of confidence in herself and her abilities, especially in math and science. It is marked by a scathingly critical attitude toward her body and a blossoming sense of personal inadequacy.

---

[7] Orenstein, *SchoolGirls,* 93.

[8] American Association of University Women, *Shortchanging Girls, Shortchanging America: A Call to Action* (Washington, D.C.: American Association of University Women, 1991).

In spite of the changes in women's roles in society, in spite of the changes in their own mothers' lives, many of today's girls fall into traditional patterns of low self-image, self-doubt, and self-censorship of their creative and intellectual potential. Although all children experience confusion and a faltering sense of self at adolescence, girls' self-regard drops further than boys' and never catches up. They emerge from their teenage years with reduced expectations and have less confidence in themselves and their abilities than do boys. Teenage girls are more vulnerable to feelings of depression and hopelessness and are four times more likely to attempt suicide.[9]

HOLISTIC THEOLOGY

To be concerned about a young person involves being concerned with the social systems that shape her life. Theology for those ministering to youth must address family issues, schools, the media, the community, peer groups, employment, and the kind of society in which these youth are about to assume adult roles.

We use insights gained from the social sciences, but we need more. Youth workers hear stories of incredible hurt and astonishing rage. Listening to some young people or watching them writhing and slam dancing in a mosh pit, we can sense enough anger to blow up a building. Living in the youth culture can drive one to angry justification of antisocial behavior—or to critical condemnation—unless one turns to Christ, who died to reach young people as vulnerable as bent reeds or explosive as the smoldering wick on a dynamite charge. There in Christ we all find healing, liberation, and the hope of a just society.

HOLISTIC YOUTH MINISTRY

We have considered a practical theology that takes individuals, culture, and social systems seriously—a holistic

---

[9] Orenstein, *SchoolGirls*, xvi.

theology. Ministry flowing from such theology will be relevant and holistic—giving attention to the physical, emotional, academic, social, economic, and spiritual needs of young people. Whether youth leaders are beginning a new work or taking up where others have left off, they should see youth ministry as a process. Leaders and students around the world have attested to the usefulness of the following nine stages of youth ministry in describing this process. These steps or dimensions have been used both in planning and in evaluating youth programs.

1. Building a support base:
- flowing from a faith community;
- mandated by pastor and denominational leadership;
- supported by committee or board;
- surrounded by a leadership team.

2. Research:
- discovering needs and resources for relevant ministry;
- community research and topical research;
- research owned by the whole support base.

3. Contact:
- becoming friends of young people on their turf;
- incarnational ministry, ministry of presence;
- hanging out with a purpose.

4. Activities and trips:
- becoming leaders of young people;
- bonding of youth group in this stage.

5. Counseling:
- referral and case management;
- informal counseling or advising on the run.

6. Proclaiming the gospel:
- flowing out of earning the right to be heard (being there, respecting, listening, responding, being trusted);
- making the whole story clear (see below).

7. Nurturing young faith:
- encouraging young disciples.

8. Leadership development and service:
* youth serving church and community.

9. Development of growing youth program:
* planning and management of new structures.

Process returns to step 1.

PROCLAIMING OUR THEOLOGY

Youth ministry these days is providing young people with a safe place where caring mentors allow them to hear others tell their stories until they have the courage to tell their own story, be affirmed in their personhood, and in that context hear the great story of God's love. Hearts open to youth will always ask, What in the world could be good news to these young people? Being with them, feeling their pain, and sensing their hopes drives us back to Scripture. There we rediscover a story that exactly fits all manner of lives and situations. The gospel we share as we talk intimately to a young friend, or search for answers in dynamic small groups, or present speeches to larger gatherings is *the whole story of God* from Genesis to Revelation. It follows an outline something like this:

Doctrine	Place of Christ	Corporate and Individual Issues
Creation	God the Creator	Beauty and goodness of nature Self-worth and self-esteem
Incarnation	Person of Christ	Love of God Human ideals Relationships of Christ Deeds (miracles) of Christ Teaching of Christ Claims of Christ
Sin and Fall (hurt)	Need of Christ	How systems have hurt How we hurt ourselves How we hurt others Divisions and violence Alienation and rebellion
Atonement	Work of Christ	Resolution of moral dilemmas

The cross and resurrection		God's holy judgment and mercy Healing of personal hurts Forgiveness and reconciliation
Repentance and faith	Appropriation of Christ	Personal and corporate repentance Nature of faith Confidence and assurance
Kingdom and church	Lordship of Christ	Cost of discipleship Christ in the world Faith community Prayer and Bible study Worship
Eschatology	Coming Rule of Christ	God making all things right

Those who love and understand young people on one hand and this wonderful news on the other find it to be God's response to the quest for personal and social truth. They find all manner of young people hungry for this story. We have said that youth ministry should provide young people today with a safe place to hear others telling their stories until they have the courage to tell their own story and then find the intersection of God's story within a supportive community. This story is capable of becoming good news in all situations.

GOOD NEWS: A LIBERATING AND EMPOWERING THEOLOGY

Youth ministry must also attend to the healing of hurts, to the liberation of the oppressed, and to the empowerment of those made marginal. The model for all this is Jesus Christ. Our whole ministry, our idea of adolescent spirituality, and our apologetic with young people must be christocentric.[10] The Christ of youth ministry is very human as well as fully divine, interested in material life as well as spiritual life, and concerned about systems as well as individuals.

---

[10] See Charles Shelton, *Adolescent Spirituality: Pastoral Ministry for High School and College Youth* (Chicago: Loyola University Press, 1983) 9, 337.

The Christ of the Gospels went about doing good; he taught and preached the good news to the poor, the imprisoned, the blind, the oppressed, and even the rich. Our theology and our ministry must recognize and touch the hurt of young people first of all. Our gospel and service are strong on liberation and empowerment. Central in all this is a recognition and proclamation of Jesus as Savior and Lord. Although youth ministry has been marked by divisions between those who are socially concerned and those who are pietistically focused, between those who teach the ethics of Jesus and those who announce his salvation, holistic ministry must be faithful to Scripture and to the full range of human needs.

Young people around the world are wondering if they really are the church and the world of tomorrow. For the sake of the world and the church they must be not only listened to but also involved in what is going on today. We need them, and they need us, now as a vital part of today's church and today's world.

Thirteen teenagers, members of an Episcopal Diocesan Youth Council, carefully pondered their relationship with the adult church. Let's listen to what they said to adults attending a Diocesan convention:

> We are young people in the ambiguous place between childhood and adulthood, we need to be recognized as such. Though we face the devastating issues inherent in today's society, we don't have the experience to deal with them without people more mature than we are . . . YOUTH—we are told we are difficult to deal with. Although we are regarded as "just children" we are facing very adult issues. We often must make very mature decisions about: Drugs, Sexuality, Prejudice, Child Abuse, Parental Battering, Peer Pressure, Faith. These are certainly not childlike issues and we face them on a daily basis. We need all the understanding and help that you can give us. . . . We want support. We want your trust, your respect—your love. We want to develop coping mechanisms, and decision-making skills. . . . We believe that through faith, understanding, communication with

and support from OUR church, we all can fulfill our mission to love and serve the Lord.[11]

These keen young people are asking, first of all, for our love. Then, with young people everywhere, they need our understanding and support. Finally, they want a mentor to give them wisdom for significant service. That is what this book has been about. It is urging you to get closer to young people and the youth culture, to seek a fuller vision of God, and to develop a theology that takes into account the perspective of, and is relevant to, adolescence.

CONCLUSION

Good theology among youth and adults should lead to healing and faith commitment, to forgiveness and empowerment, to liberation and development. Our studied reflections should provide theology for people in all manner of situations. If we theologize truthfully, relevantly, and vulnerably, with clarity and simplicity, we can bring young people with us into the theological task. Such a result should be helpful to academics and laity, young and old, rich and poor, in all cultures around the world.

I hope we all become more committed to growing theologically. As we learn more and more about adolescent development, we need a corresponding deepening of our theology of growth. The more we deal with failure and the pain of adolescence, the more we need a theology of suffering and the cross. The longer we persevere in this ministry, the more we develop a theology of resurrection and hope.

More important than an intellectual understanding about God and God's ways is our personal experience of God and the community of faith in which we live, worship, and serve. Our theology is celebrated in worship. Youth and adults come to church needing to "dump their garbage" (confession), hear the Word and affirm their faith (creed), and offer the firstfruits of their lives (communion). Worship

---

[11] Conference Notes, Episcopal Diocese of Massachusetts, 1990.

is a necessary celebration of personal, communal, and, most importantly, divine stories. A realization of Christian celebration is needed today so that eucharistic Christians (God's future kingdom people living now) will go out from church in dynamic service for the common good of all. The emphasis on the Eucharist or Communion is important. Young people (and all others) need to know they have something necessary and dynamic to contribute to Sunday worship, whether they have a special assigned task to perform or not. Church is about bringing personal and corporate offerings to a special place.[12] On the Lord's Day, God waits to bless the best of what we are about (the firstfruits of our lives) so that, in union with Christ and with one another, we can change the world. Without the offerings of young and old, there can be no Communion service.

The central paradigm of worship in the New Testament (the miracle and discourse of John 6) puts Christ's disciples on the spot. They were asked to feed the world (the crowd). All they could find was a young boy with a little food. Christ took the boy's best—as pathetic an offering as it was, as ridiculous a solution as it appeared—and offered it up to the Father, who fed the world (the five thousand). This is how we should view the Eucharist and youth ministry, as offerings of ourselves and efforts which in Christ will nourish us and serve the world.

If your theological efforts are offered up to the Lord and then to the world, if they are informed by the Word of God and the community of faith, and if they are celebrated at the altar of God, then they will exceed intellectual exercise and produce more than self-serving defenses. Such theology will lead to love and service, growth and maturity. It is the driving force of servant leaders. If this is becoming true for you at this point, then our study has not been in vain. Our work together here is no end in itself; it is all for the glory of God and for the benefit of the young people we serve.

---

[12] See Deuteronomy 26:1ff. along with John 6 and Romans 12:1.

QUESTIONS FOR REFLECTION AND DISCUSSION

1. What have you heard from young people in this chapter that you want to take with you? What cries have you heard from young people lately? How have they touched your heart and how will you respond?
2. What, for you, is the central challenge of this chapter?
3. How do you understand God's story, the story of the Bible, the gospel story? Is it, can it be, good news to young people you know?
4. How might you take the suggestions of this chapter to young friends in personal ways and story form?
5. What help has this chapter given you in translating theology to strategic youth programs?
6. As you think over this entire book, how are you doing theology? How are you reading the stories of your culture and the media? How are you reading the stories of young people today? How are you reading the Word of God?
7. As you look back on question 3 above and think through the chapters you have read, do you see yourself developing a theological base for ministry? Are you and your colleagues in youth ministry assisting young minds to be theologically established? How will you continue your theological development?
8. In what ways has this book given you new insights and new hope?

SELECT BIBLIOGRAPHY

ADOLESCENCE

Anonymous. *Go Ask Alice*. Englewood Cliffs, N.J.: Prentice-Hall, 1971.

Anson, Robert Sam. *Best Intentions: The Education and Killing of Edmund Perry*. New York: Vintage, 1987.

Bibby, Reginald W., and Donald C. Posterski. *Teen Trends: A Nation in Motion*. Toronto: Stoddart, 1992.

Brierley, Peter. *Reaching and Keeping Teenagers*. Turnbridge Wells, England: MARC, 1993.

Buechner, Frederick. "Adolescence and the Stewardship of Pain." In *The Clown and the Belfry: Writings on Faith and Fiction*. Pages 83–104. San Francisco: HarperCollins, 1992.

Campbell, Anne. *The Girls in the Gang: A Report from New York City*. 2d ed. Cambridge, Mass.: Blackwell, 1991.

Canada, Geoffrey. *Fist Stick Knife Gun: A Personal History of Violence in America*. Boston: Beacon, 1995.

Carlip, Hillary. *Girlpower: Young Women Speak Out!* New York: Time Warner, 1995.

Dorius, Guy L., Tim B. Heaton, and Patrick Steffen. "Adolescent Life Events and Their Association with the Onset of Sexual Intercourse." *Youth and Society* 25, no. 1 (1993) 3–23.

Dryfoos, Joy G. *Adolescents at Risk: Prevalence and Prevention*. New York: Oxford University Press, 1990.

Elkind, David. *All Grown Up and No Place to Go: Teenagers in Crisis*. Reading, Mass.: Addison-Wesley, 1984.

Feldman, S. Shirley, and Glen R. Elliott. *At the Threshold: The Developing Adolescent*. Cambridge: Harvard University Press, 1990.

French, Thomas. *South of Heaven: Welcome to High School at the End of the Twentieth Century*. New York: Doubleday, 1993.

Garbarino, James. *No Place to Be a Child: Growing Up in a War Zone.* New York: Free Press, 1991.

_____, et al. *Troubled Youth, Troubled Families: Understanding Families At-Risk for Adolescent Maltreatment.* New York: Aldine, 1986.

Howe, Neil, and Bill Strauss. *13th Gen: Abort, Retry, Ignore, Fail?* New York: Vintage, 1993.

Hyde, Kenneth. *Religion in Childhood and Adolescence: A Comprehensive Review of Research.* Birmingham, Ala.: Religious Education Press, 1990.

Ianni, Francis A. J. *The Search for Structure: A Report on American Youth Today.* New York: Free Press, 1989.

Israel, Betsy. *Grown-Up Fast.* New York: Poseidon, 1988.

Kozol, Jonathan. *Amazing Grace: The Lives of Children and the Conscience of a Nation.* New York: Crown, 1995.

Langone, Michael D. *Recovery from Cults: Help for Victims of Psychological and Spiritual Abuse.* New York: Norton, 1993.

_____. *Satanism and Occult-Related Violence.* Bonita Springs, Fla.: American Family Foundation, 1990.

MacLeod, Jay. *Ain't No Makin' It: Leveled Aspirations in a Low-Income Neighborhood.* Exp. ed. Boulder: Westview, 1995.

Offer, Daniel. *The Teenage World: Adolescent Self-Image in Ten Countries.* New York: Plenum, 1988.

Orenstein, Peggy. *SchoolGirls: Young Women, Self-Esteem, and the Confidence Gap.* New York: Doubleday, 1994.

Pipher, Mary. *Reviving Ophelia: Saving the Selves of Adolescent Girls.* New York: Ballantine, 1994.

Prothrow-Stith, Deborah. *Deadly Consequences: How Violence Is Destroying Our Teenage Population and a Plan to Begin Solving the Problem.* New York: HarperCollins, 1991.

St. Clair, David. *Say You Love Satan.* New York: Dell, 1987.

Sebald, Hans. *Adolescence: A Social Psychological Analysis.* 4th ed. New York: Prentice-Hall, 1992.

Shakur, Sanyika. *Monster: The Autobiography of an L. A. Gang Member.* New York: Atlantic Monthly Press, 1993.

CULTURE

Bellah, Robert N., et al. *Habits of the Heart: Individualism and Commitment in American Life.* Berkeley: University of California Press, 1985.

Bloom, Allan. *The Closing of the American Mind.* New York: Simon & Schuster, 1987.

Brake, Michael. *Comparative Youth Culture: The Sociology of Youth Culture and Subcultures in America, Britain and Canada.* New York: Routledge, 1985.

Chambers, Iain. *Popular Culture: The Metropolitan Experience.* New York: Methuen, 1986.

———. *Urban Rhythms: Pop Music and Popular Culture.* New York: St. Martin's, 1985.

Cone, James. *The Spirituals and the Blues.* New York: Seabury, 1972.

de Tocqueville, Alexis. *Democracy in America.* 1840. Trans. George Lawrence. Garden City, N.Y.: Doubleday, 1969.

Ekstrom, Reynolds R. *Media and Culture.* New Rochelle, N.Y.: Don Bosco Multimedia, 1992.

Frith, Simon. *Sound Effects: Youth, Leisure, and the Politics of Rock'n'Roll.* New York: Pantheon, 1981.

Kraft, Charles. *Christianity in Culture: A Study in Dynamic Biblical Theologizing in Cross-Cultural Perspective.* Maryknoll, N.Y.: Orbis, 1977.

Lull, James, ed. *Popular Music and Communication.* 2d ed. Newbury Park, Calif.: Sage, 1992.

Mander, Jerry. *Four Reasons for the Elimination of Television.* New York: Quill, 1978.

Mueller, Walt. *Understanding Today's Youth Culture.* Wheaton, Ill.: Tyndale, 1994.

Nelson, John Wiley. *Your God Is Alive and Well and Appearing in Popular Culture.* Philadelphia: Westminster, 1976.

Niebuhr, H. Richard. *Christ and Culture.* New York: Harper & Row, 1951.

Patterson, James, and Peter Kim. *The Day America Told the Truth: What People Really Believe about Everything That Really Matters.* New York: Prentice-Hall, 1992.

Postman, Neil. *Amusing Ourselves to Death: Public Discourse in the Age of Show Business.* New York: Penguin, 1985.

Schultze, Quentin J. *Dancing in the Dark: Youth, Popular Culture, and the Electronic Media.* Grand Rapids: Eerdmans, 1991.

Sexton, Adam, ed. *Rap on Rap: Straight-Up Talk on Hip-Hop Culture.* New York: Delta, 1995.

Storr, Anthony. *Music and the Mind.* New York: Free Press, 1992.

Tillman, James A., with Mary Norman Tillman. *Why America Needs Racism and Poverty: An Examination of the Group Exclusivity Compulsion in America as the Natural Enemy of*

Rational Social Change in Race and Poverty Relations. Rev. ed. New York: Four Winds, 1973.

Turner, Steve. *Hungry for Heaven: Rock 'n' Roll and the Search for Redemption.* Downers Grove, Ill.: InterVarsity, 1995.

Twitchell, James B. *ADCULT USA: The Triumph of Advertising in American Culture.* New York: Columbia University Press, 1996.

Wink, Walter. *Engaging the Powers: Discernment and Resistance in a World of Domination.* Minneapolis: Fortress, 1992.

EXEGESIS

Adler, Mortimer, and Charles Van Doren. *How To Read a Book.* Rev. ed. New York: Simon & Schuster, 1972.

Bausch, William J. *Storytelling: Imagination and Faith.* Mystic, Conn.: Twenty-Third Publications, 1989.

Brown, Raymond E. "Hermeneutics." In *Jerome Biblical Commentary.* Ed. Raymond E. Brown, Joseph A. Fitzmyer, and Roland E. Murphy. Pages 605–23. Englewood Cliffs, N.J.: Prentice-Hall, 1968.

Fee, Gordon D., and Douglas Stuart. *How To Read the Bible for All Its Worth: A Guide to Understanding the Bible.* Grand Rapids: Zondervan, 1982.

Terrien, Samuel. "History of the Interpretation of the Bible: Modern Period." In *The Interpreter's Bible.* Ed. G. A. Buttrick. 1.127–41. New York: Abingdon-Cokesbury, 1952.

HUMAN DEVELOPMENT

Brown, Lyn Mikel, and Carol Gilligan. *Meeting at the Crossroads: Women's Psychology and Girls' Development.* Cambridge: Harvard University Press, 1992.

Burns, Jim. *Surviving Adolescence.* Ventura, Calif.: Regal, 1997.

Erikson, Eric. *Childhood and Society.* New York: Norton, 1950.

_____. *Identity, Youth, and Crisis.* New York: Norton, 1968.

Fowler, James W. *Stages of Faith.* New York: Harper & Row, 1981.

Gilligan, Carol. *In a Different Voice: Psychological Theory and Women's Development.* Cambridge: Harvard University Press, 1982.

Rice, Wayne. "Part Two: From Children to Adults." In *Junior High Ministry.* Rev. ed. Pages 49–140. Grand Rapids: Zondervan, 1990.

Shelton, Charles. "Adolescence, Developmental Theory, and Spirituality." In *Adolescent Spirituality: Pastoral Ministry for*

High School and College Youth. Pages 29–120. Chicago: Loyola University Press, 1983.

Specht, Riva, and Grace J. Craig. *Human Development: A Social Work Perspective.* Englewood Cliffs, N.J.: Prentice-Hall, 1987.

PERSONAL GROWTH

Crabb, Larry. *Real Change Is Possible If You're Willing to Start from the Inside Out.* Colorado Springs: NavPress, 1988.

_____. *Understanding People: Deep Longings for Relationships.* Grand Rapids: Zondervan, 1987.

O'Connor, Elizabeth. *Our Many Selves.* New York: Harper & Row, 1971.

Peace, Richard. *Learning to Love Ourselves.* Colorado Springs: NavPress, 1994.

THEOLOGY AND MISSIOLOGY

Ateek, Naim Stifan. *Justice, and Only Justice: A Palestinian Theology of Liberation.* Maryknoll, N.Y.: Orbis, 1989.

Costas, Orlando. *Christ Outside the Gate: Mission Beyond Christendom.* Maryknoll, N.Y.: Orbis, 1982.

Dyrness, William. *How America Hears the Gospel.* Grand Rapids: Eerdmans, 1989.

_____. *Learning About Theology from the Third World.* Grand Rapids: Zondervan, 1990.

_____, ed. *Emerging Voices in Global Christian Theology.* Grand Rapids: Zondervan, 1994.

Fabella, Virginia M. M., and Sun Ai Lee Park, eds. *We Dare to Dream: Doing Theology as Asian Women.* Maryknoll, N.Y.: Orbis, 1989.

Gutierrez, Gustavo. *A Theology of Liberation: History, Politics, and Salvation.* Rev. ed. Trans. and ed. Caridad Inda and John Eagleson. Maryknoll, N.Y.: Orbis, 1988.

Hanks, Thomas D. *God So Loved the Third World: The Bible, the Reformation, and Liberation Theologies.* Maryknoll, N.Y.: Orbis, 1984.

Hearkness, Georgia. *Conflicts in Religious Thought.* New York: Holt, 1929.

Miguez Bonino, José. *Doing Theology in a Revolutionary Situation.* Philadelphia: Fortress, 1975.

Mugambi, J. N. K. *African Christian Theology: An Introduction.* Nairobi: East African Educational Publishers, 1992.

————, and Laurenti Magesa, eds. *The Church in African Christianity: Innovative Essays in Ecclesiology.* Nairobi: Initiatives, 1990.

Nasimiyu-Wasike, A., and D. W. Waruta, eds. *Mission in African Christianity: Critical Essays in Missiology.* Nairobi: Uzima, 1993.

Song, C. S. *Theology from the Womb of Asia.* Maryknoll, N.Y.: Orbis, 1986.

Sugden, Christopher. *Radical Discipleship.* Hants, England: Marshalls, 1981.

Sugirtharajah, R. S., and Cecil Hargreaves, eds. *Readings in Indian Christian Theology.* London: SPCK, 1993.

Villafañe, Eldin, et al. *Seek the Peace of the City: Reflections on Urban Ministry.* Grand Rapids: Eerdmans, 1995.

YOUTH MINISTRY

Benson, Warren S., and Mark H. Senter III. *The Complete Book of Youth Ministry.* Chicago: Moody, 1987.

Borthwick, Paul. *Organizing Your Youth Ministry.* Grand Rapids: Zondervan, 1988.

Burns, Jim. *The Youth Builder: Today's Resource for Relational Youth Ministry.* Eugene, Ore.: Harvest, 1988.

Campolo, Anthony. *The Church and the American Teenager: What Works and What Doesn't Work in Youth Ministry.* Grand Rapids, Mich.: Zondervan, 1993.

Copeland, Nelson E. Jr. *The Heroic Revolution: A New Agenda for Urban Youthwork.* Nashville: Winston, 1995.

Crudele, John, and Richard Erickson. *Making Sense of Adolescence: How to Parent from the Heart.* Liguori, Mo.: Triumph, 1995.

Dettoni, John M. *Introduction to Youth Ministry.* Grand Rapids: Zondervan, 1993.

DeVries, Mark. *Family-Based Youth Ministry: Reaching the Been-There, Done-That Generation.* Downers Grove, Ill.: InterVarsity, 1994.

Downs, Perry G. *Teaching for Spiritual Growth: An Introduction to Christian Education.* Grand Rapids: Zondervan, 1994.

Kujawa, Sheryl A., and Lois Sibley. *Resource Book for Ministries with Youth and Young Adults.* New York: Episcopal Church Center, 1995.

Kunjufu, Jawanza. *Hip-Hop vs. MAAT: A Psycho/Social Analysis of Values.* Chicago: African American Images, 1993.

Nelson, C. Ellis. *Helping Teenagers Grow Morally: A Guide for Adults.* Louisville: Westminster/John Knox, 1992.

Nyomi, Setri, ed. *Ecumenical Youth Ministries in Africa: A Handbook.* Accra, Ghana: Assemblies of God Literature Centre, 1993.

Ratcliff, Donald, and James A. Davies, eds. *Handbook of Youth Ministries.* Birmingham, Ala.: Religious Education Press, 1991.

Robbins, Duffy. *The Ministry of Nurture: How to Build Real-Life Faith into Your Kids.* Grand Rapids: Zondervan, 1990.

Roberto, John, ed. *Early Adolescent Ministry.* New Rochelle, N.Y.: Don Bosco Multimedia, 1991.

Rydberg, Denny. *Youth Group Trust Builders.* Loveland, Colo.: Group, 1993.

Senter, Mark H. III. *The Coming Revolution in Youth Ministry.* Wheaton, Ill.: Victor, 1992.

Shelton, Charles. *Adolescent Spirituality: Pastoral Ministry for High School and College Youth.* New York: Crossroads, 1983.

————. *Pastoral Counseling with Adolescents and Young Adults.* New York: Crossroads, 1995.

Ward, Pete. *Worship and Youth Culture: A Guide to Making Services Radical and Relevant.* London: Marshall Pickering, 1993.

————. *Youth Culture and the Gospel.* Grand Rapids: Zondervan, 1992.

————, Sam Adams, and Jude Levermore. *Youthwork: And How to Do It.* Oxford: Lynx Communications, 1994.